D0916806

THE FRENCH FAUST
HENRI DE SAINT-SIMON

THE FRENCH FAUST
HENRI DE SAINT-SIMON

by MATHURIN DONDO

PHILOSOPHICAL LIBRARY · NEW YORK

CONTENTS

FOREWORD

In Georg Brandes' monumental work, *Main Currents in Nineteenth Century Literature,* appears this startling remark: "France, which showed so little interest in the drama of *Faust,* herself produced a nineteenth century Faust in the matter of restless genius and irresistible craving of both theoretical and practical knowledge of everything in the universe."[1]

The man to whom Brandes referred in the above quotation is Claude-Henri de Rouvroy, comte de Saint-Simon, whose life forms the subject of the present study. His name is little known in this country, although he boasted of being one of the founders of the United States of America. One writer agreed with him: "The first American was a Frenchman. His name was Saint-Simon."[2]

The assumption was based on the fact that he had taken part in the War for American Independence.

Few men have been so paradoxically characterized as Comte Henri de Saint-Simon. He has been diversely designated as a rationalist, a mystic, a feudal philanthropist, an advocate of capitalism, the father of socialism, the originator of positivism, the founder of sociology. The doctrine attached to his name introduced a new word into the English language. The Century dictionary defines *Saint-Simonism* as "the socialistic system founded by Claude Henri de Rouvroy, Comte de Saint-Simon. . . ."

It is not the purpose of this study to discuss in detail the writings of Saint-Simon nor the social theories derived from them. Saint-Simonism has been adequately analysed and criticised by a number of able sociologists, whose names are listed in the bibliography appended to this book. Our task is more specifically limited to the reconstruction and interpretation of the life of Saint-Simon.

1

There is a regrettable lack of biographical studies of the man. Saint-Simon left a number of autobiographical fragments, but few are entirely trustworthy, since they were written with the purpose of creating a favorable impression. Other sources of information may be found in the writings of admiring disciples and sympathizers more anxious to build up a pious legend than to furnish an unbiased narrative. For this reason it has not been easy to separate pleasing inventions from sober truth.

In segregating fantasy from reality it was necessary to restore certain phases of Saint-Simon's life which had been more or less consciously kept in oblivion by his zealous devotees. The scattered documents are for the most part buried under files of dusty papers, often unclassified. In our research we spent considerable time in the libraries and archives of Paris. We also visited the towns and villages in Picardy where Saint-Simon had resided at one time or another, and where valuable data were brought to light with the patient collaboration of the local archivists.

Our wanderings through the highways and byways of Picardy was made possible through the kindness of Dr. Patty Gurd Willson, who graciously placed herself and her automobile at our disposal. We visited the towns of Péronne, St. Quentin, and Amiens, as well as the villages of Berny, Falvy, Saint-Simon, Rouvroy.

At Berny, where the Saint-Simons had owned a château and considerable lands, we found barely a trace of the old family home. What had remained of it had been destroyed in the First World War, together with most of the village. The church, school, and farm houses had been rebuilt, only to be razed to the ground again during the Second World War. In search of information we addressed ourselves to *monsieur le maire* who at the moment was busy mending a broken wagon wheel, and who referred us to his aged father, better versed in the history of the locality.

"The château of the Saint-Simons?" said M. Duclaux, Sr. "Why, yes, I'll show you where it stood," and he led us to what remained of the once imposing edifice. "It was partly destroyed

2

during the Revolution. The entrance gate and part of the building were intact before the First World War. Here are some of the foundations. That big farmhouse was part of the estate."

A short distance from there, at Falvy, a commune to which the domain of Saint-Simon extended, we met a resident who boasted of owning a parcel of that land. This village also had suffered cruelly during the recent wars, as did the adjacent hamlets of Saint-Simon and Rouvroy. The latter are sleepy places, consisting of a score of farm houses, a church, an elementary school, and a modest city hall. All that remains of the splendors of the former château are a number of large cut stones scattered throughout the field, and here and there a depression in the ground, indicating subterranean cellars. A profusion of wild hawthorn and eglantine fill the cavities once occupied by casks and bottles of fine wine.

At Péronne we had the good fortune to be the guests of the principal of the *Collège Henri de Saint-Simon,* M. Henri Chauvergne, and his wife. This institution is a public secondary school where boys between the ages of eleven and eighteen receive instruction. M. Chauvergne introduced us to the amiable archivist, M. Gustave Devraine, to whom we are grateful for the help he gave us in locating important documents.

From Péronne our quest led us to Amiens, the chief town of the department of the Somme which administers the localities mentioned above. In this war-battered town, Monsieur Estienne, archivist, an enthusiastic scholar, gave us invaluable assistance in the search for documents.

In Paris at the Bibliothèque Nationale, Madame Calvé offered expert advice, and Madame Briet gave permission to use a typewriter in transcribing of notes, a highly esteemed privilege. Monsieur Boussard at the Bibliothèque de l'Arsenal, was most gracious and placed all available material at our disposal.

We owe to Monsieur Arnaud our sincere thanks for his persevering aid in hunting elusive documents. We are indebted to Professor Frederic Ernst of New York University, for his painstaking perusal of our manuscript and his scholarly criticism. The first person plural used throughout this study is not

3

limited in its implication to the customary editorial application of this personal pronoun. A large part of the research has been done in collaboration with my wife, who acted as my able and indispensable secretary, and without whose aid and critical judgment these pages would not have been submitted to the public.

Mathurin Dondo

CHAPTER ONE

Henri de Rouvroy, Comte de Saint-Simon, whose adventurous life forms the subject of this study, attempted repeatedly to impress his readers with the antiquity of his lineage and the greatness of his name. At every opportunity in the course of his writings, he would boast of his glorious origin and his descent from Charlemagne.

In a letter addressed to his nephew, Henri-Jean-Victor, marquis de Saint-Simon, he thus traced the origin of the family:

"Louis XIII said: 'I decree that the land of Saint-Simon be raised to a duchy-peerage, in favor of Claude de Saint-Simon, descended in direct line from the counts of Vermandois.' You will find this phrase in the genealogical and chronological history of the peers of France, written by Father Anselme, by order of Louis XIV, a history which is even to-day the classic work of that type. See page 389, tome IV.

"The counts of Vermandois, as everybody knows, were descended from Charlemagne.

"The Council of Castille has examined, received and registered the genealogical documents which prove that the Saint-Simons are descended from Charlemagne."[1]

The true or fictitious descent from Charlemagne was a source of inordinate pride to all the Saint-Simons, but for Henri this belief turned into an exalted mental condition of a psychopathic nature. Studied from this point of view, in spite of seeming contradictions his life, his thought, his writings present a constant process of development and even his most erratic ways can find thereby, if not an excuse, at least a motivated explanation.

The figure of the great emperor stood before him, illumined his visions, beckoned him to climb higher and higher the steep road to glory. It was a long and arduous road, strewn with pit-

5

falls and insuperable obstacles which caused the ambitious pilgrim many a downfall. Painfully bruised and at times crushed by utter despair, with renewed energy he rose and went forward toward the ultimate goal. The goal Henri had set for himself was to gain in the realm of thought the prodigious eminence Charlemagne had acquired by the sword.

He exults in the pride of his lineage in this letter to his nephew Victor:

"We once possessed the Western Empire; we were reduced first to the Kingdom of France, and afterwards to the county of Vermandois; after being dispossessed of this sovereignty, we were reduced to a secondary place; but we still were in the first ranks among the governed. Related to the House of Bourbon, we had obtained from that dynasty a duchy-peerage and a grandeeship of Spain. To-day we have no connection with the throne, we have descended from the height of grandeur to the deepest abyss of oblivion; the Revolution shoved us into the lowest ranks of the governed, and the memory of past grandeur has become an obstacle to our ascent. Under such circumstances, my nephew, one must risk doubly, trebly one's skin; one must be proud to the point of arrogance."[2]

Henri drew also deep gratification from his kinship to Louis de Rouvroy, duc de Saint-Simon, (1675-1755) the celebrated author of the *Memoirs of the Reign of Louis XIV and the Regency*. Louis, proud of his glorious ancestry, became embittered when the royal court failed to bestow upon him the rank and favors which he felt were his due. He avenged himself by recording with cynical remarks the intrigues and the gossip of the court at Versailles. When the *Memoirs* were published after his death, (1788), the author was compared to Tacitus and hailed as one of the greatest writers of France. Macaulay adapted several passages of these writings, at times translating literally, and was given credit for some brilliant descriptions of men and events.

In one of his autobiographical sketches, Henri blamed his father for quarrelling with Louis and therefore losing his claim to a rich heritage:

"I was the nearest relative of the noted author, the duc de

Saint-Simon. His duchy-peerage, his grandeeship of Spain and an income of five hundred thousand francs which the duke possessed should have been passed on to me. He quarreled with my father whom he disinherited. Thus I lost the title and the fortune of the duc de Saint-Simon, but I have inherited his desire for glory."[3]

Since the duke died without leaving any male heirs, Henri had hoped to have the duchy revived in his favor, as he was the nearest relative. The loss of five hundred thousand francs assuredly was cause for grief, but few besides Henri would attach great value to the title of a Spanish Grandee. At the court of the Spanish kings, it did represent the highest honor to which the nobility could aspire, since it conferred on the bearer the privilege of wearing his hat in the royal presence. In France, however, on the eve of the Revolution, such privilege was of doubtful value, if not a source of suspicion and danger.

Michelet, the renowned French historian, repudiating Saint-Simon's extravagant claims to a descent from Charlemagne, attributed to that family a less fabulous origin:

"This new family, which claims to get back to Charlemagne, has done quite well to have produced one of the greatest writers of the seventeenth century and the boldest thinker of ours.

"The Saint-Simons deluded themselves with the thought that they were descended from Charlemagne but in reality owed their origin to the little favorite of Louis XIII."[4]

Henri's father, Balthazar-Henri, comte de Saint-Simon, was born November 27, 1721. Of his early youth we have no record. He must have embraced a military career since he is described by Father Anselme as a "captain of cavalry." In the archives of Amiens, the capital of the department of Somme, in which the landed estates of the Saint-Simons were located, he is thus recorded:

"Balthazar-Henri de Rouvroy de Saint-Simon, governor and chief magistrate of Senlis, brigadier of the King's armies, grand master of ceremonies to his Majesty, the King of Poland, duke of Lorraine, head of the guardsmen of the King of Poland, residing in Paris on rue du Bac, parish of Saint-Sulpice, and at that time in his château at Berny."[5]

7

The high sounding title of master of ceremonies to the King of Poland requires an explanation. Stanislas Leczinski, the deposed king of Poland, whose daughter Louis XV married, was given the duchy of Lorraine to compensate for the loss of his kingdom. He transformed the city of Nancy into an imitation of Versailles, and reigned with all the splendor he could acquire with frequent borrowings from the French royal treasure. Like all kings, great and small, Stanislas bestowed favors on a scale commensurate with his revenues. And the favor seekers were numerous, among them Balthazar-Henri.

At the age of thirty-six, Balthazar-Henri married his cousin, Blanche-Elizabeth de Saint-Simon, aged twenty-one. The young wife brought a dowry of sixty thousand francs, which proved of great help to the land-poor husband. As Henri said:

"My father was a younger son of small means."

In spite of their claims to ancestral empire, kingdom and duchy, the Saint-Simons were average landowners of Picardy, land-poor, dissatisfied, always in debt, begging for pensions and income-bearing offices as did most of the aristocrats of the time. J. Balde gave the following estimate of the family:

"The Saint-Simons, who claim to descend from Charlemagne, enveloping their origin in a legend which is the cause for their glorification, are possessed of a terrific pride, stubbornness and greatness. But this aristocracy is at bottom peasant! They were Picards who lived poorly and died nearly all impoverished and in debt, in spite of the 'fine estates' along the Somme, a commission in the army, pensions from the king and self-seeking alliances."[6]

However a contrary statement was made by Louis, the duc de Saint-Simon in his *Memoirs,* when he claimed that the Sandricourt branch owned large estates in Picardy which brought a yearly revenue of 50,000 francs. In those days such an income represented, if not great wealth, at least comfortable means even for a family of high rank.

The name *Sandricourt* was derived from the ownership of lands in and about the village of Sandricourt, located in Picardy. For the same reason the name of Saint-Simon originated from the appellation of a family estate, as explained by Father Anselme:

"Saint-Simon, an important village in Vermandois, Picardy, on the Somme river, between Saint-Quentin and Ham, gave its name to the ancient lords of Saint-Simon."

Henri's father held the title of lord of Falvy, Berny, Lanvin, Rouvroy; in other words, he owned property in each of these villages, within a radius of about twenty-five miles. The residence of the family was at Berny. The château, of considerable size, had architectural distinction in the French classic style. The main building opened on a formal garden with a rectilinear alley leading to a semi-circular arcade, shrubs and flower beds geometrically arranged on each side in varying patterns, the whole surrounded by high walls and stately trees. The plan of the park and château is preserved on a cadestral map in the archives of the Somme at Amiens.

The village of Berny is only a few miles distant from Péronne. It is reached through an unfrequented country road meandering among the wheat fields. Here and there pink roofs hide in sheltered groves.

During the summer months Balthazar-Henri de Rouvroy, Comte de Saint-Simon, lived in these rustic surroundings with his numerous family. In winter, residence was taken up at the townhouse in Paris on rue du Bac.

Rue du Bac means the street of the ferry, as it ends at the river's edge where in former days people were ferried across the Seine. To-day a beautiful bridge leads one from the left to the right bank of the river. Rue du Bac was once a fashionable part of the aristocratic Faubourg Saint-Germain. In the time of Balthazar-Henri de Saint-Simon, a number of wealthy and distinguished people owned townhouses on this thoroughfare. There dwelt the Prince of Salm, the Marquis d'Aubusson, the Duchess of Chatillon, and to add a graceful touch to this imposing gallery, there was mademoiselle Bourgoin, the mistress of the duc de Berry. She was an actress whose talents were not limited to the theatre, since she won the flattering title of "la déesse de la joie et la joie des plaisirs."

To be sure rue du Bac did not boast as fine palaces with monumental porte-cochère as the rue de Grenelle, or the rue de Varenne, where resided the higher aristocracy of the Faubourg Saint-Germain. But Balthazar-Henri, a true Picard, had no doubt the same attitude towards wealth as the peasant of that region of France, who prayed in all humility:

"Oh, Lord, I do not ask for riches, but grant me the favor of living near rich neighbors."

The progeny of Balthazar-Henri and Blanche-Elizabeth consisted of nine children: six sons and three daughters. One of the boys died in infancy and another Eude-Claude Henri lived only to the age of nineteen. The names of the children in order of their birth were: Adélaïde-Blanche-Marie, Claude-Henri, Claude-Henri-René, Marie-Louise, Eudes-Claude-Henri, Adrienne-Emilie-Joséphine, Claude-Louis-Jean, André-Louis, and Hubert.

Claude-Henri, who signed his name as Henri, was the oldest of the boys. He was born on October 17, 1760. Most of his biographers state that he was born in Paris, but there are three documents which lead us to believe that Henri saw the light of day at the château in Berny. In one pamphlet bearing his signature, which we found while rummaging through the dusty bundles of papers at the *Archives nationales,* we came across this statement:

"The arrondissement of Péronne, département of the Somme, where I was born. . . ."[7]

It may be assumed that he had no particular interest in misinforming the reader as to the place of his birth.

The popular song writer, Béranger, prefaced a poem in praise of Saint-Simon with this comment:

"Comte Henri de Saint-Simon was born in the château of Berny, a few miles from Péronne."

Béranger, also a Picard, was at Péronne at the time Saint-Simon resided in that locality, during the troubled days of the Revolution. He was personally acquainted with the man, who was then the most prominent resident of the town, and whose ancestral name was known all over the county.

We have also consulted the death certificate of Henri de Saint-Simon, in which it is stated that he was "born in Péronne, Somme."

In the pleasant countryside of Berny, Henri spent his early childhood among trees and flowers, breathing the fragrant air of that bucolic land, soothed by the song of birds and the lowing of herds on their way to green and lush pastures.

Henri was two years old when the epoch making theories on child education were published in Rousseau's *Emile,* but it is doubtful whether the new principles were applied to the boy's upbringing. Little authentic information about his childhood is available, other than a few anecdotes repeated by one biographer after another, which may be purely legendary. No doubt Henri was self-willed and stubborn whereas his father was the severe disciplinarian characteristic of the age.

One tale represents Henri at the age of thirteen refusing to accept holy communion on the ground that it was irreverent to receive the sacrament without conviction. This attitude would be in keeping with the irreligious tendency of the day. The Voltairian spirit may have affected the mind of the 'teenager. The father, infuriated by his son's rebellion, had him confined in the prison of Saint-Lazare in Paris, as a fit punishment for his sin. Young Henri however was not cowed by high walls, bolted doors and barred windows. He commanded the guard to free him and when the latter refused, the boy threw himself on the jailer, wrenched the keys from him and escaped. He sought refuge with an aunt of less austere disposition, who brought about a reconciliation between father and son.

It was not infrequent for parents in those days to resort to imprisonment in dealing with unmanageable children. About the time Henri was locked up in jail, another youth destined to fame, was imprisoned on the isle of Ré at parental request. The boy was Honoré Gabriel, son of Victor Riqueti, marquis de Mirabeau.

Another anecdote, cited by biographers to illustrate the stubbornness of the boy, relates the incident of Henri's refusal to let a carter pass in the alley where he was playing. When the driver insisted on his right of way, the lad threw himself across the road, daring the carter to run him over.

His exceptional will power inspired one more story. One day, so we are told, young Henri was bitten by a mad dog. He took

11

a lump of red hot coal and cauterized the wound. Then intending to shoot himself if hydrophobia should develop, he calmly waited with loaded pistol by his side.

In his mature years Henri was fond of relating an incident of his childhood which he must have told with particular relish. One of his secretaries, who preferred to remain anonymous, recorded the mischievous episode as follows:

"His early education was neglected as far as schooling was concerned, and that was a general habit among people of noble birth. He often told how, when he was fourteen years old, he had run away from home, after having thrust his penknife into the lower and posterior part of the torso of an incautious tutor who had attempted to submit him to the humiliating punishment of the whip in order to stimulate his studious efforts."[8]

This boyish prank reveals the true character of our young aristocrat, the budding scion descended from Charlemagne. Not yet able to brandish the sword of the paladins, he could at least wield with skill a smaller, but well-tempered blade to protect the honor of his noble blood. Most of the Saint-Simons were notorious for their quick temper and obstinacy, as witness the life and memoirs of the duke. Michelet, describing their characteristics, qualified them as violent, choleric, and bilious.

We need not scrutinize too closely the kind of education given our future philosopher. It followed the customary procedure to which all children of noble parentage were subjected. Private tutors were employed, not because of the lack of good schools in Paris and the provinces, but for reasons of economy. Only wealthy families could afford to send their sons to college. It was well nigh impossible for the average nobleman to provide adequate schooling for his children, who as a rule, were numerous. Some examples of the cost of education at that period might explain the situation.

Monsieur de Boëry, lord of Bouillaguet, paid 700 livres a year for board and tuition for one of his sons at the Collège de Sorèze, and 600 livres for the education of his two daughters at the convent. It took almost his entire income. Another gentleman in Brittany complained that, although born of high lineage, he would have preferred having been born a simple peasant. At least in that case, he sighed:

"My children would constitute my wealth, instead of being my care and the cause of my poverty." [9]

It is evident that the education of eight children, as in the case of the Saint-Simons, would have cost a sum beyond their income. Tutoring was the economical way of giving instruction to a large brood. And of tutors there were many and sundry.

"My education," wrote Henri, "was thoroughly but badly directed. I was overwhelmed with masters without being given time to reflect upon what they taught, so that the scientific seeds which my mind received could not grow until many long years after they had been sown." [10]

Pupils were supposed to cram Greek and Roman history, literature, mathematics, a scattering of the physical and natural sciences. The boys had to master the arts essential to the making of a gentleman: horseback riding, fencing, dancing, and other accomplishments. In one letter from America, Henri thanked his father for having given him a thorough physical education, which enabled him to endure the fatigue of the Yorktown campaign.

We can judge the efficacy of the instruction given at that time by referring to some of Henri's illustrious contemporaries:

"I was supposed to study up to midday; most of the time I did nothing," wrote Chateaubriand, describing his gloomy youth at the château of Combourg.[11]

"I had masters in all kinds of subjects, for ten years I studied arithmetic, geography, history, music, drawing—and I never knew a word of all that," said Madame de Genlis.[12]

Voltaire summed up his grievances on this matter by saying that on leaving college "I knew some Latin and some silly things."[13]

In later years Henri boasted that he had been tutored by one of the most distinguished philosophers of the time:

"My early education was directed by d'Alembert, an education which had woven for me such a close-knitted net that no important fact could pass through." [14]

This statement is in direct contradiction to the complaint he made of having too many tutors and too little time to digest their superficial teaching. His complaint was well founded, but our credulity is taxed when we are asked to believe that his education had been directed by d'Alembert. D'Alembert, the encyclopedist, the foremost mathematician member of the Academy of Sciences, secretary of the French Academy, author of numerous scientific and philosophical treaties, who refused the offer of Catherine of Russia to tutor the grand duke at a remuneration of 100,000 livres, was not likely to have taken the son of Balthazar-Henri de Rouvroy de Saint-Simon for a private pupil. The chronicle of his private secretary makes no mention of d'Alembert. On the contrary Henri's education was considered inadequate by this keen observer:

"Monsieur de Saint-Simon . . . had entered military service in 1776, that is to say at the age of sixteen; now it was impossible at that age, especially in those days, for a young man to achieve any real learning, and that was the very thing he lacked in order to attain a higher degree in a scientific career."

We are inclined to accept the judgment of the anonymous secretary. We need not blame Henri's inability to spell for that failing was the fault of greater minds than his. Chateaubriand even boasted:

"I have never been able to spell," he confessed to a correspondent to whom he made excuses for dictating the letter instead of writing it in his own hand. As for other types of learning, one might ascribe to Henri the nonchalant words which Molière put in the mouth of Mascarille:

"A gentleman knows everything without the need of study."

Yet, what an opportunity this period offered to a studious mind! Great works appeared in every field of human endeavor. The last volume of the Encyclopédie was published in 1772; Buffon had just completed his *Natural History;* the writings of Montesquieu, Voltaire, and Rousseau occupied prominent places in every library. There never had been so much curiosity for learning, so much craving for enlightenment, so much eagerness for knowledge, even among women. Ladies of distinction stood in line for hours waiting to borrow Rousseau's *Nouvelle*

Héloise. Madame du Châtelet had her own physics laboratory. Madame de Tencin, d'Alembert's mother, was an eager student of astronomy.

However though deficient in knowledge and moral discipline, as he confessed, young Henri did not lack ambition. If we are to give credence to another oft repeated story, at the age of fifteen he had his valet wake him every morning with the words:

"Arise, monsieur le Comte! You have great things to do today!"

Henri, as the oldest son of noble parents, had the choice of serving either the king or the church. He chose the military career, and his father was able to purchase an officer's commission for him.

Louis XVI had recently ascended the throne. His advent had been welcomed by cries of enthusiasm, which were less a demonstration of love than a protest against the turpitude of the preceding reign. Turgot and Malesherbes, able and conscientious men, had been called to power. Their economic and political conceptions might have saved the regime had they been permitted to put them into practice.

Henri's father had applied in 1776 for a second lieutenancy for his son. Prince de Montbaray, minister of war, granted the request on January 1777, but Balthazar-Henri delayed the acceptance of the post for another year, as Henri was only sixteen. The following year the father, anxious to get rid of the unruly boy, renewed his request in the letter which we quote:

"The desire to make him more worthy to enter the King's service, and the fear of putting him too soon on his own, has prevented his father from accepting on the 15th of January 1777, a second lieutenancy which Monsieur the Prince of Montbaray had the goodness to grant him. He had the honor, yesterday, the 15th of January 1778, to present to this minister a memorandum from the colonel of the infantry regiment of Touraine, in which he requests the commission of second lieutenant in the said regiment dated January 15, 1777, for the count Henri de Saint-Simon." [15]

Thus Henri, at the age of seventeen, with the rank of second lieutenant, joined the regiment of Touraine, of which his cousin, the Marquis Claude-Anne de Saint-Simon Montbléru was colonel. The regiment was stationed at Arras until early 1779, when it left for Brest in Brittany.

Promotion followed rapidly for young men of noble birth. On June 3, 1779, Henri was appointed lieutenant, and a few months later, November 14, he was advanced to the rank of captain.

CHAPTER TWO

While Louis XVI hesitated about giving aid to the American insurgents, French volunteers crossed the ocean on their own responsibility. Count de Ségur noted in his memoirs: "The three first Frenchmen, distinguished by their rank at court, to offer the help of their swords to the Americans were the Marquis de Lafayette, the Vicomte de Noailles, and myself." [1]

Though the French government remained nominally at peace with England, it gave secret encouragement to the rebellious colonies and made little attempt to enforce neutrality. Finally, the ministers were able to persuade the king that it would be proper to enter into commercial relations with the colonies. The treaty of commerce concluded on December 17, 1777, provided for the sending of goods and arms to the new world. The British strongly resented this act and, without formally declaring war on France, seized French merchant ships and attacked French possessions in India. The break between the two countries came as a result of the seizure of the French frigate *la Belle-Poule* by the British warship *Arethusa*.

The French government no longer hesitated to espouse the cause of the American Revolutionists and to recognize their newly-formed government. On Friday, February 6, 1778, four plenipotentiaries met in Paris. They were: Benjamin Franklin, Silas Deane, and Arthur Lee, delegates of the newly constituted United States of America, and Conrad Gérard de Rayneval, minister to the King of France, Louis XVI. They drew up a treaty of alliance between France and the United States for the purpose of ensuring the liberty, sovereignty, and political independence of the American Republic. Until this independence was won and recognized, France engaged herself not to lay down her arms, nor to claim any territory on continental North America in return for her promised aid.

17

Although she had been in possession of Canada and Louisiana until 1763, France nevertheless bound herself in this treaty of alliance to abstain from acquiring territory. These terms were so unique as to be almost unbelievable. How could a country act with such liberality and disinterestedness? There must be secret clauses, thought the skeptics. Surely France did not mean to hold to her engagements. But France did abide by her treaty. There were no secret clauses and after the victorious campaign for liberation, France did not claim the least parcel of land.

What was the reason for this singular conduct? It was commonly attributed to motives of revenge against England, who had encroached upon French possessions in the Indies and in America. Among certain statesmen this attitude no doubt prevailed, but, as far as the French nation was concerned, such an interpretation is erroneous.

As a matter of fact the French people admired, imitated and adopted from their neighbors across the channel, manners, literature, philosophy, sports, and even parliamentary institutions. De Ségur wrote in his memoirs that the French people looked to England "to learn how to think," and he added that they showed great interest "in the freedom enjoyed by the majority of citizens of Great Britain." For landscaping a garden, for ruling an empire, for philosophical thinking, it was England that furnished the model. In short, Anglomania was characteristic of the period. The year of the proclamation of the independence of the United States was also the year Letourneur translated the complete works of Shakespeare into French. His success was unparalleled. Far from being hostile to England, the admiration of France verged on worship. One must seek elsewhere for the motive that led France to declare herself for the cause of the American colonies.

That motive might be found in the fact that the French approved enthusiastically the desire of a people for political liberty. The French favored the colonists, not because they wanted to shake off the yoke of British tyranny, but because they wanted to get rid of tyranny itself. De Ségur described the American delegates in Paris as "sages contemporary of Plato, or republicans of the time of Cato and Fabius. . . . This unexpected spectacle delighted us the more because it was new, and occurred at a time when literature and philosophy aroused in us the desire for reform . . . and a deep love for liberty." [2]

The writings of Montesquieu, Voltaire, Rousseau had not been read in vain. The whole French nation was deeply imbued with the idea of liberty.

In 1778 the French government despatched to the aid of the colonies a squadron under the command of Admiral comte d'Estaing, who brought with him Conrad Alexandre Gérard, first ambassador to the United States. Further help followed in such impressive strength that comte de Ségur could remark with legitimate pride:

"To the great surprise of Europe who did not believe that our navy, destroyed in the last war, could revive so promptly, one saw besides d'Estaing's fleet a naval force of 32 vessels and 15 frigates sail out of the port of Brest under the orders of comte d'Orvilliers." [3]

In 1779 comte de Grasse left Brest at the head of four men-of-war and a number of frigates escorting a convoy of men and bringing money to the United States. On the flagship *La Couronne* were Captain Henri de Saint-Simon and his cousin, the marquis de Saint-Simon, colonel of the regiment of Touraine. Two other regiments, the Agenais and the Gatinais had embarked on the ships composing the fleet.

The destination was Cap Français in San Domingo. An attempt was made to take the island of Barbados and to free one thousand French prisoners held there, but it failed of achievement. Captain Henri de Saint-Simon took part in a number of naval engagements under the command of the marquis de Bouillé. There was a good deal of jealousy between Henri and his cousin, each probably trying to impress his commander with his worth.

Generals Washington and Rochambeau called on Admiral de Grasse for coöperation in blockading the James and York rivers where Cornwallis had entrenched himself in Yorktown, Virginia. On August 31, 1781, the squadron of twenty-eight ships and six frigates landed at Cape Henry, and two days later the troops were transported from Lynnhaven Roads to Jamestown

19

Island. Captain Henri was aboard the flagship *Le Cormoran*. Many years later, he described the landing of the flagship:

"During the memorable war of which the independence of America was the result, we went by sea to Virginia to besiege the town of York. We were on board a ship named *Le Cormoran*; and we ran aground on a sandbank in the bay of Clusapeack [Chesapeake].

"For several hours the greatest disorder reigned on board the vessel. No one dared set the sails for fear of breaking up the ship, which was known to be in bad condition. Some carried an anchor forward to turn the craft in that direction; others in the stern carried out the same maneuver in the opposite direction. There was shoving with boathooks in all directions. Prodigious efforts were expanded in all sorts of ways; and since they opposed one another, they succeeded in cancelling one another almost completely.

"But at length the tide came in and got us out of the difficulty and to it we owed our rescue, which neither the captain, nor his lieutenants, nor the crew could have accomplished without its aid, or at least without the preponderance of action which it exerted upon all the efforts that were made." [4]

On September 8, 1781, the marquis de Saint-Simon announced the encampment of his troops:

"My junction with the troops commanded by the marquis de la Fayette took place to-day. We are camped together behind Williamsburgh. . . . The body of troops under my command is made up from leading regiments of the French infantry, and I have an effective force of 3,100 men. I have eight pieces of field cannon served by a detachment of the Royal Artillery Corps. They are provided with ammunition, which in truth is not considerable, but they can manage for some time without needing help of this kind.   St. Simon

Williamsburgh." [5]

By land and by sea the British were bottled up in Yorktown. From a contemporary account, the diary of James Thacher, we learn of the disposition of the troops:

"September 28, 1781—The French troops have arrived and encamped on our left. . . . . His (Lord Cornwallis) communica-

20

tion by water is entirely cut off by the French ships of war stationed at the mouth of the river, preventing both his escape and receiving succor from Sir Henry Clinton at New York. . . . The Americans form the right and the French the left wing of the combined forces, each extending to the borders of the river, by which the besiegers form a half-circle round the town. His Excellency General Washington commands in person, and is assisted by Major-General Lincoln, Baron Steuben, the Marquis de la Fayette, General Knox, etc. The French troops are commanded by the General Count Rochambeau." [6]

Captain Henri de Saint-Simon had 166 artillerymen under his command. One of these participants recorded in his journal:

"October 9, 1781. Our batteries began to fire during the night; on the morning of the 10th the firing became very brisk and continued so all day long. We have first-class artillery, and the Americans too have big guns and are very active, but they do not approach the perfection of our cannoneers, who have aroused the admiration of Washington. . . .

"In busying myself to-day about something connected with my functions, I had occasion to enter the trenches, in a place where a mortar-battery had been established which was firing upon one of the redoubts of the enemy; they replied with some howitzers which did no damage. In the trench I met M. de Saint-Simon, who commanded it, and to whom I had had occasion to write some days before a pretty strong letter; we exchanged explanations." [7]

Lord Cornwallis surrendered on October 19, 1781.

A word of explanation may throw light on the superiority of the French artillery and its preponderant role in the capture of Yorktown on October 19, 1781. This branch of warfare had been completely transformed by General Gribeauval, a talented officer who originated a new system of cannon-firing. France at the end of the eighteenth century was in advance of all other nations in the accuracy and efficacy of gunfire. The artillery at the siege of Yorktown was commanded by Colonel d'Aboville. He obtained the most withering effects from his batteries by employing for the first time massed concentration fire, a process again utilized with great advantage in the Napoleonic wars.

Lord Cornwallis admitted that he owed his defeat to d'Aboville's ability. When the Vicomte de Noailles came to settle the terms of the capitulation, the British general said it would be more appropriate that he surrender his sword to the general of artillery.

The loss of life was not great. Of the French, fifty men were killed and one hundred and twenty-three wounded. Judging from the size of the engagement one might be tempted to minimize its importance, were it not for the fact that with the capture of Yorktown the end of the American Revolutionary War was in sight. The English fleet was driven away by the French, and the struggle virtually ended.

Writing to his wife three days later, Lafayette had this to say:

"The close of this campaign is truly brilliant for the allied troops; our movements have been all remarkably well combined, and I must indeed be difficult to please, if I were not completely satisfied with the close of my Virginian campaign. . . . I count as among the happiest moments of my life the time when the division of M. de St. Simon remained united to my army, and when I alternately commanded the three field marshals with the troops under their orders." [8]

A few days after the surrender of Cornwallis, General Washington sent a letter to the marquis de Saint-Simon, in which he thanked all the officers of his division for the aid they had given. To Admiral de Grasse, Washington wrote at the end of the war:

"Your capable intervention has secured the independence and liberty of America. May I express the gratitude of the United States." [9]

Washington's words were corroborated by Tom Paine who said:

"It is to France alone that the United States of America owe that support which enabled them to shake off the unjust and tyrannical yoke of Britain." [10]

Some thirty-odd years later, Henri de Saint-Simon boasted:

"I found myself at the siege of York; and I contributed in a rather important manner to the capture of General Cornwallis and his army. So I may regard myself as one of the founders of the liberty of the United States; for it was that operation which, in determining the conditions of peace, fixed irrevocably the independence of America."

Except for the exaggeration common to war veterans, Henri de Saint-Simon had reason to be proud of his participation in that historic event.

On October 24th, five days after the victory of Yorktown, the French fleet under de Grasse sailed to its base in the West Indies, transporting the troops that had fought in Virginia. Henri had reached his twenty-first year.

The following year, February 12, 1782, under the command of the marquis de Bouillé, he took part in the capture of Brinston Hill on the island of Saint Christopher, now known as St. Kitts. While camped at Brinston Hill, Henri wrote to his father, describing the campaign in which he was engaged. This letter revealed the strained relations that existed between father and son, as a result, no doubt, of the latter's extravagant way of living. The letter deserves to be quoted at length for its historic value.

"Camp of brinston-hille (*sic*)
February 20, 1782.

". . . I can't tell you, my dear papa and friend, how anxious I am about your health and that of my mother and of all my brothers and sisters. For a year I have not received any news of you. I cannot blame it on my laziness, since for a long time I have not missed a single occasion to give you news about myself. My situation has greatly changed since the letter I wrote to you from York. The Marquis de Saint-Simon has begun treating me a little better since then. He is leaving at this moment for France on the frigate carrying the news of the success of our arms at St. Christophe. He is quite peeved at not having been granted the chief command of the French troops for the planned expedition. He claims that you neglected him, and that if you had shown the least interest in him by recommending him to the ministers, you might have spared him this disappointment he considers very great. Not everybody thinks as he does, far from it. It is generally considered that the command was

23

rightfully due to M. le marquis de Bouillé, who had already many claims to it and who keeps acquiring new ones every day by his brilliant expeditions. Consequently none of the reasons which had induced me up to now to serve under my cousin in the seventh regiment of Touraine exist any longer. On the contrary I have many reasons to break away from it, among others the uncertainty which concerns the future activities of that regiment. Caution does not permit me to describe them to you, but I believe that when you hear of them you will give me your approval. For this reason I have begged M. le marquis de Saint-Simon to ask M. de Bouillé to take me as aide-de-camp, a favor which I have been granted. He has even promised to employ me on the general staff of his army, which will have from eight to nine thousand men when his troops join those of Saint-Domaingue [Santo Domingo]. This will place me in a position to train for my profession much better than if I had remained attached to the seventh with a rank which furnishes too few occasions to distinguish oneself. We leave here the day after to-morrow for Martinique, where I do not think we shall stay long. From there we shall go to Saint-Domaingue to join 14,000 Spaniards who have been waiting for us there for several months under the orders of M. de Galves. We do not know what will be our destination from there, but we have every reason to suppose that it will be Saint-Augustin or Jamaica, perhaps both, but I do not believe that we shall go to Jamaica first because the season is already well advanced.

"I hope, my dear Papa and friend, that the better disposition I have made of my personal affairs for the last year will cause you to forget the thoughtless acts that I had committed. M. le marquis de Saint-Simon can testify to my behavior, of which he has been a witness, so that you will be inclined to give me back your friendship, which had been partly lost through my youthful errors. Nothing in the world is dearer to me, and you may be assured that I will henceforth never again neglect to conserve it and even to better it. My expenses, notwithstanding the fact that I have put them in order, may look to you very considerable, and perhaps even beyond your means, I know it perfectly. But I know also your way of thinking, and

I know that you will never begrudge the money if it can be used to the advantage of your children. This campaign will add greatly to my own, and consequently to that of all my brothers, for you would not doubt my friendship for them . . . .

"In spite of this reduction in my expenses everything is so exorbitantly dear in this country that I reckon it will cost you 10,000 francs in French money during this year merely to place me on the level of persons of the same rank with whom I am going to serve, without permitting myself any extravagance. I hope that now I shall be able to deal with you directly, because a third party, no matter who it is, serves only to chill your friendship for me, although I do my best to deserve it.

"You should have received the detailed report that I sent you about our campaign, since our departure from the Cape[11] until our arrival at Fort Royal.[12] You have seen how fatiguing it was both on land and on sea, but owing to the care that you gave to my physical education, I have held up perfectly, and I even feel better now than ever. I wish that the care you took of my moral education had succeeded as well; but *mea culpa!* I am not going to regret the time lost, but make amends to the best of my ability. I come back to my journal where I left off.

"We left Fort Royal on the third of January and we sailed for St. Christophe, where we arrived on the 11th, after having been delayed by contrary winds. We cast anchor at Basse-Terre, the capital of that island, where we disembarked at nightfall without any opposition on the part of the enemy. Our squadron was composed of thirty warships, and the land army of 6,000 men. At eleven o'clock in the evening, when all the troops had been landed on shore, we set out for the fort called by the English Brinston-Hill, a distance of three or four leagues. We did not find any obstacle to our march, the enemy not being strong enough to oppose our passage. At daybreak the circumvallation was set at half cannon range. This fort, in the most advantageous position which nature can offer, is situated on the seashore on the summit of a steep mountain which dominates the country half a league around. After spending two days at bivouac, we put up our camp sheltered from the cannons. We set up a battery of nine mortars during the night and we dug a trench to protect it from the sorties which the enemy might make. M. de Bouillé had divided his forces in two parts, one of which he took under his command, and he gave the other to M. de Saint-Simon, who had not made as much advance on his side. The *Lion Brittanique,* a merchant ship loaded with artillery had run aground, and we spent several days removing the contents. On the 16th, the batteries of M. de Saint-Simon commenced firing and those of M. de Bouillé on the 19th. After a few days we were short of munitions. The general had not counted on such a vigorous resistance. He sent for munitions to Goudelope [13] and to Sainte-Eustache. On the 24th we began the bombardment again with all our might. On the same day M. de Grace[14] who had been notified that the English squadron composed of 22 line vessels which up to then had remained at Barbade,[15] had just arrived at Antigues, set sail to meet them. On the 25th, after a slight naval battle, the enemy squadron cast anchor at about the same place as the one we had left on the 26th. M. de Grace attacked twice, but unsuccessfully in spite of his superiority in numbers. On the 28th, the English landed 1,500 men at Salinas. M. le comte de Fléchin, maestre de camp en second,[16] of the seventh of Touraine, who was at Basse-Terre with 300 grenadiers and chasseurs, went to attack them as soon as he was informed of their landing. He killed seventy-seven of their men and wounded about a hundred, but seeing that he was surrounded on all sides, he was obliged to make his retreat to the town where he had his entrenchment. Thinking that the enemy would pursue him there, M. de Bouillé came at once to his aid with 2,500 men, but the enemy had not waited for us. They had reembarked immediately after the attack. We had in this action thirty men killed and thirty-nine wounded, among them five officers. The troops were the grenadiers and chasseurs of Agenois and the chasseurs of Touraine. The general, after leaving to M. de Fléchin 800 men to oppose the disembarkment which the enemy might attempt, returned to the camp with the rest. These operations had not interrupted the bombardment. On the 30th, the munitions failed completely. But we had perfect luck, for that very day we discovered at the base of the fort a considerable depot of bombs and cannon balls which the enemy had not had time to take along. During the night we removed a great part of it, and this put us in a position to continue our firing which we had been obliged to stop completely. M. de Bouillé seeing then that the siege was being protracted, decided to make use of the big cannon in spite of the disadvantage of the terrain. On the 4th of February, M. de Grace sent us the *Caton,* a vessel of the first class which set its artillery on land, with which we built three strong batteries. On the 6th, we found eight brass cannons of 24 and six small mortars which the English had hidden in the sand. M. de Saint-Simon had them moved away. On the 10th, the batteries of cannon began to play and continued the most lively fire up to the 12th, so that the enemy, fearing an assault, capitulated. On the 13th, the garrison marched past our troops with all the honors of war. It was composed, at the time of our arrival, of 800 men of the regular forces and 200 militiamen. One hundred of their men had been killed and 200 wounded. M. de Bouillé showed on this occasion his customary generosity for which the English worshipped him. He treated them with perfect consideration; he granted general Schirlai[17] and Fraser who commanded the fort, both of them governors, the one of the colony, and the other of all the English possessions in the Antibes, the liberty to continue their services wherever they chose. We have been very fortunate in this siege. We had only 100 men killed and wounded in spite of the fact that we had been engaged for a full month in perilous and fatiguing works. On the 14th, the English squadron, having seen the white flag on the fort, weighed anchor during the night unnoticed by M. de Grace, although he had been anchored for two days no more than one league away from it. Thus ended this affair. We are now occupied reembarking our artillery and we shall depart at once to go and meet our convoy which we await with the greatest impatience. I forgot to tell you that M. de Vaudreuil had joined our squadron on the 30th of January with only two vessels. He brought letters for everybody. I believe that I am the only one in the army who did not receive any. You understand how painful this is for a son who wants above all to deserve being your friend and who is determined by his conduct to have you acknowledge him as such. In short, my dear Papa

27

and friend, if some of my thoughtless acts have caused me to lose entirely your esteem and have extinguished in your heart the paternal sentiments which I have always known to be yours, persuade at least, I beg of you, my brothers and sisters to treat me with a little less severity and to give me news of you and of our dear ill one, whose condition I fear may have grown worse. They can reproach me for laziness, but they are punishing me too severely. I haven't the time to write to them all, but I beg the Vesse[18] to give them news of me and to tell them that never will they find a brother who loves them more affectionately or tenderly. Eude[19] has now reached the age for entering the service. If I dare take the liberty to give you advice, it would be to send him to this country. I believe, judging by experience, that one year of war would form him better than ten years of peace in France. Here he would cost you much more, but you would be fully compensated by the promotion that it would secure him either now or in the future, and by the impossibility . . . of committing any of the foolish acts customary to young men who enter society.

"I have been employed in this siege in a rather uninteresting, but a very instructive way. As the detachment of artillery was not numerous enough to perform the service which was very fatiguing, I was attached to it as an auxiliary with 150 infantry gunners. I have ridden along with the lieutenants and sublieutenants of the main corps to command the batteries and do the work which was rather laborious. This placed me in a position of being in constant danger of bombs from the English during all the siege.

". . . Having been every day and almost every night under fire, either for duty's sake or by curiosity, my ears have become quite accustomed to the noise of bombs, balls and bullets which startle one a little in the beginning. I pulled through very well with only a few contusions caused by fragments of shell bursts, but which are not worth mentioning. Some men of my detachment were not so lucky, there were seven killed or wounded. But I feel, dear Papa and friend, that the pleasure of chatting with you by writing, since I cannot enjoy that of seeing you, carries me away to the point of forgetting that the frigate is about to sail. Please excuse my scribbling, at camp one is not too comfortable. I beg you, give back to a son who loves you very tenderly your esteem and your friendship and you will make him the happiest of all men. I am not asking you to take any steps toward my promotion, but I am working hard to deserve that you recommend it. . . .

Your son and friend,

Henri"

Thus ends the letter of a boy who, exposed to the hardships of war by land and sea, was thinking of home three thousand miles away. The young officer who had not heard from his family for a year, naturally yearned for news from those dear to him. When the mail arrived, he was the only one in his regiment who had not received a letter, and his disappointment can be imagined. Henri went for a solitary walk brooding over his loneliness, while his comrades opened their packets and poured over their contents. The main anxiety of the young officer seemed to have been the winning the affection, or as he put it, the friendship of his father. The principal cause of the estrangement was the heavy debts contracted by the prodigal son. Officers had to defray their own expenses, which were proportionate to their rank and their inclinations. But, after all, was it not a sign of good breeding to accumulate debts? Montesquieu defined a gentleman as "a man who has ancestors, debts and pensions." Of these three requisites, Henri lacked only the pensions.

Henri's biographers have made much of this letter to his father, or rather parts of it, for it is published here in full for the first time. What a tender heart, they claimed, what a touching affection for all the members of his family, particularly his father. There is no intention on our part to call him an unnatural or even insensitive son. Nevertheless the desire to obtain a more generous allowance from "the governor" was probably in his mind.

In a previous letter to his father, Henri complained that it was impossible for him to live on an allowance of twelve hundred francs a year, and he asked that his debts be paid off. With four other sons to provide for, Balthazar-Henri had more than his share of worries.

Of the cause for which he was fighting, of the idealism which drew so many young aristocrats to the rebellious colonies, his letters do not breathe a word. How different the letters of La Fayette, for example, who on May 30, 1777, wrote to his wife from the ship which was taking him to America:

"Defender of that liberty which I worship, myself more free than anybody in coming as a friend to offer my services to this most interesting Republic, I bring to it only my sincerity and my good will, no ambition, no interest." [20]

La Fayette was then twenty years old, had left a charming wife and a two year old daughter.

The French fleet did not always meet with success in its encounters with the British. On April 12, 1782, the important Battle of the Saints took place off the island of Santo Domingo, with De Grasse commanding the French, and Rodney, the British.

The Battle of the Saints, what a golden source of epic narration for an imaginative veteran and his worshipful admirers! Tales of terrific blows, of armed vessels in death grapple, of men wielding cutlass and boarding hatchet, of blood stained decks littered with the dying and the wounded, of ships sinking under the roar of cannon, of crews clinging to bits of wreckage, of ferocious slaughter and heroic sacrifices.

The opportunity was not wasted. A favorite legend among biographers told of Henri's participation in this famous battle aboard the flagship *Ville de Paris,* which was forced to give up after eleven and a half hours of combat. During the action, a sailor to whom Henri was giving orders, was killed by an enemy bullet, and the impact threw Henri down and made him unconscious. He was taken for dead and was about to be thrown overboard with the other corpses. One legend has it that he was actually thrown into the sea; another that he was left undisturbed on deck. On recovering semiconsciousness he was able to move his hand and give sign of life. In lifting his hand he accidently touched the brains of the man who was lying dead alongside of him. Henri reflected: "How is it that a human being, while alive, can touch his own brains?" This, one may surmise, was one of the horror stories which Henri delighted in telling the elegant ladies gracing his dinner table in the days of opulence which came later.

The battle ended with defeat for the French, De Grasse was taken prisoner and brought to London. Henri and the rest of the French survivors were imprisoned on the island of Jamaica. Of this captivity, Hubbard in his *Life and Works of Saint-Simon* has this to say:

"He did not suffer during this short period of captivity; he was freed through the intercession of a [British] navy officer to whom he had rendered significant service during the war. This marine officer, together with a captain of engineers, had sometime previously been captured while reconnoitering the military works and disposition of the French troops. According to usual war procedure they were to be shot. Saint-Simon, deeply impressed by the sangfroid of the two men before the court martial, asked to be put in charge of carrying out the sentence. He obtained a reprieve from the marquis de Saint-Simon, who had presided over the trial. This reprieve was most fortunate for the prisoner, for soon circumstances changed, and his life was spared and he recovered his freedom." [21]

Thus Henri, in return for his generous conduct, became the recipient of a similar courtesy when he fell into the hands of the enemy.

He must have left Jamaica soon after his release, for the letter addressed to his father in September of that year was written at Martinique. A large portion of this documentary piece merits to be quoted:

"Fort Saint-Pierre at Martinique,
September 16, 1782.

". . . I am once more frustrated, my dear father and friend, of the opportunity to converse with you about matters of mutual interest to us in the same spirit of frankness and confidence which I had already shown. Although I have received your letter, I am not completely reassured about your health, and I fear that, in the first moments of your convalescence, the low state in which I put your morale might do great harm to your physical condition. I believe I am telling you the truth when I say that physical health depends on taking care of the morale. Therefore, my dear

31

friend, I beg you to be affected as little as possible and to seek distraction in the numerous and agreeable society which you abandoned for the sake of your children, and to which it would be to your advantage to return the sooner the better. My sister Louise has written a charming letter to me. With an outpouring of her heart, which brought tears to my eyes, she told me of her regret for not having behaved well enough to please you. I am convinced that she has already redressed her wrongs and that she will give you a thousand times more pleasure than the grief she has caused you. Considering her great sensibility, I believe that she needs, the more so in her young years, the support of your paternal kindness in order to acquire confidence in you such as I now enjoy, a thing which makes me as happy as one can be at eighteen hundred leagues distance from the best of friends.

". . . The arrival of the convoy has kept me so busy that only very late yesterday was I able to return from Fort Royal where I went with M. de Burmel to help distribute the recruits in the various regiments. The general who is always exceedingly kind to me has just given me the order to leave at once for Dominique,[22] where I am going in my position as *aide-maréchal-général des logis* on a reconnaissance of the roads and fortifications, to have billets ready for the troops and to prepare myself by a knowledge of the island in order to serve as guide to the troops to be convoyed for its defense in case of attack. M. de Bouillé strives with an incredible activity to put all these colonies in a proper condition of defense. The island of Guadeloupe is threatened the most. I am afraid however that the English might not leave us alone. They expect at this moment ten thousand men they had withdrawn from New York and Charleston, which it is reported are being evacuated.

"The Count de Gouvernets, aide-de-camp to M. le marquis de Bouillé, who has not yet heard a single gun shot, received a letter from M. de Castrien in which this minister who is very fond of him grants him the pay of Colonel-in-second, although he is only a captain, and gives him the hope that he will be raised in rank at the first promotion. You must agree with me, my dear friend, that it is rather hard on me, who am starting on my fourth campaign and who have been wounded, not to be treated

32

as well as he. Rest assured, dear friend, that no matter how unfairly I am treated by the court, I shall nevertheless be grateful for all the trouble you have taken for my advancement.

"M. du Chatelet and the Chevalier de Luçon present you with their respects and they often tell me how kindly they had been treated by you.

"With much regret I finish and embrace you. We are setting sail. Your son and friend, Henri [23]

"May I ask you to be kind enough to ask all the rest of my family to excuse me if I do not have time to write to them." [24]

From this second letter it appears that there was a reconciliation between the young man and his father. The latter however does not seem to have exerted any influence in favor of his son, who complained that a less deserving comrade was promoted over his head. Promotion of a fellow officer without military experience in preference to him who was embarking on a fourth campaign, and who had been wounded on the field of battle, was for Henri a cruel disappointment. But in those days, advancement in the army, as well as in other professions, was due not so much to merit as to favors from above.

Most likely this was the last letter written by Henri to his father. It took weeks, often months, for the post to reach its destination and this letter was marked "received January 24, 1783." One month later, Balthazar-Henri de Saint-Simon drew his last breath, on February 23rd, at the age of 61.

His biographers claim that during his sojourn in America, Henri was more interested in political than military science. They base their statements on Saint-Simon's writings published in 1817, thirty-five years after the event. "During my sojourn in America I occupied myself much more with political science than with military tactics," he boasted. From the letters above quoted, no such conclusion can be reached. Henri, like normal boys of his age, was interested in military life, eager for promotion, inclined to live extravagantly, optimistically hoping that his father would pay his debts.

A pretentious assertion made by him twenty-five years after the American campaign became a source for another legend. In 1808 he wrote:

"I entered the army in 1777. I left for America in 1779; there I served under the orders of M. de Bouillé and of Washington. When peace was declared, I presented to the viceroy of Mexico a plan the object of which was to establish between the two oceans a communication which would be made possible by rendering navigable the river *in partido,* one mouth of which flows into our ocean and the other flows into the southern sea. My project having been coldly received, I abandoned it." [25]

Saint-Simon received extravagant praise from his admirers for having proposed as early as 1783 a project which foreshadowed the Panama Canal. How or where he communicated with the viceroy of Mexico, he did not say. There was no mention of the matter in the communications to his father, and if we are to judge from the contents of his letters, Henri was preoccupied chiefly with military affairs. But it is quite possible that, during the long and inactive months in the Antilles, he heard his fellow officers or local acquaintances discuss the feasibility of an interoceanic canal. It was an old project that went back to the conqueror of Mexico, Hernando Cortez, to whom belongs the honor of first proposing the construction of this waterway. Interest in an interoceanic route was revived from time to time in Europe as well as in America.

One recent biographer has Henri visit Louisiana, later Mexico. [26] We find no evidence of such a visit nor any record that Henri at that time was at all interested in a canal that would join the two oceans. The river to which Saint-Simon alluded by the incredible name of *in partido* might refer to a certain water course which was mentioned as being navigable in part for the purpose of a canal. Twenty-five years later, Saint-Simon did concern himself with the planning of a canal to join the two oceans. In 1808 he addressed to the Bureau of Longitudes, a body of renowned scientists whom he was anxious to impress with his scientific qualifications, a memorandum in which he described the possibility of such an enterprise. Saint-Simon was then interpreting public opinion which favored the building of such a canal to counteract the blockade of Europe by the Napoleonic wars.

When the Treaty of Peace was signed in Paris by the delegates of the United States and Britain on September 3, 1783, the American War for Independence was won, and Henri was free to return to his native land. With his regiment he sailed for France in the fall of that year. In a succinct outline of his life, he wrote at one time:

"I entered the service in 1778; in 1779 I was made a captain of cavalry. I preferred the infantry in order to be able to go to America. There I served five years under the orders of Washington and de Bouillé, and for three years I was aide-major-général to the latter."[27]

The sojourn of Henri in America had lasted from 1779 until 1783, of which only two months had been spent on the continent, while taking part in the siege of Yorktown. These were the most impressionable years in the life of the young man. Nourished, at least superficially, with the progressive ideas of the French philosophers, he could not help being influenced by his experience in the new world. It is not likely, however, that the ideas and concepts which later in life he attributed to this influence were conceived at this time, in spite of his claims to the contrary.

As Professor Larrabbee has pointed out in his well documented article *Henri de Saint-Simon at Yorktown,* it would be presumptuous to suppose that from his brief stay on the American continent, Saint-Simon had acquired from personal observation a detailed knowledge of the life and customs of the people in the colonies. When he wrote his observations on the United States in 1817, under the title of *Lettres à un Américain,* he was fifty-seven years old. In 1824 he wrote *Notes sur les Etats-Unis.* Thus the *Lettres à un Américain* appeared thirty-four years, and the *Notes sur les Etats-Unis* forty-one years after his return from America. What he said on those two occasions could not be ascribed by any stretch of the imagination to the experiences and observations of a lad of twenty. In 1817 his mind was set on founding a society on an industrial basis, and he wanted to impress his readers with the fact that all his life he had been devoted to social studies. Therefore he posed as an expert on American Society.

It was pardonable for an old veteran of the American Revolutionary War to exaggerate his part in the capture of Cornwallis. He who had lived through five campaigns and seen lively

35

action on land and sea had the right to recall with not a little pride that "so much had been done by so few." We need not begrudge Saint-Simon the claim of being one of the founders of American liberty, since he had fought so valiantly at Yorktown. But it is not necessary to share the hyperbolic laudation of some devotees in reference to Saint-Simon's American campaign. As an illustration of the absurd heights to which blind admiration may rise, we give here a sample of such rhapsody:

"The first American was a Frenchman. His name was Saint-Simon.

"He fought through five campaigns of the Revolutionary War, and was present when Lord Cornwallis surrendered at Yorktown.

"Lafayette and he were comrades.

"His bravery on the field was so conspicuous that he received decorations from both the American and the French governments.

"Yet when the war ended he was but twenty-one, three years younger than Lafayette.

"He was the first American because he was the only one among those who fought for the Republic who understood what it meant.

"His mind was the only one that comprehended the idea of America.

"George Washington was for colonial rights.

"Lafayette fought for a political Republic.

"Saint-Simon fought for a political and industrial Democracy." [23]

CHAPTER III

"On my return to France," wrote Henri in his autobiography, "I was a colonel. . . . I obtained the command of a regiment. I was not yet twenty-three years old."

It was the marquis de Chastellux, inspector of the armies, who had recommended him as "a good officer, of much zeal and intelligence." He was made *maestre de camp en second* on January 1, 1784, and received a pension of 1,500 livres.

Henri de Saint-Simon was invited to become a member of the French branch of the Society of Cincinnati, and on September 3, 1784, he joined that distinguished group. The society was founded May 13, 1783. George Washington was elected its president and held that office during his lifetime. The purpose of the society was to maintain friendship, to give mutual aid, and to perpetuate the memory of the Revolution among the officers who had taken part in it. The insignia, given to each member, was a golden eagle holding a medallion on which was depicted the scene of Roman senators offering a sword to Cincinnatus. It had been designed by Major Pierre-Charles L'Enfant, the noted French architect who made the plan for the city of Washington.

Chapters of the Society of Cincinnati were founded in the original thirteen states and in France. The French group held its first meeting January 7, 1784, at the home of the Count de Rochambeau, 40 rue du Cherche-Midi. The building still stands and on each side of its monumental door is a plaque commemorating the event. One bears the inscription:

"Jean Baptiste Donatien de Vimeur, Comte de Rochambeau, marshal of France 1725-1807, lived in this residence when he received the command of the army sent by King Louis XVI to America, 1780, to aid the United States in gaining their independence."

37

On the other plaque are engraved the words:

"The French section of the Society of Cincinnati was founded in this residence January 7-16, 1784, in memory of the War for American Independence."

The following account is given by Edgar Erskine Hume:

"The Society of the Cincinnati was immediately popular in France. . . . It was decided that French officers of the grade of Colonel or higher would be eligible. . . .

"The French members included . . . Marshal of France the Count de Rochambeau, Commander of the French Auxiliary Army in America; Admiral the Count de Grasse, naval commander without whom there could have been no victory at Yorktown; Lieutenant-General the Count d'Estaing, Commander of the French Cooperating Army in America, the first President of the French Cincinnati; . . . General the Count d'Aboville, commandant of artillery in the French Expeditionary Force; . . . Prince Victor de Broglie, Deputy of Alsace to the States General . . . whose descendant and representative, the Duke de Broglie is now President of La Société des Cincinnati de France; . . . Berthier, future Prince de Wagram and one of Napoleon's generals; the Marquis de Chastellux, one of the celebrated philosophers of the eighteenth century and an 'Immortal' of the French Academy; . . . the Count de Custine, General in Chief during the French Revolution; . . . the Count de Ségur; . . . the Marquis and the Count de Saint-Simon; . . . the Marquis de Bouillé, Governor of the Antilles; the Count de Vioménil, Marshal of France under the Restoration; and many more."

The only president of the French branch of the Society of the Cincinnati prior to its dispersion during the Terror was Comte d'Estaing. Although the National Assembly had exempted the Society from the decree of June 19, 1790, which suppressed all titles of nobility, yet membership in the Society could rouse suspicion. For instance, Desmoulins in attacking Lafayette reproached the latter for being a member of the Society of Cincinnati. During the Restoration, membership again became a matter of pride, but the activities of the group languished until 1925 when the *Société des Cincinnati* was fully restored as the fourteenth branch, those of the original thirteen states forming the other branches. Maurice de Broglie was elected president of the French group, which now numbers over one hundred and fifty members, and he is still its distinguished president. De Broglie is a well known physicist and a member of the French Academy.[1]

On Henri's return to France, according to one biographer, he was named commandant of the town of Metz, and during his stay attended courses of instruction given by the celebrated mathematician, Gaspard Monge. We can find no data to support that statement. Monge had left Metz for Paris in 1783 and therefore could not have given lectures during the years of 1784 and 1785. Besides, Henri at that time was more interested in a military career than in improving his education. He even confessed that it bored him to drill during the summer and to act as courtier during the winter. What he wanted was action and opportunities to distinguish himself. He thought such a chance presented itself in Holland:

"A favorable occasion was offered. . . . I took advantage of it at once. A great political change had taken place in Holland. The duke de la Vauguyon, French ambassador in Holland, had triumphed over the English party there, and M. de Verrac, his successor, had convinced the government of Holland to unite its forces with those of France in order to oust the English from India. M. de Bouillé was to have been put in command of that expedition. I was to be given an honorable post in it, and I went to Holland to follow the development of this affair, which failed through the blundering of M. de Vergennes."[2]

What a prospect for a young officer! He welcomed the opportunity to try his luck again against the English who, more than once, had handled roughly the French fleet in the waters of the West Indies. To win back for France the vast empire of India, which great men like Dupleix and La Bourdonnais had once built for their king and country, that was indeed a prospect worthy of a descendant of Charlemagne.

Vergennes, minister of foreign affairs under Louis XVI, had formed the Franco-Spanish-Dutch alliance with the purpose of ending British naval supremacy. But the participation of France in the War for American Independence had been ruinous to the treasury. The government was making desperate efforts to extricate itself from its financial embarrassment. To undertake an expedition against the British at that critical moment would have been folly and an invitation to disaster. Saint-Simon returned to France in 1786, discomfited and bitterly disappointed.

An anecdote often quoted relates to this period. One day while driving to Versailles in his carriage and dressed in formal attire, he met a carter whose overloaded vehicle had overturned in the muddy road. Passers-by made no attempt to help, but Saint-Simon without an instant's hesitation got out of the carriage and helped push the cart out of the ruts. His clothes were damaged, but Henri paid little attention to that. Interested in the conversation of the carter, he joined him for a drink at a nearby inn. He sent his carriage back to Paris. Removing his soiled garments and donning a peasant's blouse, he accompanied the carter as far as Orléans, a journey long enough to afford the two companions ample time for discourse. The story may be authentic, although we are inclined to suspect that it was fitted to the conception of Saint-Simon as he appeared to his admirers in later years.

Henri was ambitious and sought means whereby he could gain further military promotions and pensions. In times of peace, advancement was slow, and vegetating in a garrison was not worthy of a valiant paladin, whose main purpose in life was to achieve fame and glory. Rumor had reached Henri that the Spanish government was considering the project of a canal to extend from Madrid to the sea. He took leave of his regiment and left for Spain in 1787. Arriving in Madrid, he consulted Comte de Cabarrus, the French financier, director of the bank of Saint-Charles. Saint-Simon and Cabarrus formulated a plan for the building of the canal which they submitted to the Spanish government. Saint-Simon's account of this matter is given here:

"Having returned to France in 1786, it was not long before I was bored with the inaction in which I again found myself. I left for Spain in 1787. The Spanish government had undertaken to build a canal designed to link Madrid with the sea; this undertaking was languishing because the government lacked workers and funds. I consulted with M. le comte de Cabarrus, now minister of finance, and we presented to the government the following plan: M. le comte François de Cabarrus proposed in the name of the bank of Saint-Charles, of which he was director, to furnish the government the necessary funds for the construction of the canal, if the bank were given the right to collect toll rates. I proposed to raise a legion of 6,000 foreigners, of whom 2,000 would always remain in garrison, while the other 4,000 would work on the canal. The clothing and hospital expenses only would be charged to the government. . . . With an extremely moderate sum the king of Spain could thus have built the most beautiful and most useful canal in Europe; he could have increased his army by 6,000 men, and enlarged his estate with a class of people who would necessarily have become laborious and industrious. The French Revolution came and prevented the execution of the project."[3]

It was indeed a practical, albeit grandiose scheme, that would have done honor to a scion of the Frankish King, whose name still echoed within the walls of Saragossa and the mountain gorge of Ronceval. But once more fate intervened and his dreams were shattered.

One may wonder how Saint-Simon, with meager resources, managed to make a living commensurate with his social position. According to one account, he promoted a stagecoach business somewhere in Andalusia, a venture that may or may not have been profitable. But nowhere can one find confirmation of that report. An aristocrat of high rank, he did not lack ways of solving his financial troubles, the easiest of which was to borrow money.

During his stay in Madrid, Saint-Simon made the acquaintance of Sigismond Ehrenreich, count de Redern, who was then serving as diplomatic representative of Saxony. Both were young, of an active turn of mind, eager for intellectual not less than social companionship in a foreign land. Saint-Simon was then twenty-eight and Redern thirty-three years old. They became friends and spent much time together. Both were fond of good cheer and high living. But the French officer could ill afford luxuries, except by borrowing. Count de Redern lent him a sum

41

of 28,000 francs. As a matter of fact, it was not a loan, for Henri had no intention of repaying it, nor did Redern expect to be reimbursed.

The meeting with Redern was one of the most consequential events in the life of Saint-Simon. Apparently they had separated for good when the Saxon diplomat was appointed to a post in London and the French officer returned to France to find the Revolution in full sway. However fate was to bring them together again and link their lives in strange ways.

When Saint-Simon left for Madrid about two years later, little did he dream of the changes he was to find on his return to France. Neither did any one else at that time. On the fateful day of July 14, 1789, Louis XVI wrote a single word in his diary: "Nothing." Yet great events were shaping on the day of the fall of the Bastille, events of such magnitude that their meaning could not be grasped by the limited outlook of the king, no more than by the reformers themselves. The most extreme among these did not expect a radical change of regime, least of all a revolution.

The wealth of the country had shifted from the nobility to the bourgeoisie. This class composed of landowners, financiers, entrepreneurs, physicians, lawyers, merchants, manufacturers, was in general intelligent, well educated, and progressive. Brought up on the writings of Montesquieu, Voltaire, and Rousseau, imbued with the liberal spirit of the Encyclopedists, the bourgeois aimed at protecting their interests against the arbitrary actions of the government. The revolution was their work, but not their wish.

In spite of difficulties, optimism prevailed and belief in progress was a common dogma. Such a cheery attitude was moreover well founded. By the end of the eighteenth century, France was the wealthiest and the most densely populated country in Europe. By making good use of her abundant water power she became foremost in industry. It was only after Watt's steam engine made possible the utilization of coal of which England had plenty, that the latter country leaped ahead of France. The rich, enlightened French bourgeois had no desire to bring chaos and destruction to the order of things. What they particularly wanted was that they should not alone bear the whole burden of taxation.

The participation of France in the American War for Independence had emptied the royal treasury and it could not be refilled by any magic formula or succession of ministers. Faced with a difficult situation, the king summoned the Estates-General on May 1, 1789, and the conflict between the representatives of the privileged classes and those of the third estate began. Some of the nobility were liberal enough to join with the people's party. For example, the vicomte de Noailles, one of the deputies representing the nobility, proposed during the famous night of August 4th equal partition of taxes, abolition of feudal rights, and suppression of serfdom. Another aristocratic delegate, the duc de Montmorency, renounced his privileges on that occasion. However most of the representatives of the clergy and nobility refused to accede to the demands of the third estate, and they had the support of the king. The will of the people being stronger than the obstinacy of the reactionaries, the third estate won control of the government.

What attitude would Henri de Saint-Simon assume while events were taking such rapid and unexpected turns? He was colonel in the French army. Would he desert with the majority of the officers who left their country to join the ranks of the enemy? He might follow the examples of his commanders in the American expedition. The marquis de Bouillé prepared the flight of Louis XVI and fled to England. Henri's cousin, the marquis de Saint-Simon, crossed the frontier into Spain. The marquis de Lafayette plotted the restoration of the king and fled to Austria. Henri's three brothers, knights of Malta, sought refuge on that Mediterranean island, the seat of the order.

Henri de Saint-Simon remained in France. He who dreamt of high deeds in the pursuit of fame, did he await a chance to play a leading role in the political drama? He who claimed descent from the great emperor of the Occident, would he give up his birthright for the sake of egalitarian principles?

We have no means of knowing Saint-Simon's sentiments at the outbreak of the Revolution. His continued interest in a military career is attested to by the fact that in May 1790 he

43

applied for the cross of Saint-Louis. In this request he stated that he had taken part in the American campaigns of 1779, 1780, 1781, 1782, and 1783; that he had participated in nine combats at sea, and had been wounded twice. The distinction of Chevalier of Saint-Louis was conferred upon him on June 24, 1790. This was an order created in 1693 by Louis XIV, and its insignia was awarded to army and navy officers for valor and distinguished service.

Several years after the events, Saint-Simon defined his political attitude:

"The French Revolution had begun when I returned to France. I did not want to get involved in it because, on the one hand, I was convinced that the ancient regime could not be prolonged, and, on the other hand, I was opposed to destruction, and one could plunge into a political career only by attaching oneself to the party of the court which wished to destroy national representation, or to the revolutionary party which wanted to destroy royal power."[4]

The neutral position which Henri claimed to have taken in the revolutionary movement might have been true as far as his sentiments were concerned. His actions however do not fully accord with his own statement. He left turbulent Paris and betook himself to his country estate of Falvy in Picardy. The family owned considerable properties in that region, and Comte Henri de Saint-Simon became one of the leading citizens of that community. On February 7, 1790, invited to preside at the local council, he addressed the members in these terms:

"I am greatly flattered, gentlemen, to have been given the honor of presiding over you. The pleasure I feel is only disturbed by one thing. I fear that in choosing me you intended to show deference to your lord, and that your vote was not determined by my personal qualifications. There are no more lords, gentlemen, here we are all equal. To dispel the error that with the title of count I might have superior rights to yours, I hereby renounce for ever the title of count which I regard as inferior to that of citizen. To confirm my renunciation, I request that it be inserted in the minutes of the assembly."[5]

Saint-Simon, now a plain citizen, was offered the office of

mayor of Falvy by its city council. This honor he refused as he wished to be free to give his attention to activities of a different nature. Before he left, he helped to compose a letter addressed to the National Constituent Assembly in Paris:

"With great admiration for each article of the Constitution, filled with pride at the thought that our will has created the greatest code of justice and reason, imbued with the deepest respect for the National Constituent Assembly, . . . the electors of the canton of Marchélepot[6] have unanimously decided to devote the first moments of their political life to congratulate the Assembly on the lofty use which it is making of its supreme power. . . .

"We have the greatest contempt for those worldly sanctimonious people who call on God to help them retain their riches, pretending to fear for religion at the moment when twenty-five million men remind the world by their example that the Eternal God has created them all in his image without distinction, and they cease at last to insult His Almighty Majesty with the impious distinctions of birth and they declare that all citizens are equally admissible for all functions, posts and public offices, according to their capacity, and without other distinctions than those of their faculties and talents. . . . Now that justice established on a firm basis no longer fears the efforts of a few adversaries, will not our august legislators realize that the happy moment has at last arrived when they can erase even the least traces of the *ancien régime?*"[7]

Saint-Simon made his home in the district of Péronne until November 1793, with frequent visits to Paris and other parts of the country. Péronne, the capital of Picardy, was the center for the purchase of national lands in that region. The impecunious Henri discovered here a new source of wealth, and a quick way to make a fortune.

The National Constituent Assembly decreed on November 2, 1789, the confiscation of properties belonging to the clergy, which comprised nearly one-fifth of the territory of France. Later the domains of the crown as well as the estates of the *émigrés* were also expropriated. The purpose of the government was twofold. Land values were to be used as collateral for the issue of assignats. Land ownership was to be more widely distributed by the breaking up of large estates. Nationalized properties were being put up for sale in 1791. Every inducement was given to purchasers by permitting them to make small down payments. These ranged from twelve to thirty percent of the total price, the balance to be paid off in twelve or more installments at five percent interest.

Saint-Simon decided to engage in the purchase and sale of national lands, but, as usual, he was without funds. He went to Paris and approached several financiers, including the celebrated chemist Lavoisier. But they all declined. The historian Michelet was of the opinion that Lavoisier was afraid of compromising himself in favor of the Revolution, for the buying of national lands meant a tacit acceptance of the reforms promulgated by the National Assembly. Had Lavoisier joined Saint-Simon in his scheme, he might have escaped the fate of twenty-seven other farmers-generals and saved his neck from the guillotine.

Just as Saint-Simon was wondering where to turn to get the necessary funds, he met by chance his friend Redern whom he had not seen since he left Spain. Redern was in the French capital on a vacation from his post of ambassador of Prussia in London. Henri exposed his plans to his former companion who approved them and was willing to advance the necessary funds. Before he returned to London in January, 1791, he left with his banker, M. Perrégaux, assets valued at 500,000 francs at the disposal of Saint-Simon. The latter was to receive 12,000 francs a year salary for managing the enterprise and retain a share of the profits.

The financing of his project being assured, Henri began at once purchasing parcels of land. His procedure was as follows: down payment of twelve percent of the cost, then a portion of the newly acquired property was sold. As he explained: "the resale of a small portion was sufficient to pay off the property which was acquired by auction."

The confiscated properties had been sold by the central government to the municipalities in which the lands were located. The municipal officers in turn resold in smaller portions in order to redistribute the property among a larger number of people. Public auctions were held and bids entertained. Saint-Simon, careful to keep his name in the background, used several agents to do the bidding for him, often in the name of a fictitious person.

There was some dissatisfaction on the part of the government officials as to the way the national lands were being sold in the district of Péronne. The complaint was made that "the properties had not been divided as much as the authorities had wished and the country people with restricted means were prevented from bidding at the auctions."[8] Saint-Simon's methods of doing business aroused suspicion. He made frequent use of a device called a counterdeed, a secret and private agreement with provisions which differed materially from the publicly recorded deed. The Committee of Public Safety sent a letter to the local authorities on June 23, 1793, requesting them to place Saint-Simon under surveillance. The administrative officer replied that there was no cause to suspect him.

Not long after, suspicion was again directed against Saint-Simon. An item in the archives of Péronne at Amiens reads:

"Cabour . . . placed on the desk a letter from citizen St.-Simon, undated, addressed to cit. Torchon, formerly manager of the stagecoach service at Marchélepot; it deals with various political matters and the commissary believes it contains somewhat intemperate expressions in reference to the activities of the National Assembly previous to the war, and a scheme for handling of assignats. The rest of the papers consists of the correspondence of St.-Simon and contains various suggestions on the purchase and resale of national properties, on the greatest profit to be derived from goods bought at a low price and many other items in which are interested the aforesaid St.-Simon, Coutte, public notary at Péronne, and count de Redern, a Prussian. The board of directors having ascertained that Cabour's mission is ended . . . decrees that there is no ground for indicting St-Simon, considering that 'a man who had held erroneous ideas two and a half years ago may not be a bad citizen, especially since he has given evidence afterwards of a non-equivocal attachment to the Revolution and republican principles, that no citizen can be required to have always kept an unwavering attitude toward the Republic, it being sufficient that he recognizes its merits and practices its virtues.'"[9]

As a patriot and former colonel, Saint-Simon's zeal in defending the Republic was not particularly fervid if we are to judge by his negligence in fulfilling his duties in the National Guard. This military force was organized after the declaration of war on April 20, 1792, against Prussia and Austria who were threatening to invade France. A state of danger was proclaimed and 20,000 volunteers were needed to reinforce the regular army. Saint-Simon joined the National Guard of Péronne with the rank of colonel. On July 14, 1793, a day of special ceremonies in commemoration of the fall of the Bastille, colonel Saint-Simon was designated to take command of the guard, an honor granted to him since he was the highest ranking officer and a prominent citizen. But Saint-Simon did not show up at his post before one o'clock and then disappeared soon after. He gave as excuse that he had taken a cathartic and felt indisposed. But the excuse was not accepted and he had to appear before the local tribunal. The police record reads as follows:

"The tribunal, considering that citizen Saint-Simon did not produce a medical certificate proving his indisposition, condemns him to pay 30 *sol* for his substitute and 30 *sol* for the benefit of the battalion."[10]

The urge to attain military glory promptly vanished as soon as the prospect of riches loomed before his eyes. He now directed his ambition to reaping quick profits, seizing every opportunity that might come his way. In the summer of 1792 Saint-Simon attempted to corner the local coal supply. Cart atfer cart filled with coal unloaded in front of his house on the 21st of August. The sight attracted the attention of the residents and the public solicitor was notified. In the police records we find this notation:

"Citizen Saint-Simon cannot use the entire quantity for his own consumption and there is reason to believe that he intends to corner this indispensable commodity. The tribunal acceded to the solicitor's demand and the coal was sold on the public market."[11]

Saint-Simon realized that he must make some demonstration of patriotism if he were to retain the confidence of his neighbors.

48

Since the beginning of the Revolution it had become the custom to change one's name, particularly when it happened to be of aristocratic origin. The custom was confirmed later by a decree of the Republic which permitted citizens to take a name of their choice by conforming to the formalities prescribed by law. The duke d'Orléans, the king's brother, set the example by choosing the name of citizen Egalité.

On September 20, 1793, Saint-Simon presented himself before the City Council of Péronne, with the request that he be granted permission to change his name to a new one. The following is a record of the proceeding:

"City Council of the Commune of Péronne

meeting on Friday 20 September 1793.

"Citizen Claude Henri Saint-Simon, ex-noble, residing in this town, comes before the Council declaring he wishes to purify by a republican baptism the stain of his original sin. He asks to abrogate a name which reminds him of an inequality which reason had proscribed long before our constitution had condemned it. He requests the Council to give him a new name. The Council acquiesces to this demand, and he announces that he chooses the name of Claude Henri Bonhomme. The Council, after hearing citizen Sauvage acting as public attorney, decides that the former Saint-Simon will henceforward be called citizen Bonhomme and that he will be listed under that name on the official register of the Commune.

"Citizen Bonhomme informs the Council that, if by his birth he had lost rather than acquired the rights of citizenship, he has redeemed them by one of those acts which the Constitution regards as worthy of those precious rights; he states that for about two years he has been taking care of an old woman at Cambrai, the aunt of a young patriot by the name of Legras who had been providing for her needs until he was killed by the aristocrats as the result of an affray they had instigated in the theatre; he states also that, wishing to take advantage of the rights which the Constitution grants for the adoption of a father or a son, he intends to adopt an old man and begs the Council to designate the aged citizen of whom he will be happy to take care.

49

"The Council accepts the propositions of the aforesaid Bonhomme and designates citizens Lange, Dinaud and Lemaire, asking him to choose one of the three for adoption. He will inform the Council within three days of his decision."[12]

The adoption of dependents was considered by the Republic a highly commendable civic virtue.

By adopting the name of Bonhomme, Claude-Henri de Rouvroy, comte de Saint-Simon, descendant of Charlemagne, could not have chosen a more lowly appellation. During all the centuries of feudal serfdom the French peasant had been referred to as Jacques Bonhomme.

Henri not only divested himself of his name, but a few days after his republican baptism, on the 26th of September, he also gave up all the insignia of his military career: officers' commissions, certificates of membership in the Society of the Cincinnati and that of Chevalier of Saint-Louis, together with all decorations. The City Council ordered the papers to be burned and the crosses and medals deposited with the recorder.

The biographer, Maxime Leroy, stated that Saint-Simon changed his name on September 20, 1790. This date is obviously erroneous. At that time, being still free from suspicion, he did not need to take such a step. It was three years later, when his shady speculations began to make his stay in Péronne dangerous, that Saint-Simon resorted to a theatrical demonstration of patriotism, and took the lowly name of Bonhomme. In the archives of Péronne the incident is recorded on the register of the commune for the year 1793.

At the moment he forsook his aristocratic origin, when he gave up the honors bestowed upon him for services in the armies of the king and for participation in the War for American Independence, Saint-Simon was fully aware of the fact that France was in mortal danger. The powerful nations of Europe had allied themselves against the nascent Republic, and the enemy had already crossed the frontiers. Every Frenchman, rich or poor, with the least trace of patriotism in his blood, had volunteered. Barefooted and ragged, in nondescript uniforms, they marched by the thousands, singing the Marseillaise, determined to win or to die.

In these critical and momentous days, Henri de Saint-Simon, colonel of the National Guard of Péronne, who dreamt of rivalling the exploits of Charlemagne, devoted himself to no more glorious task than speculating on national properties and making enormous profits by means not altogether commendable.

Three days before he assumed the name of Bonhomme, Péronne learned that the foreign armies were approaching Cambrai, in the adjoining department. The inhabitants of the threatened towns and villages were already crowding the highways, fleeing before the invaders. On the 18th of September, the municipal council of Péronne addressed a letter to the Convention confirming the patriotism of the residents of their district:

"The citizens of our communes, following the examples of their neighbors, have risen *en masse* to the defense. A whole legion, composed of heads of families and farmers have gone forth to meet the slaves of Austria."[13]

To the dangers from outside were added internal dissensions. Provence and Vendée rose in arms against the Republic. The English landed at Toulon. The Girondins were arrested. The Committee of Public Safety ruled supreme and the Reign of Terror was inaugurated. The promulgation of the *loi des suspects* made possible the issuing of warrants for the arrest of persons accused or suspected. Delegates of the Committee of Public Safety were sent to the provinces to see that the local officials perform their duties.

Notwithstanding the insistence with which biographers dwell on the sincerity of Henri's conversion to republican ideals, the fact remains that he was looked upon with suspicion by the citizens of Péronne. When the deputy of the revolutionary government, André Dumond, arrived in that town on October 8, 1793, he called a meeting of its citizens for the purpose of drawing up a list of suspects. Here is the record of that meeting:

"The citizens assembled in the said church listen with liveliest enthusiasm to the republican speech of deputy Dumond, frequently interrupted by applause. He tells them he cannot stay longer with them, that he is going to Amiens, and before his departure he is glad to see the fire of patriotism burning again at Péronne in the hearts of the citizens worthy of liberty. He

51

invited the assembled citizens to proceed with severity, albeit with justice, and to take a purifying poll of all the inhabitants of the commune.

"He left amidst applause and evident marks of devotion on the part of the assembly for the unity and indivisibility of the Republic."

An expurgatory vote was taken of all the citizens of the commune. From the minutes of the poll we learn that the following persons were to be referred to the Committee of Surveillance:

"1. Claude Henri Bonhomme, former noble.
2. Armand Chopart. . . .
3. Mattias Furcy Pillot, age 68.
4. Pierre François Devaux, age 67.
5. Jean-Louis Moine, age 23.
6. Charles Beaufort, official solicitor of the District.
7. Pierre-Marie Froment, junior, age 18, for attempt to evade the last levy.
8. All the clerks employed in the supply and administration of the armies, with the exception of citizen Furcy Degachagny, a native of this town, warehouse-keeper of military supplies, who had been admitted among the republican citizens of this commune."[14]

At the very head of the list was Henri's name. All his attempts to get into the good graces of the public had failed. He left for Paris hoping to escape attention.

On November 4th the papers of Mr. Torchon were placed under seal. He was accused of having business relations with Mr. Hulot, agent of Redern, who had bought considerable parcels of national properties. Part of these properties had been resold secretly in order to avoid sequestration. However the results of the seizure were "negative," that is, there seemed to be no reason for indictment.

In spite of the attempts of local officials to exonerate Saint-Simon, an order for his arrest was issued, and on November 19, 1793, he was placed in the prison of Sainte-Pélagie. The official record of his arrest was found among the documents of the National Archives by Albert Mathiez who published it in the *"An-*

nales Historiques de la Révolution Française," from which we have translated the following:

"The case of Saint-Simon Bonhomme
Committee of Revolutionary Surveillance
The 29 brumaire, year II[15] of the Republic,
one and indivisible.

"This day, at six o'clock in the morning, citizens Boyer and Semé appeared with an order from the joint committee of Public Safety and General Security . . . requesting a member of our Committee to go with them and arrest citizen Simon. Citizen Desfieux, a member of our Committee, came at once with a retinue of armed men. We went to rue de La Loy to the furnished house run by citizen Armand. We summoned him to show us the apartment of citizen Simon. He answered, pointing to his register as proof, that citizen Saint-Simon, now Bonhomme, had left twelve days ago for Péronne. According to information given by persons who might know citizen Bonhomme, we have discovered that he had been in town for two days, that he lived on rue de La Loy, number 55. We went there. We did not find the said Bonhomme, we affixed seals on the doors of the apartment on the third floor and posted a sentry. We made further visits to several citizens who had been designated to us as acquainted with the said Bonhomme. After due search, not having found him, we returned at noon to the Committee to draw up an official report. Citizen Bonhomme entered alone and said: 'I learned that you were looking for me. I come to the Committee to learn what is desired of me. Here I am.' We read to him the order of his arrest, accompanied him to his lodgings and searched his papers. We found many records of purchases and sales of national properties and of several *procurations* (sales by proxy), which are kept under seal together with other documents. We found in a small portfolio diverse papers which we placed in an envelope to be sent to the Committee of General Security, and citizen Bonhomme was handed over to citizens Boyer and Semé to be led to Sainte-Pélagie prison according to orders." [16]

What were the reasons for his arrest? Because he had been born an aristocrat? Because he was the business associate of a

Prussian? Years later he attributed his arrest and imprisonment to the fact that he was working for Redern:

"I am going to show that your (Redern's) association was very harmful to me. Since you were ambassador of Prussia to England at the time of my most important business operations, my connection with you appeared suspicious; it cost me eleven months of detention and solitary confinement; it came very near sending me to death."[17]

But this is not what he admitted in his letter to the Committee of Public Safety:

"I believe that I was arrested instead of another, for the name Simon appearing in the order of arrest by the Committee was not exactly the one I bore before calling myself Bonhomme, and the description of 'Simon living on his revenues' which is in the police order does not refer to me either."[18]

In his protests to government officials, Henri asserted that his main activity since the beginning of the Revolution had been the acquisition and administration of national lands for Redern, whom he had influenced to transfer his fortune and home to France. These transactions were advantageous to the Republic since it prevented capital from leaving the country, and also caused a foreign investor to contribute to the good of the national treasury.

Some biographers believed that Henri might have been a victim of the *Conspiration de l'Etranger* (Conspiracy of Foreigners). Two of his friends were imprisoned at the same time, Proli, a Belgian banker, and the marquis de Champgrand, whose daughter Henri married a few years later. These two men belonged to a group who were loudest in their protestations of loyalty to the Revolution, but were suspected of doing so in order to cover their financial manipulations, some of them fraudulent. They were aptly termed *patriotes d'industrie,* that is to say "sharpers." Perhaps Henri shared the suspicions cast on men who were interested in acquiring wealth under cover of patriotism. He might have been arrested partly because he was associated with "industrial patriots" and partly because his partner was a foreigner.

Michelet offered another reason for Henri's imprisonment. The churches of Paris had been ordered closed in November 1793, and put up for sale. The roof of the cathedral of Notre-Dame was made of lead, and our bold speculator offered to buy that valuable metal and have it stripped off. But since the municipal government of Paris had declared that the churches were for sale, of what offense could he have been guilty? Michelet gave the answer.

The sale of churches was violently opposed by Robespierre, who was a fervent theist. He denounced the action of the Commune as part of the foreign conspiracy to discredit the Republic. Henri became the victim of the conflict between the "incorruptible" Robespierre and the atheistic commune. As proof of the statement that the offer to buy the lead from the roof of the church was the cause of Henri's arrest, Michelet wrote:

"I have it from three persons worthy of trust, from three different sources and yet all in agreement: from a disciple of Enfantin, a disciple of Bazard, and a Fourierist who once belonged to the Saint-Simonian sect and who had often heard this fact mentioned."[19]

Of such rumors, many degrees removed from the original bearer of the tale, and many years after the event, was the biography of Saint-Simon compounded.

In the review of his life which he made in 1812, Saint-Simon justified himself for the part he played in the buying and selling of national properties:

"I saw the Revolution reduce my mother's fortune. Before the Revolution, my mother enjoyed an income of one hundred thousand livres. To-day her income is reduced to twelve or fifteen thousand livres. My father was a younger son of small means. He had married his cousin, the heiress of one of the Saint-Simon branches and of two wealthy uncles, to whose inheritance I was entitled. I sought compensation in speculating in church properties. I felt the need to make up the losses I suffered. At the same time I realized that the loftiest scientific project without the necessary funds to carry it on, was like a soul without a body. Such is the reason, or rather the excuse for my financial activities during the stormy days of the French Revolution."[20]

That Henri did not inherit anything on the death of his father, was borne out by the document we found in the Archives of Amiens, dated December 1, 1798. It stated that the widow Blanche-Elizabeth Rouvroy Saint-Simon was the mother of seven children and of these "Saint-Simon, the oldest son, was obliged to renounce the considerable advantages which were guaranteed him by the laws and customs in existence at the time his father's estate was probated, leaving all the family properties in the hands of his mother."

The document specifically declared that "the oldest son was obliged to renounce" his share, which, according to custom, would have been the major portion of the estate. But why was he obliged to give up his birthright? Were his debts so large that his share of the inheritance had to be traded to cover the amount? Was he judged legally unfit to administer a nobleman's estate? Saint-Simon more than once referred to his severance from the family estate, but nowhere does he give the reason for such an extraordinary situation.

The rest of the above document furnished interesting data about the family:

"Considering the declaration handed to the secretary's office on the seventh of this month by citizeness Blanche-Elizabeth Rouvroy St.-Simon, in reference to her properties personal and real, consisting of the houses and lands of Berny, . . . four houses in Paris, the deponent is owner of a capital of 112,560 francs producing an income of 5,628, for which sum the deponent is listed on the Register, to wit . . . 112,560 francs. Total assets 338,974 francs, debts 201,100 francs.

"The same declaration states that citizeness St. Simon has seven children: Claude-Henry, Adélaïde-Blanche-Marie, Marie-Louise, Adrienne-Emilie-Joséphine, Claude-Louis-Jean, André-Louis and Hubert St. Simon, these last three absent and accused of emigration."

The three youngest sons became Knights of Malta. Membership in the Order of Malta was sought by the younger sons of the aristocracy, not only for the sake of the title but also for the pensions attached to it. These three brothers were classed as *émigrés* as they had left their country in time of need. Their properties were placed under seal.

Within three weeks after Henri's imprisonment, his oldest

sister was arrested, December 9, 1793. She was accused of being the sister of an *émigré* and that several "aristocratic brochures" had been found in her residence. The official report of the search stated:

"We examined all the writing desks, cabinets, bureaus, book-cases, and after the said citizeness opened these for us, we found nothing against the principles of the Revolution except in the bookcase where we found five brochures which in our judgment should be confiscated."[21]

Adélaïde-Blanche-Marie however was not long detained in prison. Blanche-Elizabeth, the mother, was subject to all kinds of vexations from the local and state officials. On November 19, 1793, the day Henri was arrested, an inventory was made at the château of Berny of the personal property which belonged to the *émigrés*. The mother tried to save her sons' properties from confiscation by asserting that they were sent to Malta for their education and consequently they were not *émigrés*. The matter dragged on for a while but two years later, on July 21, 1795, the municipal council of Péronne ordered "the widow Rouvroy Saint-Simon of Berny" to pay a fine amounting to 8,633 livres because of the emigration of her sons.

Although she was spared arrest and imprisonment, the mother had more care and adversity than she could endure, to the point that her mind broke under the strain. According to one document:

"Dame Saint-Simon, mother of *émigrés*, was obliged to divide her estate among her future heirs. As she was incapable of taking care of her affairs, she was provided with an agent who was given power of attorney to represent her."

Further evidence of the mental derangement of the widow Saint-Simon was furnished by a letter written by her son Hubert to a notary at Péronne. Hubert was trying to recover certain properties, and as the mother's signature was required for the transaction, he explained the difficulty as follows:

"My mother, declared legally irresponsible on account of the state of her health, has not been able to manage her estate for many years and consequently her signature has no legal value."[22]

It would hardly seem à propos to dwell on this regrettable

misfortune were it not that certain traits of Saint-Simon could be attributed only to a strain of insanity. Not only did Henri, at least at one time, succumb to a mental disorder, but the behavior of his brother Hubert, on the occasion of the latter's marriage, could hardly be explained as the act of a sane person.

The youngest brother, Hubert, when he felt that he was not safe in Malta, had left for Spain. Soon after the Restoration, he returned to France, less for his attachment to his native land, than for his desire to marry a rich heiress, the daughter of a Parisian jeweler. The marriage was celebrated with appropriate pomp and splendor, and the happy bride was seated with her aristocratic spouse at the wedding table surrounded by merry guests. During the height of the festivities, Hubert left secretly and hastened to the notary's office to grab the bounteous dowry.

The bride and the guests waited in vain for the ritual toast. Meanwhile the bridegroom was speeding at full gallop on the road to Naples, where a young actress of the San Carlos theater had given him a rendez-vous.

CHAPTER FOUR

We have no exact knowledge of Saint-Simon's life during the eleven months of his imprisonment. In his autobiographical fragments he remained silent about these most trying days of his existence. However one may gain an accurate picture of prison life under the Terror from the accounts of other liberated prisoners. Several such reports may be found in the *Almanach des Prisons* which started publication early in 1795. The following description of the prison of Sainte-Pélagie, which closed its gates on Saint-Simon, November 19, 1793, is by one of its former inmates:

"In this prison, humid and unwholesome, were confined about 350 prisoners. All were kept there without knowing why, for the jail entry was not read to them . . . The poor wretch was shut up in a cell six foot square, lighted by a narrow window with strong iron bars. A miserable straw mattress, a worn out blanket were the only furnishings of this sad abode permanently infected by the excrements of the occupant, who was not permitted to leave his cell to satisfy the needs of nature. On his arrival, he was approached by a turnkey with a broad face and heavy moustache, who asked him in a raucous voice and menacing tone: 'Have you any money?' If he answered yes, he was given a bowl and water pitcher, and some broken dishes for which he paid three times their value. But should the unfortunate fellow happen to have an empty purse, he was told: 'Too bad, brother, but here you get nothing for nothing.'

"During the months of April and May 1794 the prisoners received only a pound and a half of bad bread and a dish of very tough beans cooked in rank grease or tallow. The wealthy prisoners could secure other food at enormous prices; but the poor had nothing to satisfy their hunger but that foul and dirty dish.

"However physical suffering was nothing compared to the moral torment endured by prisoners whose life hung by a thread and who could not tell on awakening in the morning whether it was to be their last day on earth. Here, at Sainte-Pélagie, came the Girondin deputies awaiting the guillotine. Here also was locked up proud madame Roland, whose hatred of the Montagnards sent her to the gallows."[1]

Faced with the prospect of a death sentence, Saint-Simon used every means of self-defense. We have given the letter he wrote to the Committee of Public Safety in which he tried to convince the committee that his arrest must have been due to mistaken identity. He wrote again giving assurance that he had been "one of the ardent partisans of the Revolution . . . The misfortune of being born into a proscribed caste should not create an unfavorable prejudice against me on the part of the impartial judges. That wrong was involuntary. I have atoned for it."

Reviewing his life to the time of imprisonment, he went on:

"I was a soldier before the Revolution and I had occasion to defend the cause of liberty in the American war in which I was wounded. Since then I served no other master but my country. I solicited so little the favour of the Court that, wearied of the idleness to which the former nobles were condemned by imbecile prejudices and not having a sou of inheritance, I left my post to go to Spain to usefully employ my time and services. I was at the head of a considerable project, when the first hours of liberty blazed forth in France. I returned to my country at once. I have resided at Falvy, commune of the department of Péronne, from the month of November 1789 to October 1790, and since that time until my arrest I lived constantly at Péronne, excepting the months of May, June, July and August 1791 during which time I was at Cambrai.

"I have had no communication whatever with the former nobles of Péronne, nor with any other since the Revolution, I have not even seen my relatives. I am honored by the fact that the former nobility have expressed hatred for me."[2]

He stated further that his "customary pursuits since the Revolution have been directed toward the acquisition and to the administering of national lands for a Saxon whom I had influenced from the beginning of the Revolution to transfer his fortune and his home to France, who had confided to me the task of finding for him some investments, and for whom exclusively I have bought some national lands. This transaction was advantageous to the Republic in that it prevented foreign capital from leaving the country and the income was turned over to the national treasury. My relations with this foreigner had been investigated last October by three commissioners of the Committee of Public Safety to whom I had been denounced and who, after an exhaustive examination of our correspondence, withdrew the order of arrest that had been issued against me."

Henri Bonhomme, as he was then known, was anxious to prove that he had resided at Péronne prior to his arrest. For that purpose he requested a certificate of residence from the officials of that town. This was forwarded in 1794 in a form which gave full identification of the applicant:

"We, the undersigned, the mayor, municipal officers and members of the general council of the commune of Péronne do certify that Claude Henri Saint-Simon, former colonel of infantry in the service of France, now landowner habitually living at Péronne, age thirty-four, height five feet nine inches, hair and eyebrows auburn, eyes brown, nose aquiline, mouth average, chin round, forehead high, visage full . . . has resided without interruption at Péronne, in a house belonging to him from the first of January 1791 to the 25th of Brumaire, year II of the Republic (November 12, 1793) ." [3]

On March 10, 1794, the city fathers of Falvy wrote a letter of commendation for their "ex-seigneur, named Bonhomme, former Saint-Simon," and the letter stated that "he had shown the greatest attachment for the cause of liberty and equality." The Revolutionary Committee of Cambrai also testified April 15, 1794, that the conduct of citizen Bonhomme in our commune was that of a true citizen; to our knowledge he had done nothing which might lead one to suspect his civic integrity." And the Patriotic Society of Péronne declared Bonhomme to be "one of our brothers, a persecuted patriot, a courageous as well as an enlightened friend of liberty. His patriotism did not waver at any period of the Revolution."

These belated testimonials made little impression on Fouquier-Tinville, the inexorable prosecuting attorney for the Revolutionary Tribunal. He may have had serious doubts about Saint-Simon's patriotic sentiments since the prisoner was apparently straddling both sides. In a letter addressed to his banker Perrégaux, which must have been smuggled out of prison, Saint-Simon wrote:

"It seems to me evident that for the present, and for a long time to come, a monarchical government is the only one desirable for Parisians, and therefore the French people."[4]

It was during Saint-Simon's incarceration at Sainte-Pélagie that the Ronsin plot took place. Henri Ronsin, a general in the army of the Republic, supported by Hébert and his partisans, was accused of planning the overthrow of Robespierre. Hébert and a number of his followers were arrested. A Belgian refugee, Charles Jaubert, notified Fouquier-Tinville that Ronsin was hatching a plot within the prison walls, attempting to win support of the imprisoned political suspects by promising them release. He wrote:

"Citizen, I believe it of the highest importance to obtain the testimony of citizens Mollin, Seymandi, Robinet imprisoned in Saint-Lazare and particularly citizen Bonhomme, imprisoned in Sainte-Pélagie, in the affair Ronsin. These citizens may tell important things and particularly confirm all the facts I have already brought in as evidence."[5]

According to that letter citizen Bonhomme seemed to have been implicated in that conspiracy, but at the trial of Ronsin he was exonerated, as the evidence showed that he had refused to join the Hébertists. This was fortunate for Saint-Simon. Ronsin and Hébert and his followers were sent to the guillotine.

Saint-Simon had been in Sainte-Pélagie for over five months waiting from day to day to be called before the Revolutionary Tribunal. Winter had given way to spring. The month of May brought life and hope even to the stunted acacia tree reaching upward for a ray of sunshine in the gloomy shadow of the high prison walls. But the days did not turn brighter for the unfortunates behind the bars.

From Sainte-Pélagie Saint-Simon was transferred to the Lux-

embourg prison on May 4, 1794. The change, however, w
thing but cheerful. Transfer to the Luxembourg meant
the antechamber of death. Of the hundreds of people co
there, only seven were not inscribed on the death list.

The vast Luxembourg palace, once the residence of Marie de
Medicis, had been transformed into a gaol, and its many apart-
ments into as many cells containing ten to twelve prisoners.
These belonged to various political groups and social conditions.
They were of both sexes and of all ages. Many were young, and
in the presence of death they felt life's attractions with greater
potency than ever. All wanted to drive the fatal hour from their
minds and banish from their thoughts the fear of the morrow.
Knowing they were fated to die, they heedlessly gave their last
moments to pleasure.

The women took great care of their *toilettes,* as if they were
still living in their former fashionable surroundings. In the
morning they would be seen in the halls wearing négligé gowns,
artfully négligé. At noon they appeared in the dining hall,
rouged and powdered, in elaborate coiffures, and elegantly
dressed. In the evening, for dinner, the gowns were more bold,
and the conversation became even more so. The sex instinct held
in restraint under normal conditions now ran riot, untram-
meled, unashamed. For a woman there was one last hope. Being
with child might furnish a chance of escape from the guillotine.

The *Prison's Almanach* contains many entertaining anecdotes
concerning the life in the Luxembourg. One lady of high rank
was caught by the jailor hiding behind a screen with a young
man who had managed to sneak into the prison. The *grande
dame* did not lose her head, but, uttering a piercing cry, pre-
tended to be forcibly raped and simulated a faint. During the
commotion the young man disappeared.

Moral behavior was extremely lax inside the prison, so much
so that the administrator of the police felt compelled to admon-
ish the inmates: "Do you know what people are saying about
you in town? They say the Luxembourg is the biggest bordello
in Paris, that you are a bunch of whores, and that we act as
your pimps."

On the other hand, many traits of heroic fortitude are also

63

related of some of the victims. One of the most touching examples was that of Louise-Joséphine Cailles. Her lover was condemned to death. Determined to follow him, she wrote a letter to Fouquier-Tinville in which she declared herself a royalist and an enemy of the Republic. Her letter was intercepted by a friend and prevented from reaching its destination. Not getting a reply, Louise-Joséphine addressed a second letter to the fierce prosecuting attorney, who this time received her message and had her placed in prison. On that very day she learned that her lover had been executed. At night she gathered all his letters and read them over and over. At daybreak she was called before the Revolutionary Tribunal. Exultant with joy, she bade good-by to her fellow prisoners, saying: "I am happy. I am going to join my lover." Then she cut her hair as was customary among the women victims in order to be spared the touch of the executioner's hand, and offered her blond locks to her friends. Having distributed her jewels among the poorer prisoners, she marched with firm steps to the tribunal. The trial was short, just one question and one answer.

"Did you write this letter?"

"I did. You separated me from my fiancé and I want to rejoin him."

She climbed the gallows without a tremor and addressing the executioner:

"Yesterday," she said, "you killed the man who was dearest to me on earth. To-day you will add my blood to his."

Then without help or coercion, she stepped forward and placed her neck under the knife.

Social distinctions were as strictly maintained within the prison walls as in the world of free and careless days. The nobles kept away from the commoners and the fiery republicans. They maintained the strictest etiquette, addressing one another by the proper title of *monsieur le prince, monsieur le duc, monsieur le comte, monsieur le marquis,* and treating seriously matters of precedence. The commoners laughed among themselves at this humbug and made fun of such absurd prejudices.

When Henri Bonhomme was transferred to the Luxembourg, the warden, M. Benoit, a kind old man in his seventies, tried to make life pleasant for his charges. He permitted the inmates to form groups according to their interests, or social rank, or age. A few would get together to discourse philosophy, others would play at cards, some would make love, sing, or play musical instruments. But this pleasant state was rudely interrupted when Benoit was dismissed and the "ferocious" Guiard took his place.

No longer was it permissible to come to the window and breathe in fresh air since two prisoners had one day jumped to their death to the street below. During the night armed guards accompanied by enormous dogs, wakened the prisoners in order to count them. All night long the sentries kept yelling insults and threats.

What was the attitude of Saint-Simon under these harrowing conditions? Did he ponder over the social and political problems which absorbed his interest in later life? It is inconceivable that such an active mind as his would remain passive and inert during eleven months of confinement. However, he may have assumed the stoic indifference of the eighteenth century aristocrat, drinking the cup of life to the bitter dregs, discarding all thought of the future, jesting even at death.

In all his writings, Saint-Simon made only two references to this period of his life. In the first one, mentioned in the previous chapter, he blamed Redern for his arrest and for his being kept eleven months in solitary confinement. The second reference is found in the dedicatory letter to his nephew Victor, which appeared as a preface to the volume entitled *Nouvelle Encyclopédie:*

"At the most cruel time of the Revolution, during one night of my detention in the Luxembourg prison, Charlemagne appeared to me and said: 'Since the beginning of the world, no family had enjoyed the honor of producing a hero and a philosopher of the first order; this honor was reserved to my lineage. My son, your success as a philosopher shall equal those I obtained as a military and political leader,' and he disappeared."

This brief mention of his imprisonment was made years later, at a time when his pursuit of glory led him to the study of science and philosophy. The vision to which he referred may not have been merely a figure of speech. The horror of those days and nights, the prospect of death, the over stimulation of a fevered brain were enough to explain a state of hallucination.

More than one fellow prisoner kept his mind alert during those trying days. Madame Roland wrote her famous *Memoirs* in Sainte-Pélagie while she awaited death by the guillotine. André Chénier, expecting a similar fate, composed his best known verses. His last poem was interrupted in the middle of a line when he was called to climb onto the death cart. Thomas Paine wrote the second part of the *Age of Reason* in the Luxembourg prison, where he was detained from December 28, 1793, until November 4, 1794. This period corresponds to the time Saint-Simon was there. It is not improbable that the two met and discussed the American and French Revolutions in which both had participated.

When Danton fell, he too was brought to the Luxembourg together with Camille Desmoulins. The arrival of the two leading revolutionaries on March 31, 1794, created no little stir among the prisoners. Camille entered "somber and melancholy," carrying under his arm the book of Young's *Night Thoughts*. The fiery pamphleteer remained silent and distant. Danton was more sociable towards his new companions. Seeing Thomas Paine, he greeted him in English, saying:

"What you did for the happiness and freedom of your country I tried in vain to do for my own. I was less fortunate but no less innocent . . . They will send me to the gallows; well, my friend, I'll go cheerfully."

One of the most touching marks of family devotion is to be found in the letters Camille Desmoulins wrote to his adored wife Lucile, whose welfare and that of his infant son Horace, gave him the greatest anxiety. His last letter, dated March 22, 1794, 5 o'clock in the morning, we transcribe here in part:

"Beneficent slumber interrupted my sufferings. One is free when one sleeps . . . Heavens took pity on me; only a moment ago I saw you in a dream. I was kissing you and Horace. Dearest Lucile, here I am taken back to the days of our first love, when somebody interested me by the very fact that he had seen you. Yesterday, when the man who brought you my first letter had come back, I asked: 'Well? have you seen her?' as I used to ask my friend Landeville in those happy days, as if something of your person, something of you had remained on his garments, on his whole being.

"My name has just been called. . . . At this moment the commissaries of the Revolutionary Tribunal have come to question me. (This is the 4th of April; this letter has been interrupted). I know the fate awaiting me. Adieu, my dear Lucile, my dear Lolotte, my sweetheart. Say adieu to my father. . . . Oh my dear Lucile! I was born to write poetry, to defend the unfortunates, to make you happy. My Lucile! my sweet, my good Loulou! You must tell him, what he cannot yet understand, that I would have loved him so much! . . . Adieu, Loulou, adieu, my life, my soul, my divinity on earth! Adieu, Horace, Annette, Adèle. Adieu, father!"[6]

It became evident that the Revolutionary Tribunal wished to get rid of the prisoners as fast as the functioning of the guillotine would permit. In order to speed up the work they would foment plots among the inmates. Spies were posted within the jail and the victims were tempted by treasonable suggestions. If a prisoner brought before the tribunal could not be accused of any specific crime, Fouquier-Tinville would remark: "Just have him wait until the next conspiracy." Every time a plot was concocted thirty to fifty persons were beheaded. One horrible night one hundred and sixty-five prisoners were rudely awakened from their sleep, and carted away to their death. After that, terror gripped the hearts of those remaining. They dared not step out of their rooms, they stopped asking news of their friends, they even avoided looking at each other. The food became vile and many fell ill, with no recourse to medical care.

On the night of July 27, 1794, the tocsin rang from the bell towers. The prisoners thought that their last hour had come. They bade adieu to one another. But the bells were ringing glad tidings. Robespierre had fallen! Terror and despair changed to transports of joy, and the jubilation was indescribable.

The Revolutionary Tribunal was reorganized, its arbitrary power eliminated and its functions defined by legal procedure. Its first act was to liberate the prisoners who had been held without definite charges against them.

67

To obtain an idea of the Thermidor reaction, we quote two paragraphs from contemporary newspapers. The first is an extract from *Sans-Culotte,* August 8, 1794:

"Paris, 21 Thermidor. Since the prisons began to yield the numerous victims Robespierre and his accomplices crammed into them, people of this district present a most touching spectacle. From the prison gates to their own residences, the liberated prisoners are given the warmest welcome. Relatives, friends, even strangers, by their show of sympathy, endeavor to make them forget the misfortunes they endured and the dangers that threatened them."

The second item is taken from the *Gazette historique et politique de la France et de l'Europe,* of the 23 Thermidor (August 10, 1794) :

"Long live the Convention! Long live our worthy representatives! Yesterday those cries filled the rue de Tournon (on which the prison opened) , when Tallien went to the Luxembourg to restore to liberty a great number of patriots who were unjustly incarcerated there. Crowds of people had assembled in the street, giving them their blessings, embracing them, embracing those who had just been set free. 'Don't worry my friends,' Tallien said to those he could not yet deliver from jail, 'you will not wait long for your freedom; the criminals are the only ones who will not enjoy that favor.' And tears of joy came to the eyes of every one and they showered the Convention with their blessings. Horror and indignation filled their hearts on learning that, of the vast number of prisoners confined in the Luxembourg, only seven were to escape death; all the others had been inscribed on the fatal list which the odious Robespierre had sent to the Revolutionary Tribunal."

The decree liberating the prisoners did not include those persons who had been arrested under the *loi des suspects.* The case of Henri Bonhomme apparently came under that law. He lingered three months more in the Luxembourg. However, the prospect of deliverance and the vanishing spectre of death made existence more endurable.

At last the Committee of Public Safety issued the order to free Saint-Simon on the 18 Vendémaire, year III, (October 9, 1794) , one month before the release of Thomas Paine.

CHAPTER FIVE

Immediately after his release, Saint-Simon returned to Péronne to resume the management of his financial affairs. During his imprisonment the properties were administered by a state representative, M. Roux. Sequestration worked in favor of the owner because it delayed the payments due to the public treasury. During this interim the value of the assignats had depreciated considerably, but the price of the properties remained at the same amount. In other words, the properties were acquired at a ridiculously low sum, but were sold or leased for the highest price the market would bear.

What caused the assignats to fall forty and fifty percent of their original value? While it is true that the national treasury issued too many paper notes, the chief reason for this progressive depreciation was due to the machinations of the British prime minister William Pitt. By his order counterfeit assignats were printed in England and Holland and secretly unloaded by the shipload on the markets of France. Pitt made no secret of his hatred for the Revolution and meant to destroy it by fair means or foul.

Nor did Pitt hesitate to use questionable methods when he wanted to destroy the champion of the common man, Tom Paine. He paid five hundred pounds to a government clerk, George Chalmers, to write a scurrilous pseudo-biography of the author of the *Rights of Man*. By such treacherous means he succeeded in assassinating the good character of the defender of the American and French revolutions.

Pitt succeeded only too well in causing the assignats to become practically worthless, so much so that at one time one thousand assignats were worth six francs. But this national misfortune turned to Saint-Simon's and his associate Redern's advantage and made both enormously rich.

Never were facilities for amassing wealth greater than at that moment. The financial disarray and distress, the desperate efforts of the government to raise money, the corruption of officials, everything favored the speculators. A quick fortune awaited any person with an enterprising spirit and an elastic conscience.

After months of fear and repression there followed a spontaneous reaction, and people hastened to enjoy life with avidity. A multitude of provincial visitors and foreigners crowded into the capital with but one intention, to make merry. Saint-Simon left Péronne for Paris in 1795 and, with what seemed to him inexhaustible wealth at his command, he decided to enjoy the good things of life. Resuming the proud name of his ancestors, he leased a palatial residence in a fashionable district of the capital at 8 rue Chabanais. As Michelet noted: "he lived near the Palais-Royal, in the cynical license of a grand seigneur sans-culotte, dividing his time between pleasure and business." His sisters and brothers lived with him, and Redern joined them whenever he came to Paris.

In later years, Saint-Simon lingered with melancholy pleasure on the memory of those days of magnificence:

"We occupied the whole of the Chabanais mansion and the first floors of two contiguous residences. Each of us had for his personal use an eight-room apartment. Our maître d'hôtel was Monoyer, who had been the maître d'hôtel of the duke de Choiseul; Le Gagneur who was our chief cook had rendered famous the dinners of Marshal Duras; Tavernier, our chief butler, had been trained in Rome in the service of Cardinal de Bernis."

Twenty domestics were needed for the entertaining of men prominent in politics, science, literature, and of women noted for their beauty and charm. Among the guests were Count de Ségur, Boissy d'Anglas, former president of the Convention and later peer of France under Napoleon, Lagrange, Monge, and Poisson, celebrated mathematicians.

"My friend, M. de Fourcy," wrote Michelet, "who saw him . . . has kept a very vivid picture of him. He was a fine looking man, very gay, with a frank and smiling countenance, admirable eyes, a fine long nose, Don-Quixotish. . . . His manner of dressing was in the style of that of Anaxagoras Chaumette. No cravat, or one worn very low, tied carelessly. He wore the houppelande (cloak) of the time. . . . One could not help being attracted to him."[1]

M. de Fourcy described Saint-Simon, of whose salon he was a frequent visitor, in these words:

"His speech was loud, abundant, witty. His talk was often marked with an unrestrained cynicism; but he knew how to treat seriously serious things . . . a generous and sincere man. He made noble use of his money acquired honestly or otherwise, of which he spoke with an air of disdain which proves that he possessed wealth without being possessed by it. 'Go ahead,' he would say to those whose efforts he was encouraging, 'and when it is only a question of money, come to me, I have some of it.' He found it as simple to accept money as to give it."[2]

From 1795 until the autumn of 1797, Saint-Simon was one of the dominant and financial figures of Paris, a grand seigneur spending his income and most of his capital recklessly, without thought of the morrow, enjoying life to the full. He had his portrait painted by Madame Labille-Guiard, whose popularity as an artist rivaled that of Madame Vigié-Lebrun.

Saint-Simon's favorite haunt was the Palais-Royal, once the residence of royal princes, now the rendez-vous of fashion, of bon vivants and pleasure seekers. Cafés, restaurants, and shops lined the galleries surrounding the inner garden. The stalls of jewelers, perfumers, tailors, modistes, novelty dealers, booksellers stood side by side with the haunts of brokers, money changers, and *filles de joie*. Fops and courtesans, former nobles and fashionable ladies, *nouveaux riches*, popular actresses, journalists, politicians, swindlers, adventurers were seen lounging in the cafés, parading under the arcades or promenading in the shaded walks of the garden.

This was the period of the Directoire, which came into power on October 27, 1795. The wife of the most popular member of the government, madame Tallien, ruled as the queen of fashion. She was the daughter of Cabarrus, the financier with whom Saint-Simon associated in Madrid for the proposed building of a canal. She had taken the place of Marie-Antoinette, and went on displaying the most insolent luxury, appearing in the

71

theater loaded with diamonds, half naked, setting the example of moral laxity to Parisian society. She was referred to by her jealous rivals as the greatest whore in France. It was madame Tallien who introduced the Greco-Roman dress, the loosely draped gown of sheer muslin with generous décolleté, and gold sandals on bare feet.

Men discarded the patriotic red cap, the short jacket, and the long trousers of the sans-culottes. They wore frock coats, tight fitting breeches, large brimmed hats which were held in the hand rather than worn on the head, so as not to disturb the complicated arrangement of powdered hair.

In contrast to the luxurious life of the wealthy classes, we might mention that the average working day consisted of fifteen to sixteen hours at a wage of from one and a half to two francs a day.

Life was not all frivolity and licentiousness for Saint-Simon. His financial activities were greater than ever, and his purchases of national lands had reached such vast proportions that he was regarded as one of the biggest manipulators of the time. Profitable as this business was, his fertile mind kept planning other enterprises.

In January 1795 he put on the market a set of playing cards which he had invented and patented. Card playing was extremely popular at the moment, and the game was encouraged by the government as an effective means of propaganda. To eradicate all vestiges of the ancient régime, various sets of cards were printed on which the traditional king, queen, and knave were replaced by revolutionary symbols.

Saint-Simon felt that here was a profitable field to exploit. He launched his set of playing cards with intensive publicity. A circular began with this announcement:[3]

"Patented new cards of the French Republic.

"No more Kings, Queens, Knaves. Talent replaced the King, Liberty the Queen, Equality the Jack. Law alone is above them," that is, law took the place of the ace.

The prospectus made a strong appeal to patriotic feelings:

"There is no republican who wants, even in playing, to use expressions which continuously recall despotism and inequality."

Equality was represented by a Negro and a *sans-culotte;* Law by the emblem of fasces; the Queen of Hearts wore the red cap of the Revolution and her hand was placed on her heart; the Queen of Clubs was symbolized by a chaste Venus.

Yet, for all the bombastic eloquence of the printed circulars, it is doubtful whether Saint Simon's playing cards ever had a wide appeal. Maxime Leroy refers to the printing of these cards as further evidence of Saint-Simon's attachment to the Republic. We doubt it. He favored any government while it lasted. He lived through half a dozen régimes and condemned each in turn after its downfall. His mind was that of a promoter and his Balzacian imagination led him to sponsor many a daring venture.

Up to Thermidor, industrial production had been considerably slowed down and in some fields completely suspended. But in 1795 there was a resurgence of economic life and a marked industrial recovery. To supply the demand for goods, commerce was activated throughout the land, traveling became more general, and better facilities of transportation were needed. Saint-Simon was prompt to take advantage of the situation. A new enterprise of stagecoaches was founded that year under his name. The headquarters of the company were located in rue du Bouloi, in the business center of the city, close to the Palais-Royal. The name of Saint-Simon appeared in large letters on the façade of the building as well as on the doors of the bright colored coaches.

The years 1796 and 1797 were those of Saint-Simon's greatest activity and social eminence. In August 1797 we find him at Lille, in northern France, on a secret mission in an attempt to negotiate a treaty between the British government and the Directoire. Both countries were in need of peace and hoped for a settlement.

England who had spearheaded the coalition against revolutionary France, seemed exhausted by her war efforts. Pitt instructed Malmesbury to "swallow his pride" and to conclude immediate peace. The French delegates asked for the restitution of colonies belonging to France, Spain, and Holland. Spain was represented by Cabarrus, former associate of Saint-Simon. At first Lord Malmesbury offered to restore the French colonies, but not the Spanish nor the Dutch. The Directoire was about to stop all negotiations unless the status quo of January 1793 were restored.

In the middle of July 1797, two unexpected events changed the course of the negotiations. One was the nomination of Talleyrand to the post of foreign affairs, the other a secret intrigue between Maret and Malmesbury.

Maret, on Talleyrand's advice, started secret negotiations with Malmesbury's secretary, George Ellis. Saint-Simon was personally acquainted with Ellis whom he had met in Paris in the circle of Anglophile financiers. He was then on the best of terms with several Parisian bankers who exerted pressure on the government in favor of peace. Among these was Perrégaux who had helped him in his land speculations, and his former associate Cabarrus. It was probably the latter who suggested that Talleyrand make use of the services of Saint-Simon. At any rate his mission was confirmed by an order of the Committee of Public Safety, as shown by the following document:

"Petition by Henri St.-Simon to be permitted to have an authorized agent obtain for him a certificate of residence from the municipality of Péronne, in view of the need to absent himself by order of the Committee of Public Safety . . . the latter having requisitioned the services of the petitioner to furnish the Committee with information regarding the political and commercial relations of the Republic with foreign countries."[4]

Saint-Simon arrived at Lille at the critical moment when all hope for agreement seemed abandoned, selfish interests on both sides running through a maze of intrigue and counter intrigue. He got in touch with George Ellis, who transmitted the advice of the French banker's emissary to Lord Malmesbury. Saint-Simon exerted a personal influence on the peace deliberations, judging from the reports in the Public Record Office, which Professor Larrabee has published. Since these letters, exchanged between Malmesbury, Pitt, and Greenville, minister of foreign affairs, throw light on Saint-Simon's political acumen, they are worth reproducing in part:

"My Lord,   "Lille, August 14, 1797.

On Thursday last (the 10) a particular friend of Mr. Ellis's came from Paris to pay him a visit, and as I have reason to believe from the accuracy of all the information which came to us from this quarter when we were last in France, that the fullest reliance may be placed on the judgment and sincerity of this informant, and as the substance of all which he has communicated perfectly confirms and elucidates the intelligence which I have already in my separate dispatches transmitted to your Lordship, I shall in this dispatch confine myself to a copy of the report which Mr. Ellis wrote for my information immediately after the conversation with his friend. . . .

"I told him it was very natural that the Directory should wish for a continuance of the War. He said, I do not believe it. . . . Carnot, who is the only man amongst them capable of planning a campaign or indeed any consistent system of conduct, is decidedly a friend to peace. The others, I am persuaded, have no other reason for wishing a continuance of a war which they have neither ability nor the means to prolong with any hope of success, but that the Councils and the ministry of their own Body having declared one opinion, they chose to persevere in another. . . .

"Carnot is the only man at all fitted for his place. . . . Our whole Government is so completely null and insignificant that a Counter Revolution must happen tomorrow, but that at least one half of the lands in the Republic are in the hands of new Proprietors who are interested in supporting and will continue to support the present order of things, and that the taste for equality, which is universal throughout the great Towns, though it has not yet gained the Inhabitants of the country, makes the return of the Monarchy with all its distinctions of rank and title nearly impossible. . . . A French general has no power but in his camp, and not always there. Bonaparte has not six officers on whom he could depend and probably not one regiment; he has already lost the greatest part of the popularity he as acquired by his victories. . . .

"I asked him what were the speculations of the Publick respecting the terms of peace. He said you will of course keep something; we conclude you will keep Ceylon, and nobody can think this unfair. It is likely too that you will wish to keep the Cape. . . .

"I asked him what pecuniary resources the Directory could possibly look forward to for the further prosecution of the war. He answered to none; but bankruptcy would make very little difference in our situation; we have been very near it, for our funds lost ninety seven percent. But we have in our favor the habits of poverty; any degree of privation appears tolerable to a people who passed through a revolution as ours. I do not mean that this patience would last forever, but it might last long enough to distress the richest enemy and expose them to the same misery which we experience. . . .

Malmesbury"[5]

Pitt was impressed by the reports he received regarding the information conveyed by Saint-Simon and wrote to his representative in Lille, August 19, 1797:

"Your last separate letter put the secret intelligence into an excellent form for communication; and Mr. Ellis's friend has the merit of furnishing one of the most *interesting*, and certainly the most entertaining dialogue that ever made part of a negotiation."

In spite of Saint-Simon's optimism, the Lille negotiations failed. By the coup d'état of September 4, 1797, the Directoire got rid of the moderates and became more insistent on the restitution of all colonies. This led to a break in the negotiations. Contrary to Saint-Simon's prediction, the French people did not become excited over the matter, nor was his estimate of Napoleon correct.

Professor Larrabee's questions as to the reasons that brought Saint-Simon to Lille are left without an answer. Was he an agent of Talleyrand? Was he sent by the banker Perrégaux to present to the British the views of the powerful French financiers? He was probably an Anglophile already, as proved by his subsequent writings. At the moment, we may presume that he represented the peace appeal of the influential men with whom he was associated in business as well as in social life. At least that appeared to be his aim, for his observations were those of a man of affairs. At this date he was far from being a social reformer, utopian or dreamer. His talks with Ellis reveal a realist, a man whose positive views were deduced from a survey of

76

facts and whose conclusions were drawn with a cold if not cynical lucidity. Even Pitt, a competent judge, found the views of Saint-Simon "interesting."

When Saint-Simon returned to Paris, he found himself the butt of attacks by the *Gazette Nationale de France* in its issue of September 3, 1797:

"The service of stage coach transportation which used to be an important and lucrative branch of the government, has been encroached upon by a private concern which bears the name of Saint-Simon. The former count de Saint-Simon, who appears to be the principal owner, possessed little wealth before the Revolution. To-day his fortune is immense. One of the head clerks of his offices has been taken to the Central Police Bureau. The police wanted from him some information concerning a rather strange matter. This man invited unemployed people, who are not rare in Paris, to come and see him. They would come. After a few questions to the applicant about his abilities, honesty and general principles he was told: 'You will get a job in a few days. You will be notified. You must hold yourself ready. Meanwhile here is a sum of . . .' The name of the applicant was entered in a register and this register came to the attention of the police. It is said that it contains about two thousand names. If this fact which was reported to us is verified, it would be surprising, to say the least, to find that a private citizen wanted to employ two thousand clerks."

Saint-Simon made no reply to this accusation. The same paper declared on September 16th that he had been arrested for competing too successfully with the state postal service:

"Besides the conveyance of passengers and merchandise, he had undertaken the carrying of letters and newspapers, and the speed of his coaches was by far superior to that of the postal service. The first news received at Lyons of the events of the 18 Fructidor were brought by the *Précurseur*, a newspaper forwarded by the coaches of the marquis (sic) de Saint-Simon. It is easy to foresee the danger of such an establishment.

"In all times and under all different types of government, the conveying of letters and public papers must belong exclusively to the government. Its safety, the safety of all, depends on that.

77

The communication among citizens of the same State is a public necessity as much as the courts of justice; consequently it is necessarily a branch of public administration."

In answer to this attack Saint-Simon wrote to the editors of the journal on September 19th:

"If it was to me that some journalists intended to refer, I warn them that they were mistaken.

"1° I have not been arrested.

"2° I could not have been arrested for transporting newspapers to *départements,* because my carriages never transported newspapers.

"3° Because of my opinions and political conduct since 1789, I am not subject to arrest for any cause nor for any motive. I have only to fear the enemies of the Revolution to which not a single man in France is as strongly bound as myself.

"Saint-Simon, head of the establishment Saint-Simon,

rue du Bouloi."

The editors added the comment:

"The marquis de Saint-Simon was not arrested. Worse than that, he claims he is not subject to arrest, and that he is more of a patriot than the patriots. Well, let it be so."

Here we have a definite statement by Saint-Simon that he was engaged in the business of stagecoach transportation. But later when contention arose between Redern and him, he denied having had any part in the project:

"I must combat and destroy an opinion which spread about me in this part of the country[6] and which is entirely erroneous. It is generally believed here that I was proprietor of an agency of stage coaches. This belief is founded on the fact that for some years certain coaches passing through Alençon bore my name. I had bought two city mansions, the Hôtel des Fermes and the Hôtel du Roulage, which comprised a piece of ground of several acres in the heart of Paris. In order to utilize this important property, I had thought of establishing there a perpetual fair, a sort of Palais-Royal on a small scale, and I planned to open shops and stalls both on the street sides and court sides of the buildings. Mr. Dumorey, a contractor for stage coaches, offered me 30,000 francs rental for part of the site. I accepted his proposition, which was favorable for my project, since it made my premises more alive and thereby more advantageous for the merchants who were to establish themselves there. I had given my name to that property. For this reason M. Dumorey had it put on his establishment and on his carriages."[7]

This elaborate explanation does not annul the fact that in September 1797 he signed: Saint-Simon, head of the establishment Saint-Simon, rue du Bouloi.

Another industry that attracted Saint-Simon's inexhaustible activity was the manufacture of white linen. A great demand arose for this textile as a result of the craze for dancing which spontaneously developed as a relief after the Terror. White muslin gowns became the fashion at the uninterrupted succession of parties, weddings, and balls. Saint-Simon opened a mill in the department of the Somme, expecting that the use of white linen would soon extend to many other usages, such as sheets, table cloths, and the like. But the demand for such niceties on a large scale did not come until later, about 1818, at the end of the imperial wars. In 1795, when Saint-Simon launched this venture, people were interested chiefly in the acquisition of land. Some bought silverware, which possessed a durable value and could be sold again. Few purchased curtains, bed sheets, table-linen, to say nothing of underclothing. As a result, the textile mill was not a financial success.

His imagination was further lured by the prospect of wealth in most diverse fields. Besides the service of stagecoach transportation, and the manufacture of linen, we find him engaged in a drayage business, a commission house, and even a retail wine shop. But the promoter of so many enterprises lacked the elementary qualifications of a man of business. All his commercial undertakings ended in failure, even the purchase and sale of national lands. Soon after his return from Lille, there arose between him and his associate a long and unfortunate dissension which was to terminate their partnership and lead to his complete ruin.

One may recall that, prior to his imprisonment, Saint-Simon was busy acquiring lands with the funds left him by Redern in 1791. The latter, as Prussian ambassador to London, was away from France. Even when he resigned his diplomatic post in 1792 he did not feel it would be safe to return to France as long as that country was at war with Prussia. He sought instead refuge in the neutral state of Tuscany, residing in Florence until the declaration of peace. In January 1796 he came back to the French capital as a guest of Saint-Simon, who entertained him royally in his luxurious quarters on rue Chabanais. Redern seemed completely gratified with the way business was being conducted in his absence, so much so that he felt free to leave again, and he went on an extended visit to Germany.

Late in September 1797 Redern was back in Paris to supervise his financial interests. Since his last visit, important modifications had been made by Saint-Simon in their common holdings. A large part of their landed estates had been exchanged for city properties. Saint-Simon had bought two palatial residences in the heart of Paris: the Hôtel des Fermes and the Hôtel du Roulage, comprising an area of several acres, on which was established a drayage and stage coach business.

According to a memorandum published later by Redern, Saint-Simon had sold properties which were bringing in an annual income of about 80,000 francs and had mortgaged a large part of the remainder for 400,000 francs, on which he had to pay interest at the rate of five percent a month. He was obviously using a large part of his revenues on his princely style of living, and for benefactions which he distributed with nonchalant munificence. Such costly extravagance disturbed Redern who could see disaster ahead.

To avoid the threatened collapse Redern decided to take personal charge of the management and suggested to his associate that he leave Paris and take an extended vacation, until such time when the business was again functioning on a sound basis. Saint-Simon took the matter good naturedly, declaring that he owned nothing, that everything belonged to Redern, and therefore the latter was free to do as he pleased. Redern, however, did not want to assume all responsibility and asked one of Saint-Simon's intimate friends, M. de Béhague, to represent his partner.

With an allowance of five hundred francs a month, Saint-Simon left for Brussels, with the intention of turning over a new leaf. From the Belgian capital he wrote to Perrégaux on March 2, 1798:

"Far from being chagrined I thank heaven for this occurrence; it will serve to strengthen my soul, which was beginning to grow flabby." In the same letter he referred to a project for a new commercial firm and a bank that would be "the most unique in the world." [8]

Brussels proved too austere and boresome and after two months' absence, Saint-Simon returned to Paris. He was determined to expound the new scheme he had evolved to a group of financiers. To humor him Redern and a number of friends gathered on the evening of July 9, 1798, to listen to his plan. For five hours Saint-Simon discussed a fantastic system of ethics of which his audience could make neither head nor tail. Then he concluded by presenting a project for the acquisition of the buildings surrounding the Hôtel des Fermes. It was a matter of a mere 1,200,000 francs. His reason for the purchase was that the ownership of this central area would give the possessors control of the stock exchange. The ability to manipulate the stock exchange would in turn give power over the city of Paris. It followed that those who had Paris under their thumbs could manage France, and finally the entire European continent. This power, the author of the scheme assured his listeners, would be used solely for the benefit of humanity. But neither Redern nor the practical men of business were in the least impressed, and no one came forward with an offer of money.

Undaunted by this setback, Saint-Simon determined to set his mind on other matters. He was now thirty-seven years old. The adventurous days of his reckless youth were over. He had pursued wealth and gained it and had enjoyed all the pleasures of luxurious living. But for a man who claimed descent from Charlemagne, was that an achievement to be proud of? Such glorious ancestry imposed obligations other than the enjoyment of an empty life. Noblesse oblige. The apparition that visited him in the Luxembourg prison had not faded from his memory. He recalled the prophetic words of the Frankish Emperor: "My son, your success as a philosopher shall equal those I obtained as a military and political leader." The great vision again shone before his eyes, and he resolved to fulfill the imperial oracle.

At this critical moment he felt the need to collect his thoughts in peaceful meditation. He must leave the city and its dissipations, worldliness, and tumult. Seeking the quiet of the countryside, he retired to Montmorency, the very place where the author of the *Nouvelle Héloïse* found a few moments of happiness in his troubled life.

Was he conscious of following in the steps of Jean-Jacques Rousseau? At any rate, it was to this sylvan retreat that Saint-Simon withdrew at the turning point in his life. He brought with him the shepherd dog that was his constant companion. Long walks with this mute friend took him from glade to glade along the silent paths of the woodland valley. And now his mind became lucid and the road to glory appeared in full light.

"The desire for glory," was his refrain, "possessed me from the moment of my entrance into the world; it has dominated all my life; it still exerts upon me the most absolute command."

Until now his quest had been in vain. In his youth he had sought glory in martial adventures. Then came the search for fame through wealth and worldly eminence. All that was mirage and self deception. But Charlemagne had shown him the right direction. He will become a great philosopher, the intellectual leader of the world. Henceforward Redern can go alone "in the direction of the foul mire in the midst of which fortune has erected its temple." As for him, Saint-Simon, he will ascend "the arid and steep mountain which bears on its summit the altar of glory."[9] Such was his resolve when he left the peaceful valley of Montmorency to return to Paris.

Saint-Simon was only too willing to abandon the administration of the business to his partner, but even a philosopher must live and Redern should give him his rightful share of the profits. The dissolution of the partnership involved the two associates in endless conflicts and tergiversations. Redern accused Saint-Simon of using a large portion of the revenues for personal use and gratification, of misrepresenting the mortgages, of using dummy buyers, of falsifying accounts, of neglecting to take care of premises in need of repair. To bring the matter to a close, it was decided to submit the dispute to arbitration.

No sooner were the arbiters chosen than Saint-Simon, without waiting for their decision, settled the case in his own unexpected manner. In a letter to Redern he gave up all claims in return for a lump sum of 150,000 francs. The following day he added to this demand the payment of an annual pension of 1,800 francs to Madame Thillays by whom he had a daughter, Caroline-Charlotte, born May 29, 1795. Redern agreed to these terms, and legal papers were drawn and signed on August 6, 1799, whereby the partnership was dissolved.

Saint-Simon was to be paid the 150,000 francs in four instalments; the first one on the day the papers were signed, the second on October 17th of the same year, the third on May, 6, 1800, and the fourth on February 5, 1801. As M. de Béhague claimed that Saint-Simon owed him six thousand francs, that sum was withheld and paid to the creditor. This explains why Saint-Simon at a later time referred to the amount he received as 144,000.

It is difficult to understand why Saint-Simon transferred to his partner the entire ownership of the properties without legal guarantees for himself. His biographers credit him with a total confidence in Redern and complete disinterestedness. Knowing with what determination verging on despair Saint-Simon attempted later to arrive at a more profitable settlement, one is inclined to look for different motives.

Were his debts so large that they exceeded his share of the revenues? Was he threatened with the loss of most of his income as the result of legal entanglements of one kind or another? The fact is that during the last two years he had lived recklessly. His speculations in urban real estate had been unfortunate, his commercial ventures had ended in failure. The dissolution of partnership on the basis of a sum in ready money could be the best means of extricating himself from an embarrassing and dangerous situation. At any rate, at the time of the settlement, Saint-Simon made no protest, and appeared to be fully satisfied with the new arrangement.

"This adjustment will be entirely satisfactory to me if it makes you happy," he declared to Redern.[10]

Redern's comments on the manner in which his associate conducted business are not without interest. His transactions were carried on without discernment or sagacity; he just sold a pack of wares to the first comer; the success of his speculations was due entirely to the depreciation of paper money; the value of the original investments diminished continuously due to his extravagant prodigalities, lack of system and order, indiscriminate choice of agents; he did little himself, leaving most matters to intermediaries; he gave or promised shares to a number of men, some of whom made fortunes while all gained substantial profits. The latter remark was confirmed by Saint-Simon who made this admission to Redern:

"Several of the agents whom I employed bought lands on their own account and became wealthy; this fact is known to you. You know that M. de Béhague enjoys to-day some one hundred thousand livres of income; that M. Coutte has more than fifty thousand; M. Joanne thirty thousand, and so forth, and you know that they paid for the estates with the money they acquired by selling part of their purchases, that they made profits without putting up any capital." [11]

Redern's comments do not present Saint-Simon as a high moral exemplar. Even granting that the accusations were made in the heat of a bitter quarrel, the facts and figures contained in Redern's memorandum cannot altogether be denied. They fully confirm the judgment of Michelet who portrayed Saint-Simon as a cynical and licentious "grand seigneur sans-culotte."

As to his physical appearance at this period, a certificate of residence issued in 1798 furnished the following description:

"We the undersigned certify that Claude Henri Saint-Simon, wholesale merchant living off his income, age 37, height five feet nine inches, nose large, mouth average, chin round, hair brown, face oval and full, forehead high, eyes gray, has resided without interruption in this municipal precinct, rue Chabanais, since September 23, 1795, up to January 1798. Dated January 11, 1798."

CHAPTER SIX

Saint-Simon relieved of all business administration and financial responsibilities felt free to pursue his way of life and to indulge in his fancies. Spurred by the desire to distinguish himself in the field of knowledge, he decided on a definite plan of study, the purpose of which was to classify all known facts and draw conclusions that might solve the problems of human society.

"This undertaking," he explained, "required preliminary studies. I had to begin with the study of the physical sciences by examining their actual state, and by ascertaining by means of historical research the order in which the discoveries which had enriched them had been made. To acquire this knowledge, I did not content myself with researches in libraries. I began again my education. I attended courses of lectures given by the most famous professors. I took up residence opposite the Ecole Polytechnique. I made friends with several professors of this school. For three years I devoted myself exclusively to the study of what was known of the physical nature of inorganic matter. . . .

"I had to surmount great difficulties. My brain had already lost its suppleness; I was no longer young, but on the other hand I enjoyed great advantages: extensive voyages, the company of a great number of capable men whom I had sought and met."[1]

The Ecole Polytechnique, located at that time on the left bank of the Seine in the classic building which is now the meeting place of the National Assembly, was founded by the Convention for the training of civil and military engineers. Here mathematical and physical sciences were taught by illustrious men, as Lagrange, Monge, Hachette. Several other educational institutions were fostered by the young Republic. The Ecole

Normale Supérieure became the training center for teachers of higher education. The Ecole des Arts et Métiers and the Conservatoire de Musique offered instruction to students of liberal and applied arts. For the promotion of scientific studies a number of institutions were founded, such as the Bureau des Longitudes, to which the world owes the introduction of the metric system. The Institut de France gathered a group of the most prominent men in politics, literature, arts and sciences. Among its members were George Cabanis, Condorcet's brother-in-law, who carried on the tradition of the Encyclopedists; Cuvier, the great naturalist, who taught at the College de France; Lamarck, Darwin's predecessor, and Geoffrey Saint-Hilaire, no less famous naturalists.

Saint-Simon took advantage of the public lectures at the Ecole Polytechnique which he attended assiduously. He took up residence in the vicinity of the school so that he could mingle with students and teachers in the neighborhood. To young men of promise, Saint-Simon offered generous help, glorying in his rôle of a wealthy Maecenas. He aided the mathematician Siméon-Denis Poisson (1781-1840) in acquiring an education:

"He was only sixteen years old when I first met him; his financial position was poor; I provided for all his needs and even his whims up to the time when the post he obtained from the government brought him ease and comfort and rendered further help needless."[2]

A curious anecdote related by Pierre Leroux illustrates Saint-Simon's willingness to aid deserving students. The story is told by Dupuytren (1777-1836), a renowned surgeon who in his struggling youth had been approached by the philanthropist:

"I was 22 years old, I lived in a garret. I was working, cramming as they say in school, preparing for my examinations. There was a knock on my door. 'Come in,' I said without getting up.

"There entered a man, still young, very well dressed, attractive, with a frank and affable countenance. I got up to receive him.

"'You are M. Dupuytren,' he said to me. 'I am Saint-Simon. I am your neighbor. My residence is situated between the Ecole

86

Polytechnique and the Ecole de Médecine. Here is my address.' He gave me his card. 'I have heard you spoken of as a young man who will contribute to the progress of science. Your last speech was very brilliant. We have often mentioned you in our talks. I have come to ask you to be kind enough to be our guest. I keep open house. I am on friendly terms with many men of science. Monge is a friend of mine. Among the younger men I may mention Poisson and Arago. Don't you think that those who have done successful work in science should meet each other? Come and see us. Share your knowledge with us. We dine at five o'clock, you will always find your plate set at our table.'

"I listened to this strange fellow, and I didn't know what to answer. I found his manners engaging, but his familiarity displeased me. I told him that my time was taken; that, in order to fulfill the flattering hope which he expressed concerning me, I could not spare a single moment of time.

" He spoke to me then of the necessity of change, of not keeping the bow always bent. Besides one has to dine; it is an occasion to see one another, to exchange ideas, to step out of one's specialisation.

"After a few more words, discouraged perhaps by my cold reception, he left. I accompanied him to the stairway landing.

"But on reentering my room, what did I see on my dresser but a wallet containing a thousand francs which he had forgotten.

"I took the wallet and ran after the man. He had already walked down two flights. I ran down stairs and caught up with him.

"'Monsieur,' I said to him, 'here is a wallet full of money which belongs to you.'

"He answered, while trying to reach the doorway, that this money belonged to me.

"I lacked many things. But I was proud; and far from being moved by his offer, I felt offended. I made him understand that. He took back his money after my objections, and excusing himself, left saying I don't know what." [3]

By attending lectures at the Ecole Polytechnique, Saint-Simon acquired a broad knowledge of the physical and mathematical sciences, which he later utilised in his attempts to attract the attention of the scientific world. But the School of Medicine, in the same neighborhood, offered more advantages for the realisation of his ambitious design. The study of inorganic matter was but the first step toward his goal, "the opening of a new career to human intelligence, the physico-political career." Much more important was the delving into the secrets of organic matter, of living tissues, for there could be found the secret of life, and he who possessed that secret could formulate the rules for the conduct of man, the principles for his private as well as his social welfare.

"I got away from the Ecole Polytechnique in 1801," wrote Saint-Simon. 'I established myself near the Ecole de Médecine. I sought contact with the physiologists. I did not leave them until I had acquired full knowledge of their general ideas concerning the physical nature of organic matter."[4]

Saint-Simon became an assiduous student at the Ecole de Médecine, where he derived particular benefit from the teaching of Dr. Burdin, whose *Etudes médicales* prepared the ground for the momentous work of Claude Bernard. It was Dr. Burdin who, by revealing to Saint-Simon the importance of physiology, made a deep impression upon his mind and gave a new direction to his thoughts. Saint-Simon became convinced that this new science held the key to man's destiny and he resolved to become its exponent. With his usual generosity, he paid the expenses for the publication of the works of Dr. Burdin.

One of the important achievements of the period was the classification of all living beings, thereby pronouncing the fundamental concepts of natural history. The kinship of the world, the unity of life, this was the new dogma promulgated during the days of the Convention. Lamarck, Lavoisier, Saint-Hilaire, Haüy, Ampère were not only great scientists, they were also great philosophers. Saint-Simon strove to follow in their steps and hoped to surpass them.

The interest in scientific studies had reached an extraordinary vogue among women as well as among men. Fashionable and attractive ladies came to listen to public lectures on physics, chemistry, anatomy. They might not understand nor perhaps even care to understand these subjects, but the main thing was to be seen at these learned assemblies. To satisfy the popular curiosity for scientific knowledge, a number of institutes were founded under the name of *Lycée* and *Athénée*. They were opened to subscribers who in return for a yearly or monthly assessment had at their disposal comfortably furnished rooms and a well supplied library. In a vast hall, from nine o'clock in the morning until ten in the evening, one lecturer after another dispensed learning to eager audiences.

Saint-Simon, prone to follow the fashion, subsidized at his own expense a series of courses similar to those given at the Ecole Polytechnique and the Ecole de Médecine. He thus gave some young scientists the means for supplementing their meager revenues by teaching and the opportunity of demonstrating their knowledge in public.

In his eagerness to enrich his mind he entertained lavishly at his home distinguished scientists, the more to profit by their presence and their learned conversations. His uninterrupted series of banquets and social receptions were presided over by successive mistresses. But with the advent of Bonaparte to power, there came a reaction against the lax morality of the Directoire. Decorum and propriety found their place in social intercourse. Consequently in order to give a tone of respectability to his entertainments, Saint-Simon decided to get married.

There are several legends connected with this phase of his life. According to one story, Saint-Simon told M. Poisson of his intention to take a wife. He described the qualifications he wanted: intelligence, sympathetic understanding, good breeding, social graces. He would want the marriage to last for three years, at the end of which time, he would consent to a divorce, and turn over a sum of money to the woman he set free. Mr. Poisson suggested the name of Mademoiselle de Champgrand, the daughter of one of their friends.

Another story has it that the marquis de Champgrand, on his deathbed, had entrusted his daughter to the care of his former prison companion. Whatever his motive, Saint-Simon decided to marry Alexandrine-Sophie Goury de Champgrand. She was then twenty-seven years old and he, forty.

Alexandrine-Sophie, born October 8, 1773, was the illegitimate daughter of the marquis Charles-Jean de Champgrand and Madeleine-Virginie Vian, the operatic singer. Two years after the birth of Sophie, her mother left for Russia where she married, and presumably never again figured in her daughter's life. Sophie was legally adopted by her father.

The life of the marquis de Champgrand bears many points of resemblance to that of Saint-Simon. Born in 1732 at Strasbourg, he started his military career as an officer in the army. During the Revolution he speculated in national lands, engaged in various enterprises, yet made ostentatious display of extreme revolutionary opinions, a practice adopted by many aristocratic profiteers. His place of residence was close to that of Saint-Simon, a luxurious apartment at the Palais-Royal. There he entertained distinguished men of letters, artists, financiers, and others. Sophie grew up in that charming and cultured company.

Her biographer, Elise Gagne, gave this vivid description of the young woman:

"Her piquant and expressive face captivated attention from the very first. She was tall and slim, and knew how to dissimulate the slight imperfection of her waist with so much art that one could not have detected it without being forewarned. Her bright and limpid eyes, her dark hair, extremely fine and abundant, her teeth the whiteness of which flashed in a pleasant smile, her manners which were elegant without affectation, charming without coquetry, everything contributed to make her one of the most attractive young women one could meet."[5]

Her portrait in pastel was drawn by Baron de Gérard, when she was twenty years old. Sophie inherited her mother's musical talents. Nor were these talents neglected. Her voice was trained by two operatic singers, Elleviou and Garat. Musical composition she learned from Grétry and Boïeldieu, and the great Vestris taught her the minuet. It was Vestris who boasted:

"We are the three great men of Europe: I, Voltaire and the King of Prussia."[6]

The Terror brought an abrupt end to that life of ease and luxury. The marquis de Champgrand was arrested November 1793 and imprisoned at Sainte-Pélagie. In an effort to save him, his daughter made a pathetic appeal to the **Revolutionary Tribunal**. In a letter addressed to the members of that board Sophie claimed that her father was wrongly accused of being of noble extraction: "He had not the misfortune of being a noble," she wrote. This assertion contradicts the rank of marquis which her biographer attributed to him. However the contradiction can be easily explained. Titles of nobility, at least those of lower rank, were frequently assumed by wealthy or pretentious commoners of the ancient régime whenever such distinction could not be bought or obtained by royal dispensation. Under the Terror, when this title might lead one to danger, it was discarded with the same alacrity as it was sought in more favorable days.

Sophie, in the same letter, attempted to make her father one of the heroes of the Revolution by claiming that "he was among the conquerors of the Bastille." The rôle attributed to monsieur de Champgrand by his devoted daughter was exaggerated. But she may be excused on the ground that her intention was most commendable.

Notwithstanding the assertion of some biographers, there is no record to show that Sophie had been arrested and imprisoned. On the contrary, she claimed that during the ten months of her father's incarceration she continued to live in the apartment at the Palais Royal under the watchful eye of an invalid appointed by the authorities to keep her under surveillance. Sophie's father not only lost his freedom but his wealth as well, and Sophie was obliged to accept help from her friends. One of these, Mr. Hall, a well known painter of Swedish origin, lived with his wife and two daughters near the home of the Champgrands. The two families had cordial relations for many years and when misfortune befell Sophie, the kind neighbors came to her aid.

Sophie visited her father in the prison of Sainte-Pélagie nearly every day, ostensibly for the purpose of bringing him comfort. But her conduct was not motivated by filial duty alone. In the same prison was confined the son of the former governor of Nîmes, prince Jules de Rohan-Rochefort, whom she had known previously. She was then twenty years old and prince Jules was also young and fond of life. They fell in love in the shadow of the guillotine. Sophie's friends affirmed that a priest, a fellow prisoner, performed the marriage rites and that the marriage was kept a secret. The affair ended tragically when the young prince, accused of participating in the conspiracy of Batz, was sent to the gallows. Sophie bore a son who died a few years later.

Sophie never mentioned the episode of her secret marriage in her memoirs published under the title of "Souvenirs." If she had been legally entitled to call herself the Princess of Rohan, by what inconceivable modesty did she renounce such an illustrious and honorable name?

When the Terror ended, M. de Champgrand was released from prison, August 5, 1794, two months before the freeing of Saint-Simon. With his daughter he retired to Saint-Maur, where he owned a small home, which was all that was left to him of his large fortune. There he lived until his death in 1799.

Sophie had to find a way of making a livelihood. She came to Paris at the invitation of Grétry, a friend of the family. With the help of the famous composer and the advice of Elleviou and Boïeldieu, she wrote a number of sentimental songs. Garat, the popular singer, included them in his répertoire and thus assured their success. The royalties from these songs gave her the needed income.

"But," she wrote in her *Souvenirs,* "I was not satisfied with the writing of songs. Passionately fond of music, I wanted to compose orchestral pieces, and I decided to write melodramas."[7]

Under the pseudonym of M. François, she wrote several works of this genre, which included singing and orchestration. Sophie was busily engaged in her musical and dramatic career when Saint-Simon came offering her the prestige of his name and the advantages of wealth. Sophie possessed only her artistic talents, her winsome countenance, and her gracious manners. However, she was hesitant in accepting the proposal of a man whose singular character did not give much promise of marital security. According to her biographer she yielded to her friends' advice rather than to considerations of comfort and luxury.

The marriage took place on August 7, 1801, the official witnesses to the ceremony being André Grétry and Alexandre Duval.

What Saint-Simon acquired was not so much a wife as a gracious and cultivated hostess to preside over his salon, which continued to attract men and women of distinction. Among the habitués may be mentioned the names of the scientists Arago, Lagrange, Monge, and Poisson, the composer Grétry, the playwright Duval, the philosopher Pierre Leroux, the financier Perrégaux. The comtesse de Saint-Simon added grace, charm, and respectability to these social occasions.

Associations with talented people meant to Saint-Simon more than a pleasant way of life. By conversing with learned men and women, he hoped to assimilate knowledge without great effort and in cheerful surroundings. He said at one time:

"I utilized my money to acquire knowledge; good cheer, good wine, lavish entertainment of professors to whom my purse was open, secured for me all the facilities that I could desire."[8]

But the generous amphytrion was not always satisfied with the eminent company he entertained. Reminiscing about this period of life to Léon Halévy, he made this complaint:

"My savants and artists ate much and spoke little. After dinner, I would seat myself in a corner of the salon and listen. Most of the time, I heard nothing but twaddle, and I would fall asleep. Fortunately madame de Saint-Simon, with much grace and wit, did the honors of my salon."[9]

As a gracious hostess, the countess fulfilled her part of the marital contract, and according to an understanding the relationship was to have endured for another two years. But the eccentric husband changed his mind: "The experiment lasted one year, at the end of which I took leave of my apartment and of my wife."[10] The divorce took place by mutual consent June 24, 1802.

What motive impelled Saint-Simon to make that sudden decision? On the day he left Sophie, it is reported that he shed tears of regret. Was the demand for a divorce expressed by Sophie? Were the two utterly incompatible? Did she fear the approach of the coming downfall? Her biographer quoted her as saying:

"I would not have had the courage to leave him when the inevitable ruin overtook him."[11]

93

At the rate he was squandering money on lavish entertainments, endowing students, subsidizing courses of study, his limited capital was bound to be promptly exhausted. The fourth and final instalment of his share due from Redern, some 36,000 francs, was paid to him February 5, 1801. During his one year of married life he had spent 30,000 francs. At that rate of expenditure the end of his fortune was easily foreseeable. The prospect of a life of privation held no particular inducement to a woman who had been attracted to matrimony by a display of splendor and opulence. Aside from the impending ruin, life with a husband like Saint-Simon was not without its drawbacks. His eccentricities might even be interpreted as the manifestations of a deranged mind. For example, why did he insist on accumulating assignats that had lost all value?

"Why do you collect all these worthless notes?" Sophie asked.

"I am going to use them to set the cathedral of Notre-Dame on fire," parried Saint-Simon.

Undoubtedly a sense of humor might have saved the countess a good deal of worry.

The sentiments we attributed to madame de Saint-Simon in regard to her divorce are mere conjectures, but the attitude of Saint-Simon can be judged with more precision. Elise Gagne, the simpering biographer, remarked:

"Their parting was both sad and comical. M. de Saint-Simon, who never had but praise for his companion, could not part from her without deep regret. The only thing he had against her was that she was not willing to rise with him above all known standards." [12]

The ephemeral union was evidently a *mariage de convenance.* Saint-Simon referred to it with the cynical comment: "I made use of marriage as a means for observing the savants, a thing which seemed to me essential for the realization of my aims." [13]

On recovering her freedom, Sophie resumed her literary works which had been momentarily interrupted. However she gave up melodrama and devoted herself to the writing of novels and comedies. She wrote nine novels and eight plays and a number of miscellaneous compositions. Of the latter, the *Soirées des Jeunes Personnes* was crowned by the Académie Française.

Soon after her parting from Saint-Simon, she married Baron de Bawr, a Russian nobleman, who enjoyed a considerable income. But misfortune dogged her footsteps. In 1810 her husband was killed in a traffic accident, and again she had to fall back on her writing to make a living. Some of the comedies by madame de Bawr attained considerable success, particularly *Les Chevaliers du Lion* which ran for two full years at the Théâtre de l'Ambigu-Comique, and *La Suite d'un bal masqué,* which was performed at the Théâtre Français in 1819. With the participation of Mlle Mars, the greatest actress of the time, the latter play was revived during the last years of the nineteenth century by both national theaters, the Théâtre Français and the Théâtre de l'Odéon.

Several volumes of stories for children were also written by Sophie with the title *Nouveaux Contes pour les enfants.* Yet in spite of all her literary activities, she could hardly make ends meet. Her influential friends succeeded in obtaining for her a pension from the government of Louis XVIII, in 1818, "for her success in the drama . . . and the loyalty of her sentiments."[14] This financial security she enjoyed until her death, December 31, 1860, at the age of 87.

It is regrettable that in her *Souvenirs* she told nothing about herself. Her recollections and comments are concerned mostly with the men and women of note she had known in the course of her long life.

The most accurate account of her life is to be found in a lengthy article by Jules Janin who wrote on January 14, 1861, shortly after her death, for the *Journal des Débats,* to which she had been a contributor of long standing. The prominent literary critic described madame de Bawr as a gracious and vivacious old lady who delighted her listeners with witty anecdotes about the celebrated men and women she had known in the course of her long life. She had frequented the distinguished salons of Mme de Staël and Mme Récamier, where she had met Chateaubriand. She knew the poet Delille, the painter Vernet, men and women of distinction in the various arts, Mlle Mars who acted in her comedies, the great actor Talma, M. Bertin, founder of the *Journal des Débats,* the composer

Grétry, who taught her music, the renowned opera singer Garat, who gave her singing lessons.

Jules Janin expressed his unrestricted admiration for a woman he qualifies as "the last personification of a century which is gone forever." He condenses his appreciation of her life and works in this lapidary sentence: "She knew how to live, she knew how to write."

The Directoire which was so joyfully welcomed after the Terror now fell into discredit due to bankruptcy and military reverses. The depreciation of the assignats left the treasury empty. Pitt continued pouring counterfeit money into France to the extent that the paper notes became totally discredited. The bold attack against the British Empire which Bonaparte conceived by invading Egypt ended in disaster. The French government made itself odious by its decrees of compulsory military service and the imposition of burdensome taxes. The moment was ripe for Bonaparte, who had well planned his coup d'état and hastened his return from Egypt.

"In order that Bonaparte could become master of France," Napoleon wrote in his memoirs, "it was necessary that the Directoire fall into reverses in his absence, and that his return bring back victory under our flags." One of his first political successes was the treaty of Lunéville, 1801, concluded between France and Austria to the advantage of France. The following year he achieved further success by the treaty of Amiens, which established peace between France, England, Spain, and Holland, and was the crowning triumph of the Republic. Europe could at last enjoy some respite from wars and internal dissensions.

Saint-Simon, whose income was considerably reduced by the time of his divorce, hoped more than ever to attain fame and fortune in the field of science. He had gained all he could from his contacts with the French savants, but in foreign lands there was a possibility of discovering new sources of knowledge. Having disposed of his wife and his establishment, he was free to travel and to broaden his education.

The country that offered the greatest promise for accomplishing his design was England. This was the land of Bacon, the first scientific experimenter; of Newton, whom Saint-Simon worshipped above all philosophers; of Locke, who found the secrets of human perception; of Harvey who explained the mechanism of blood circulation. Full of hope and anticipation, Saint-Simon undertook the journey to London after the signing of the peace treaty of Amiens in 1802.

"The peace of Amiens," he wrote, "made it possible for me to leave for England. The purpose of my journey was to find out whether the English were working in the same field which I had undertaken to cultivate."[15]

It would be interesting to know who were the scientists he met during his brief stay in London. Unfortunately he mentioned no names nor gave any details in reference to that journey. Priestley he could not have met since the distinguished chemist and physicist had already left for America, where he fled to avoid the persecutions of his countrymen because of his sympathy for the French Revolution. It is possible that Saint-Simon had personal contact with Cavendish, the famous physicist and chemist. Cavendish's theories and experiments were so highly esteemed in Paris that, in 1803, the *Institut* chose him as one of its eight foreign associates. However all we learn of Saint-Simon's visit to England is that it did not contribute to his scientific education:

"I came back from that country with the conviction that its people were not directing their scientific works toward the physico-political goal, that they were not intent on the reorganization of the scientific system, and had not at their disposal any new capital idea."[16]

England was a disappointment, but Germany might be more favorable for his quest. Saint-Simon had met in Paris a German scientist, Dr. Oelsner, who assured him that a visit to Germany would be more fruitful. About this journey, Saint-Simon wrote:

"I travelled over a part of Germany, I brought back from that journey the certainty that general science was in its infancy in that country, since it is still based on mystic principles, but it will surely make great progress before long, for this great nation is ardently striving in that direction; it has not yet found the right way, but it is bound to find it . . . and will go a long way."[17]

While traveling in Germany his mind was not altogether

occupied with scientific research. His thoughts, if not his heart, remained focussed on the "first woman" in the world.

One biographer, in reference to Saint-Simon's divorced wife, stated that "in spite of the affection and esteem with which her person and character inspired him, the narrow and commonplace ideas in which she had been brought up and by which she still was dominated, prevented her from rising with him above all accepted standards; he was therefore obliged to ask her for a separation, since the first man in the world could not have any but the first woman as a wife."[18]

If we should take this statement seriously, the divorce of Henri who considered himself the first ranking man in the world, may have been precipitated by the death of the Swedish ambassador to France. His wife, Madame de Staël, had uncontestably won the reputation of the world's first woman, and Saint-Simon placed his hopes on winning the hand of the illustrious widow.

Through her writings and political activities Madame de Staël had become the most prominent woman in Europe. She aspired to be the first lady of France by the side of Bonaparte. However, her ambitions clashed openly with those of the First Consul. As a consequence she was exiled from Paris, and took up residence at Coppet, on the shores of Lake Geneva in Switzerland. Separated from her husband since 1797, she held at her villa a veritable court frequented by the most brilliant men and women of the time. Among her many admirers more than one gave proof of a devotion that was not purely platonic. At the time of her husband's death she was bestowing her favors on a young Frenchman, a sincere republican she admired for his caustic tongue and more so for his blond hair and good looks. His name was Benjamin Constant, who was to gain a distinguished place in literature with his psychological novel, *Adolphe*.

Saint-Simon considered the proper moment had come to make overtures to Anne Louise Germaine Necker, baroness de Staël, and directed his steps to Coppet. The door of that palatial mansion was never closed, neither was the heart of the celebrated hostess. Saint-Simon, according to one version, presented himself to Madame de Staël with this proposal:

"Madame, you are the most extraordinary woman in the world, and I am the most extraordinary man. The two of us could have a still more extraordinary child."[19]

Nowhere does Saint-Simon refer to Madame de Staël in any of his writings, so that we must accept the anecdote for its piquancy rather than its authenticity. Yet his proposal of marriage to Madame de Staël is conceivable. His belief in his own eminence was absolute. What if he had not yet given to the world a single proof of distinction? Was he not a descendant of Charlemagne, destined to equal the Emperor in greatness and glory? His offer of marriage to the most illustrious woman was on his part an honor and a compliment. Taken in that sense, the words attributed to Saint-Simon are in accord with his impulsive temperament and unlimited pride.

As for Madame de Staël, her fame rested on much more substantial claims. Aside from the active part she played in politics, her name ranked among the highest in the world of letters. Before 1800 she had published works of a miscellaneous kind including novels and essays. But with the publication of *De la Littérature considérée dans ses rapports avec les institutions sociales,* she became the writer of the day. She too was no less convinced of her supremacy than Saint-Simon was of his. She was devoured with the desire to surpass, to attract and dominate, to be heard and noticed, to be everything and in everything. The Goncourt brothers, describing Madame de Staël among a crowd of admirers, painted her with their usual impressionist touches:

"A woman with a leonine face, ruddy, pimpled, greedy lips, abrupt in mind and body, hurling in a boyish voice robust and pompous sentences, Madame de Staël keeps bouncing around from group to group."[20]

There is no evidence to prove that Saint-Simon had occasion to visit and talk with Madame de Staël. But if he never mentioned her name in his writings, she, on her part, made some eulogious remarks about him after his death:

"All his works aimed at the happiness of mankind; freedom, industry, philosophy in its highest conception were the continuous objects of his meditations. I believe that no human being ever had occasion to complain about him; he has received ungratefulness from many, he has also known gratitude from others, and this was the most pleasant aspect of his life."[21]

Jehan d'Ivray, who wrote the article containing the above quotation, is convinced that Madame de Staël exerted a veritable domination on the mind of the philosopher. The writer even claimed that Saint-Simon's first literary output was the direct result of his visit to Coppet.

The fact is that during his stay in Switzerland Saint-Simon wrote *Lettres d'un habitant de Genève à ses contemporains*. This essay was dedicated to Bonaparte, First Consul, and sent to him the 17th nivôse, year XI (January 7, 1803) with the following letter:

"Citizen First Consul,

"I am sending you my work; it is not voluminous, but you must not be surprised if I tell you that I have spent most of my life in planning it. I hope you will esteem it good, and I dare take the liberty of telling you that, in my opinion, you are the only one of my contemporaries capable of judging it; if you will be kind enough to let me know the judgment that you pronounce upon it, you will do me a very great pleasure.

"By signing this letter, by living on the part of the globe the inhabitants of which are directly under your orders, I take, as you see, the liberty of placing myself directly under your protection.   St.-Simon

rue Derrière-le-Rhône à Genève."

There is assuredly nothing in the tone of this letter to recommend its author to the attention of Madame de Staël. Did Saint-Simon dedicate his first writing to Bonaparte as a rebuke to the widow of Coppet for having jilted him? From his claim that the First Consul was the only one of his contemporaries capable of judging his work, it might appear that Madame de Staël did not give her approval to the *Letters of an Inhabitant of Geneva*.

There was evidently some relation between the Saint-Simon *Letters* and Madame de Staël's work published in 1800: *De la Littérature considérée dans ses rapports avec les institutions sociales*. Her main thesis was that literary progress stands in direct relation to social and political evolution. A firm believer

100

in the eighteenth century doctrine of the unlimited perfectibility of man, she concluded that in a more or less remote future the ideal state will be established. Under those future blissful conditions, works of literature will cease to be a vain and frivolous pastime. They will become part of human activities contributing to the common weal. Writers will be auxiliaries to rulers. Not only auxiliaries, for the rulers will often be chosen among the eminent writers. The man of letters has a mission, which is to discover and propagate moral ideas and safeguard liberty.

The social function of the writer, which Madame de Staël had conceived and eloquently expressed at this date, became one of the most constant principles of Saint-Simon's social philosophy. In the *Lettres d'un habitant de Genève* the new society which the author envisaged was to be governed by mathematicians, physicists, chemists, physiologists, and artists, the latter including writers, painters, sculptors, musicians. The task of the scientists was to take care of the material well-being of the community. To the artists was entrusted its mental development and emotional enjoyment.

Both writers thus agree on the rôle of art and literature in the society of the future, and both believe in the advent of an improved social order. But Madame de Staël was preoccupied with the progress and development of French literature, rather than the reform of social institutions. Saint-Simon, on the other hand, presented a plan for reorganizing society on a scientific basis. In the dedication to Bonaparte, he asserted that he had spent most of his life in planning his tenuous volume. Saint-Simon exaggerated. His concept of a future society could not have taken more than two years of gestation. The *Lettres* were the result of his conversations with Dr. Burdin and other scientists. They were also, and primarily, an attempt to prove that he was the greatest man on earth, not after Bonaparte, but on a par with the First Consul, the only genius capable of understanding the sublimity of his thought.

Another reason may have prompted Saint-Simon to dedicate his first work to the First Consul. By the time of his arrival at Geneva, his revenues were nearing the vanishing point. The money obtained from his settlement with Redern had been used up in a whirlwind of entertainments to which he referred as a source of experimentation. Instead of posing as the Maecenas of science, it was the turn of science to help him. Firmly convinced of his genius, he offered his collaboration to Bonaparte for the building of a new social order on the ruins of the old régime. Was it not legitimate to expect a reward for his great services to mankind? Being a promoter with a fertile imagination, Saint-Simon in his *Lettres* proposed another grandiose scheme to bolster his financial situation.

Newton being at that time the object of his veneration, Saint-Simon proposed that a temple be erected to the discoverer of the law of gravitation. The priests of this temple would be scientists and artists of renown. All Europeans, men and women, would elect twelve of the most illustrious men. These men of genius must be freed from all material cares so that they could devote their time and energy to the progress of mankind. For their financial support Saint-Simon recommended to Bonaparte the opening of a world wide subscription.

"Let every one subscribe for any amount he wishes. Let each subscriber name three mathematicians, three physicists, three chemists, three physiologists, three men of letters, three artists, three musicians. Renew the subscription every year; divide the amount of the subscription among the three mathematicians, the three physicists, etc. who will obtain the largest number of votes. The men of genius will then enjoy a reward worthy of themselves and of you."[22]

One can readily imagine that Saint-Simon counted himself as one of the three scientists who would be assured of the largest number of votes and a worthy reward. But Bonaparte had other things to do, and ignored the ingenious project in spite of the flattering compliments of the author.

Saint-Simon returned to Paris ready to carry on his great ambition:

"One sees that I have neglected nothing, spared nothing to insure the success of my scientific enterprises; it is after having terminated all the preparatory work of which I have given an account that I took to writing."[23]

CHAPTER SEVEN

From his travels abroad Saint-Simon returned to Paris in the course of the year 1804, enriched in knowledge but impoverished in funds. However, there was no reason to worry about financial matters when he felt certain the time had come to fulfill his sublime destiny. He firmly hoped to win fame and honor as a great scientist and fill in the government a function worthy of his intellectual capacities. He had given generously of his fortune to aid others, and when in turn he needed assistance he looked for it as a matter of course.

As no response came from Napoleon Bonaparte, who was soon to crown himself emperor, Saint-Simon applied to his friends to intercede for him. In a letter to M. Agasse, March 1804, he asked him to bring the manuscript of *Lettres d'un habitant de Genève* to the attention of Napoleon. But as his appeal was of no avail, he began to lose confidence in his plan of world reform. In another letter to M. Agasse he did not conceal his discouragement:

"I forego my project to gain recognition; I give up the hope of being useful to my contemporaries. . . . I shall work for the generations to come."[1]

Saint-Simon's revenues were reduced to a small pension which was granted to him by Redern and one of his friends. In 1805 Redern was notified by his legal representative that his former associate was in dire need. Redern authorized his agent to give him 100 francs a month with the admonition not to let him know the source of the income. The same agent obtained another monthly contribution of 120 francs from M. de Béhague, who had been involved in various transactions with Saint-Simon and who had acquired a considerable fortune of his own.

But a man with princely habits could not be satisfied with so modest a sustenance. He clung to his determination to obtain a government post to which he felt rightfully entitled. He applied to one of his comrades in the American campaign, whom he had often entertained at his table. The man was comte Louis-Philippe de Ségur, now one of the highest officials of the imperial court in his function of master of ceremonies. We read in Saint-Simon's memoirs:

"My funds being exhausted I applied for a post; I addressed myself to monsieur le comte de Ségur. He received my request graciously, and notified me after six months that he had obtained for me a job at the national pawn shop. The job was that of copyist; it brought 1,000 francs a year for nine hours of work a day. I held it for six months. My personal work was done at night." [2]

The bitter irony of these lines needs no comment. Count de Ségur, whom Stendhal characterized as base and worthless, could not have found a more humiliating job for one of his former fellow-officers.

It took more than ordinary determination for a man who worked all day at a menial task to devote his nights to writing. But even the strongest constitution could not endure the strain without serious injury to his health.

"I was spitting blood. My health was in the worst condition, when by luck I met the only man whom I can call my friend. I met Diard who had been in my service from 1790 to 1797. I had parted from him when I broke relations with count de Redern. Diard said to me: 'Monsieur, the post which you occupy is unworthy of your name, as well as of your capacities. I beg you to come to my house; you may dispose of anything which belongs to me; you will work at your ease and you will be doing justice to yourself.' I accepted the proposition of this good man, I have lived at his house, I have been living there for two years (1806-1808), and since that time he has earnestly catered to all my needs and defrayed the considerable expenses for the work which I have published." [3]

The work for which Diard, the Good Samaritan, had paid the

expenses of publication was the *Introduction aux travaux scientifiques du dix-neuvième siècle,* which appeared in 1808. Napoleon had requested from contemporary scientists an account of the progress of science since 1789. Saint-Simon's *Introduction* was an ambitious attempt to answer the Emperor's inquiry.

With renewed hope he submitted his treatise to the attention of the master of Europe. "The Emperor is the scientific as well as the political head of humanity," declared Saint-Simon. Hence Napoleon should help the author in "building a scientific monument of a dimension and magnificence which cannot be equalled by any of his successors."

But work on such a large scale would require ten years of application and a generous subsidy to carry the task to completion. Saint-Simon proposed, among other ideas, the constitution of a new spiritual power necessary to maintain social order. "The Emperor will need a scientific lieutenant capable of understanding his projects; he needs another Descartes."

This scientific lieutenant, the other Descartes, was obviously Saint-Simon himself. And the better to gain the attention of the Emperor, who was not indifferent to praise, the author indulged in the most hyperbolic adulation a conqueror ever received. Drawing his image from the bold feat of Bonaparte crossing the Alps, he exclaimed:

"In order to offer the Emperor a monument worthy of him, one should carve Mount Saint-Bernard to make his statue, the base of which would be the earth itself."

But Napoleon was more interested in good engineers and artillerymen than in philosophers, and not even such extravagant praise could attract his attention.

Saint-Simon was not content with Diard's generous assistance. Not only did he continue sending begging letters to his wealthy acquaintances, he did not even hesitate to resort to questionable means of extracting money from some of his friends. While M. de Béhague, from whom he received a monthly pension of one hundred and twenty francs, was traveling in Germany, Saint-Simon demanded a thousand louis, that is about 24,000 francs, of the financier's wife. In case of refusal, he threatened to publish some papers that would injure her husband's reputation as well as her own.

Madame de Béhague was not intimidated. When her husband returned and learned of the incident, he stopped the monthly allowance. Saint-Simon, in spite of his failure to gain any advantage, never carried out his threat. He then turned his attention to Redern in the hope of better results.

Redern had settled permanently in France, making his home on a large estate at Flers in Picardy. On May 21, 1807, Saint-Simon wrote to his former associate, claiming that he had been wronged in the division of the property. In the apportionment made in 1798, Redern had gained 150,000 francs of revenue from real property, while he, Saint-Simon, had merely received a total sum of 144,000 francs. The settlement to Redern's advantage was unfair since the latter's contribution to the business had been insignificant. The capital invested by his associate was the least important factor in assuring the success of the enterprise.

"Our benefits were derived from the depreciation of assignats," explained Saint-Simon. "Any one who acquired national domains and waited before making payments until the assignats had fallen in value, made a fortune in proportion to the amount of his acquisitions. The agents in my employ bought properties in their own names, they sold a small portion of them at a profit which enabled them to pay off the whole amount . . . Neither of them deposited a single *sou* of capital in advance. I did not need your money for my speculations, that money was of secondary help only. I should have received, in the apportionment, a larger share than you."[4]

Saint-Simon argued that during the troubled days of the revolution he took all the risks while his partner kept safely away.

"You left France in 1791; you came back in 1794. During your absence I ran the risks to which the nobles, the rich, and the enlightened men were exposed. My association with you, who were then ambassador of Prussia to England, had placed me in a most dangerous situation. During that time, on the contrary, you were safe from the persecutions to which I was constantly exposed. In your absence you were not able to contribute in any manner to the success of the partnership. Yet, let us consider what my conduct was on your return. At the very moment of your arrival I handed to you a written declaration, stating that you were the owner of all the properties I had acquired, which rendered you absolute master of our interests and free to settle them at your will."[5]

Saint-Simon admitted that, by signing the final settlement which granted him a sum of 144,000 livres, he could not have recourse to law for a revision of the case. But he contended that his share should have been larger by 150,000 or 200,000 francs. He appealed to Redern as to an old friend who should come to his aid:

"You have an income of more than 200,000 francs and you are single. It is easy for you to secure for me the means to terminate my career in easy circumstances."

A month passed and Redern had not answered. Saint-Simon, embittered and desperate, wrote a second letter. The conciliatory tone of the first missive changed to anger and threats:

"Paris, June 22, 1807

". . . I am determined to employ all necessary means to get out of the unfortunate position into which I have been led by too great a trust in you. In the apportionment that took place between us, there has been an error of a great sum, to my disadvantage. I can show proof of that error. . . . I can force you to correct it. I have ten times more means than necessary for obtaining that result."[6]

However, in ending the letter Saint-Simon assumed a more genial tone, not wishing to cause his former associate the loss of tranquility and happiness. He concluded by proposing to submit his claims to arbitration by mutual friends.

Redern's answer came on July 29, 1807. It was curt, cold, and scornful. The wealthy count addressed Saint-Simon in the third person, the better to mark his utter detachment.

"His threats are impertinent and I am indifferent to them as I am to his person. His reputation makes it impossible for him to harm other people; he cannot touch mine."[7]

This rebuff did not discourage Saint-Simon, who, on August 1st, reiterated his request to have the case arbitrated, and his determination to see it done. On August 6th, Redern sent a final note:

"All my relations with him have been broken long ago, and for ever. There is nothing to settle between us."

Since there was no hope of negotiating directly with Redern, Saint-Simon tried to interest a notable statesman in his case. On November 2, he addressed himself to Senator Boissy d'Anglas, asking his intervention in favor of a revision of the terms. Boissy d'Anglas, who had been a frequent guest of Saint-Simon in his days of opulence, commanded the respect and the admiration of all. He had been an influential member of the Convention, had worked for the fall of Robespierre, and had shown great courage and determination in the critical days of the Terror. On the first of Prairial (May 20, 1795) he was presiding over the Convention when the mob invaded the assembly hall. Unmoved by the insults and menaces of the insurgents he remained in his chair, while a young deputy, Féraud, was shot to death, his head cut off, and presented to him on the end of a spike. Boissy d'Anglas, calm and dignified, bowed to it impassively, and ordered the assembly to carry on its business. In 1801 he was made member of the Tribunate and became senator of the Empire in 1815.

Both Saint-Simon and Redern presented their arguments to the senator. The statesman wanted to get acquainted with the facts in the case and help redress the wrongs, if any had occurred. But he found that Saint-Simon's claims had no valid grounds since all transactions between him and his associate had been duly notarized and sanctioned by legal documents. Boissy d'Anglas refused to intervene in favor of his former host.

The quarrel between Redern and Saint-Simon dragged on for several years. It is the one episode in the philosopher's career that is well documented. Both men issued lengthy reviews of their business relationships in the form of printed brochures, in conformity with the custom of the day. But while he kept publishing statements about Redern and demanding contributions from his wealthy friends, Saint-Simon did not lose hope of obtaining recognition as a philosopher. He tried to impart his theories to the prominent men of science and addressed to them a series of printed letters entitled *Lettres au Bureau des Longitudes.* Convinced of having made the greatest discovery of all time, Saint-Simon presented himself to the learned members of this institute with no false modesty:

"I believe, gentlemen, that I have found an encyclopedic conception better than that of Bacon, a conception of the universe better than that of Newton and a method better than that of Locke."[8]

In his series of *Lettres,* seven in all, Saint-Simon proposed a plan for raising a colossal monument to Descartes, upon whose method was to be founded a scientific system of world government. Why did Saint-Simon replace the cult of Newton with that of Descartes? In the *Lettres d'un habitant de Genève,* Newton was enthroned as the greatest benefactor of mankind. But Newton was an Englishman. It would be unpatriotic to uphold him to his countrymen for worship now that England had become Napoleon's most stubborn enemy. For political expediency, if for no other reason, it was wise to enshrine a Frenchman in the place of worship. But Saint-Simon, as might be expected, gave his own explanation for the sudden abjuration of Newton:

"I see that Newton's influence is most harmful to the progress of science, and I cry out with all my strength to my contemporaries: it is time to take another road; it is on a *à priori* road that discoveries are to be made." The *à priori* road referred to the cartesian method in opposition to the *à posteriori* philosophy of Newton. However the scientists remained unimpressed by the boastful declaration of the author of the *Lettres.* The president of the Bureau of Longitudes sent him the following answer:

"Monsieur,

"The *Bureau des Longitudes* asks me to notify you that the nature of the work which you communicated to them in your various letters is not the kind which the Bureau is competent to examine.

"The law of its foundations requires that it occupy itself exclusively with the means of perfecting geography, navigation and astronomy: consequently the *Bureau des Longitudes* has decided not to give you any other answer than the one which I have the honor of sending you to-day.

"Since M. de Saint-Simon intends to publish his ideas on world organization, the scholar and the public will be able to judge them with impartiality.

"I have the honor to salute you,   Bouvard

"August 29, 1808."

Realizing that he had addressed himself to indifferent judges, our undaunted philosopher sought to gain a hearing from a higher tribunal by sending his communications to the *Institut des Sciences*. In order to better impress the members of the *Institut* with his scientific qualifications as well as with his financial difficulties, Saint-Simon prefaced one issue of the letters with a brief autobiography:

"I am a descendant of Charlemagne. My father was the comte de Saint-Simon. I was the nearest relative of the noted author, the Duc de Saint-Simon. His duchy-peerage, his grandeeship of Spain and five hundred thousand livres of income which he enjoyed, all these were due to be mine. He quarreled with my father, whom he disinherited. Thus I lost the titles and the fortune of the duc de Saint-Simon; but I have inherited his desire for glory.

"The death of my father, which took place in 1783, made no change in my financial status; the property came from my mother's side, who is also a Saint-Simon. My mother is living, she has been ruined by the Revolution; all hope of inheritance is gone for me. I never inherited anything from anybody; I never had any income other than the money received for my work. I made very lucrative speculations from 1790 to 1797, and I would have been opulent if my scientific studies had not made me neglect my financial interests. The count de Redern who was my associate, has profited by my negligence; he aimed at wealth, I pursued glory: I was bound to be financially his dupe and that is what happened.

"In 1798 I took up a scientific career. I possessed at that time a sum of 144,000 livres. That sum of money was but a very small part of the profit to which I was entitled."[9]

There followed the recital of his dealings with Redern and an exposé of the state of destitution to which he had been reduced by his quest for knowledge and scientific experiments.

Saint-Simon did not receive from the *Institut des Sciences* the recognition he had expected. In retrospect he realized that he had presented his ideas prematurely, being still ill-prepared for his great scientific task.

"Convinced by experience that I was not yet mature to plan and compose the work which I had conceived, I decided to publish some *Lettres*[10] in which I treated separately the questions the partial solutions of which are the principles which I shall use in the organization of the scientific system.

"The *Letters* which I published did not lead, as I had hoped, to a general discussion; but this work was very useful to me, because it furnished me with the occasion to elaborate my ideas, and because it attracted the attention of some people who have been kind enough to communicate their observations to me. . . .

"For lack of funds I was not able to continue the work; I was obliged to change my plan and adopt a new one."[11]

A period of dire poverty now began for the once wealthy grand seigneur. He even had to pawn some of the furnishings of the apartment, to which the concierge objected. He sent a number of despairing and begging letters:

"For two weeks I have been living on bread and water. I have been working without fire, and I have sold even my clothes to defray the expenses of making copies of my work. I have fallen into this state of distress because of my passion for science and public happiness, the desire to find a means of putting an end by pacific ways to the frightful crisis in which all European peoples are engaged. Therefore I can without shame confess my misery and ask for help needed to put me in condition to continue my work."[12]

To another friend he wrote: "I lack everything, despair is mounting, my position is becoming insupportable."[13]

What kept up his courage in the face of difficulties was his unshakeable faith in his greatness, and his firm resolve to achieve glory. Added to his *Introduction aux Travaux scientifiques du XIX siècle* and *Lettres au Bureau des Longitudes,* he outlined in 1810 a plan for a new encyclopedia: *Nouvelle Encyclopédie, Première livraison servant de Prospectus.* This work he dedicated to his nephew, marquis Henri-Jean-Victor, born February 12, 1782, the son of his oldest sister, Adélaïde-Blanche-Marie, and Louis-Charles de Saint-Simon of the Monbléru branch. Victor at that time was an officer in Napoleon's army fighting in Spain. His uncle felt a keen interest in the young officer who had distinguished himself on the field of battle, particularly at Iena, as aide-de-camp to Marshal Ney. He was made Chevalier de la Légion d'Honeur in 1806.

In the person of Victor the family name began to shine again with glory. Victor must be reminded of his illustrious origin in order to encourage him in his striving for fame and greatness.

"My purpose, my dear Victor," Saint-Simon wrote in the preface, "in dedicating my work to you is to urge you toward the achievement of great deeds. Think of your name, my dear nephew, let the thought of your birth be continuously present in your mind. The study of history will teach you that the most sublime things that have been done or said, have been done or said by men of noble birth. Our ancestor Charlemagne, Peter the Great, Frederick the Great, and the Emperor Napoleon were born noblemen. And the best thinkers, such as Galileo, Bacon, Descartes and Newton were also noblemen."

Saint-Simon's delusions of self importance and descent from royal lineage belong to a form of paranoia in which the patient is able to analyse his own case with perfect lucidity:

"Insanity, my dear Victor," he wrote to his nephew, "is nothing else but an extreme exaltation, and this extreme exaltation is indispensable for the achievement of great things. Those who escaped from an insane asylum are the only ones who enter the temple of glory, but not all who escape from an insane asylum can enter the temple. At the most one in a million succeeds in entering it, the others break their necks."

Saint-Simon's delusion in his quest for glory was the belief that he was the greatest philosopher of all time. Philosophy, as he conceived it, must cease to be a metaphysical speculation. It should be positive, basing its premises on science and deducing laws applicable to human society. For this reason science must not devote itself exclusively to special research. What is most needed is the formulation of a general plan, a conception of life applicable to all mankind. The time had come for making a synthesis of all positive knowledge and constructing on that basis a moral and political philosophy.

Descartes had been bold enough to champion the scientific method as opposed to the theological. The political revolution must also be accompanied by a scientific revolution. Science must take a "Napoleonic step" and that was the task Saint-Simon undertook in planning a new encyclopedia. He seriously fancied himself the "Napoleon of Science" and in the preface to the *Nouvelle Encyclopédie* boldly stated that he and the Emperor were partners in the new organization of the world.

The dedicatory preface of the Encyclopedia was addressed to his nephew:

"I enjoy a blessing of which Bacon and Newton had been deprived, that of living under the laws of the most magnanimous of all the princes and the most philosophical of all the kings who ever existed. Under the reign of the Great Napoleon, France must shine with all kinds of glory. The Emperor is the scientific chief of humanity, as well as the political chief. In one hand he holds the unerring compass, in the other the sword that exterminates the opponents of progress. Around his throne must gather the most illustrious savants as well as the most valiant captains. In the capital of the Emperor's immense dominions took place the scientific discovery which I am about to announce, a discovery which by its vastness and importance is superior to all that have been made and which the generations to come shall never be able to surpass."

Saint-Simon urged the most celebrated scientists of the world to come to Paris and work under Napoleon's orders for the organization of a compendium of all human knowledge. This achievement would make France the greatest nation on earth and thus put an end to the long antagonism between her and England.

The following year, 1811, Saint-Simon wrote *Mémoire sur la Science de l'Homme*. Lacking the necessary funds for publishing his Treatise on the Science of Man, he had only sixty copies printed for distribution among prominent scientists, in the hope of interesting them in his ideas. His claims of surpassing Bacon and of conceiving a world system superior to that of Laplace need not engage undue attention. But here again in the Introduction, his strange mentality revealed itself. Considering Laplace as his dangerous rival and personal enemy, he attacked the great astronomer-philosopher with a violence surpassing all bounds of courtesy and common decency.

Laplace had stated that the science of astronomy rendered great services to man, particularly in dissipating errors born out of ignorance of the true relation between man and nature. Those errors were the more harmful since social order is based on such relations.

"Truth and Justice," said Laplace, "are the immutable laws which cannot be violated with impunity."

Commenting on the preceding remarks, Saint-Simon wrote:

"It is evident that Monsieur Laplace's conceptions of the rapport between the astronomical sciences and human knowledge are extremely vague. The words Truth and Justice, written in bold letters in the middle of the most insignificant text, are placed there with a charlatanism which I shall unmask.

"In reading the remarks of Laplace which I have quoted, I was reminded of an incident which I witnessed on the Champs-Elysées.

"A mechanic believed he had found the means of flying like the birds. He announced that he would make a demonstration in the garden on the Champs-Elysées. I went there. In the middle of the garden stood an upright post with an arm projecting from the top, which held a pulley with a rope passed through it. This rope was used to hoist the mechanic who was fastened crosswise to his machine. This machine was equipped with four wings which the new Icarus was supposed to move with his arms and legs. When he reached the top of the post he signaled to cut the rope. Thinking that this had been done, he imagined that he was holding himself up in the air by means of his contraption, and looked down on the spectators with that air of satisfaction inspired by success, while the spectators were laughing in his face.

114

"When the mechanic had signalled to cut the rope, they had not been able to execute his order, because the ladder was not conveniently placed for that purpose. But soon the ladder was moved to the proper place. The rope was cut, and the poor devil fell like a mass of lead. He paid dearly for the little amount of satisfaction he had enjoyed.

"The mechanic Laplace fashioned with Truth and Justice two wings, with which he thought he could fly to immortality. At this moment he thinks he is soaring above his contemporaries. He is mistaken. I shall cut the rope and he will fall."

At the time Saint-Simon wrote this venomous attack, Laplace, already known the world over for his discoveries, was engaged in formulating his famous *Mécanique Céleste,* of which four volumes had already appeared. This great work not only offered a complete solution of the problems presented by the solar system, but it contained also, especially in the section called *Exposition du système du monde,* pages which are masterpieces of literary style.

Saint-Simon realised that his attack on Laplace was carried on with more than the customary violence and, anticipating rebuke by his readers, he answered their objections with what he entitled: "Episode. My opinion on the discussion." He excused his boldness on the ground that a controversy is a combat which requires courage:

"He who takes up the pen must arm himself with courage, in the same way as he who takes up a gun. The savant and the soldier who show cowardice are equally despicable. The doors of the temple of glory are open to the brave only."

And Saint-Simon added in capital letters:

"Only the men who are possessed with a passionate desire for glory are capable of discussing well."

However, his antagonism was not based solely on philosophical grounds. There were personal reasons which explain his attitude and which he stated with frankness:

"I am going to tell what arouses me personally against M. de Laplace.

"For ten years I have been acquiring every day new rights toward scientific recognition, and every day my social position

115

has grown worse. It is M. de Laplace who has poisoned these ten years of my life, and at this moment I challenge M. de Laplace in view of obtaining from him reparation for the harm he has done me. But, before presenting the plan of my challenge, I must give my own Theory of the solar system."

His final judgment on Laplace contributes not a little to an understanding of Saint-Simon's character:

"It is to M. de Laplace that we owe the most absurd arguments which the human mind ever produced. I conclude by requesting that a fool's cap replace the doctor's cap of M. de Laplace, and that the same Laplace be exposed, his head thus covered, to the hooting of school children."

Such vituperative language does little credit to a scion of Charlemagne, and least of all to a gentleman.

Napoleon steadfastly refused to recognize Saint-Simon, while he gave important posts to the great scientists of the country. The mathematician Monge was made member of the Senate with the title of count. Cuvier was elevated to the post of Minister of Interior. Lacépède became president of the Senate and grand chancellor of the Legion of Honor. As was to be expected Saint-Simon reversed his attitude toward the Emperor. He condemned the men of science for lending their talents to the nefarious designs of the conqueror:

"The human species is engaged in one of the greatest crises since the beginning of its existence. What efforts have you made to end that crisis? What means have you for reestablishing order in human society? All of Europe is slaughtering itself. What do you do to stop this butchery? Nothing. Moreover, it is you who improve the means of destruction. It is you who direct their use by all the armed forces. You are placed at the head of the artillery, you conduct the attack on fortifications. I ask you again: what are you doing to restore peace? Nothing. What could you do? Nothing. The knowledge of man is the only study that might lead to the discovery of means by which one could reconcile national interests, but you do not study that science. You have acquired only one trait in that direction, that of flattering those who are in power in order to obtain their favors and share in their bounty. Give up the direction of scientific activities. Let us warm our hearts frozen under your leadership and turn our attention to studies which can restore peace by reorganizing society."

It ill behooved Saint-Simon to accuse men of science of flattering "those who are in power in order to obtain their favors," for his bombastic adulation of the Emperor could hardly be surpassed. On the other hand, one cannot help giving him credit for condemning science when it lends its resources to the destruction instead of the salvation of mankind. And no less praiseworthy was his desire to restore peace and stop war by a reorganization of European society. Political and social reforms became with more and more insistence the object of his thoughts. Vague and wavering as might be his theories, there is no denying that his aim was fixed and his determination set.

Although ingratitude is a human trait only too common among all classes, it may appear strange that, apart from the good servant Diard, Saint-Simon could not find a helping hand among the prominent and wealthy men he had associated with in his days of opulence. But he must have estranged his former friends by his extravagant ways and dubious morality.

Saint-Simon, aware of having created an unfavorable impression by his mode of life, found a ready excuse for his conduct. Being a superman, he was not subject to petty conventions and moral impediments as an ordinary mortal, and consequently his conduct could not be judged by the same standards. Instead of condemning his transgressions, the world should consider them as the valuable and necessary experiments of a genius in quest of great discoveries. In an autobiographical statement Saint-Simon lays particular stress on this aspect of his life. It constitutes a remarkable psychological document and for this reason it is worth quoting at length:

"My life presents a series of falls, and yet my life is not a failure, for, far from descending, I have kept on ascending, that is to say, none of my falls caused me to fall back to the point from which I had started. The enterprises to which I devoted myself and which ended in failure, must be considered as experiments which were necessary; they must be regarded as preparatory works which have taken the active part of my life.

"In the field of discoveries my activities have been those of a flowing tide. I have receded often, but the rising force in me has always gained over the descending one. Nearly fifty years old, I have reached the age when a man goes into retirement, but I am just beginning my career. In a word, after a long and painful journey, I have just reached the starting point.

"I return to the history of my life. I do say that my acts must not be judged according to the same principles as those of the average man, because my life up to now has been a series of experiments. I shall indicate by an example the differences which seem to me to exist between the principles by which one must judge actions directed toward the ordinary aim of life and those which aim at experimentation.

"If I see a man exercise his strength or skill on an animal for the only purpose of making it suffer, I say (were the animal but a fly) that this man unfortunately did not receive from nature a sensitive organization, and I affirm without hesitation that he is following a direction which is bound to lead him to cruelty. But if I see a physiologist experiment on living animals, disemboweling bitches with young, dissecting vigorous and healthy dogs, etc., I say: here is a man busy with researches which aim at the discovery of processes useful toward the alleviation of humanity.

"If I see a man who is not interested in general science frequenting houses of gambling and debauch, seeking the society of persons known for their immorality, I would say: there is a man on the way to perdition; the habits which he is forming will debase him in his own eyes and will render him consequently supremely contemptible. But if this man is interested in theoretical philosophy, if he aims by his researches to rectify the line of demarcation which must separate actions and classify them into good and bad, if he tries to discover a remedy to cure the diseases of the mind which cause so great misfortunes to those who are victims of it, I would say: this man follows the road of vice in a direction which will necessarily lead him to the highest virtue.

"I have done all I could to learn as exactly as possible the moral habits and opinions of the various classes of society, I

118

have sought, I have seized every occasion to become acquainted with men of all characters and all kinds of morality.

"These researches have caused me great harm in the opinion of the public, but I am far from regretting them. My self-esteem has always increased in the proportion to the harm I did to my reputation; I have every reason to congratulate myself for my past behavior, since I find myself in a condition to present new and positive views to my contemporaries; the immense genius of the Emperor did not circumvent me and my admiration for him has not altered the independence of my thoughts.

"One can easily imagine that many extraordinary things must have happened to me; I could indeed relate many a piquant anecdote, but at this moment a more important work occupies my attention, absorbs all my time and faculties, I am still vigorous, I still live in the future."[14]

Notwithstanding its brevity, Saint-Simon's autobiography compares with Rousseau's *Confessions* at least on two points, the brazenness of self-justification and the boldness of self-glorification. Saint-Simon was not concerned so much in giving an accurate account of his life as in making an apology *pro domo*. His intention was to convince the reader of his greatness based on his illustrious descent and his unique achievements. He took care to justify his profligate and prodigal existence by assuming a high philosophical purpose. A philosopher must lead a full life and live through all human experiences. He is not to be judged by ordinary standards: "No, my actions cannot be judged by the same principles as others, because all my active life was one of experimentation."

CHAPTER EIGHT

Saint-Simon persuaded himself that his ancestors had been the object of continuous injustices since the death of Charlemagne. From the possessions of the whole western Empire they were reduced by an unkindly fate to the Kingdom of France, and afterwards to the county of Vermandois until the Revolution took from them the last piece of land and the last vestige of glory. As for himself, was he not personally entitled to inherit from the noted author, the duke of Saint-Simon, a duchy peerage, a grandeeship of Spain and five hundred thousand livres? All of which he lost because the duke quarreled with his father, whom he disinherited. Most of the above claims were probably the fabrication of a deluded mind.

Victim of an equally mistaken notion, Saint-Simon blamed Laplace for his failure to achieve recognition as the greatest scientist of the time, and his undignified condemnation of the illustrious astronomer must be attributed to mental vagaries and irrational speculations.

But of all his real or fancied grievances, his dispute with Redern revealed the most conspicuous phase of the persecutory mania. After squandering to the last sou the fortune he received as his share of the partnership, he accused Redern of an unjust division of property. Legally Saint-Simon had no grounds for such an accusation. In 1797 he had transferred to Redern by notarized deed, ownership to all the properties. At the time he seemed to be satisfied with the terms of the agreement, and it was not until he had dissipated most of his allotted funds that he began to pester his former associate for a more advantageous apportionment. Redern remained deaf to his pleadings, and Saint-Simon appealed to friends in the government to have them use their influence in reopening negotiations. But his efforts were in vain.

The more his financial circumstances became precarious, the more was he determined to obtain redress for a fancied wrong, and to reopen the case. Since letters had no effect, he betook himself to Alençon, the chief town of the district in which Redern occupied the château of Flers. There the erstwhile ambassador lived the life of a country gentleman, greatly esteemed as a respectable citizen of the country of his adoption, and a generous benefactor of the local community. Saint-Simon preceded his coming to Alençon with a pathetic letter to Redern:

"Paris, Tuesday, October 15, 1811.

"I am leaving to-day, to-morrow I shall be in Alençon, it is high time to put an end to this. I have not slept for three nights, which I spent repeating to myself: what will become of me! what will become of me! I told you many times, I am telling you again and I shall write it to you again when I arrive in Alençon: bread and books, that is all you are asked by your old friend who recognizes his wrongs toward you, toward his family, toward everybody, but who is confident of being able to repair his wrong towards you, his family and everybody if you give him the books he needs and bread."

On his arrival at Alençon, Saint-Simon threatened to publish a pamphlet against his former associate. This was the method he had threatened to use in his attempt to extort money from madame de Béhague. Redern notified him that if he would return immediately to Paris he would be given five hundred francs and a monthly subsidy of one hundred francs through the intermediary of a mutual friend. Saint-Simon complied, but after having received the five hundred francs he returned to Alençon bent on getting a revision of the agreement which had been concluded some fourteen years previously.

Saint-Simon's biographers place all the blame on count de Redern. To permit the reader to form an impartial judgment, we present those parts of the documents which bear directly on the case. In a letter addressed to Senator Boissy d'Anglas, Saint-Simon declared:

"I associated myself with M. de Redern in 1791. The speculations which I had in mind offered but mediocre prospects; the assignats were at par, their fall could not be foreseen. . . .

As early as 1792 matters took a new turn, the assignats fell in value, the payments for the national domains were not strictly imposed so that it became possible to make acquisitions without having any funds; this is what many people did, . . . the resale of a small portion was sufficient for acquiring title to the lands that were sold to the highest bidder.

"It was not money, it was energy which was required to promote the sale of the domains of the Priory of the Abbé Maury and to become the highest bidder for those domains. It was energy which was needed and not money to promote at Cambrai the sales of the national properties the day they learned in that town of the flight of the king. . . .

"Without my association with M. de Redern, without his capital, I could have made the same speculation, the same profits, and in all likelihood I would not have spent eleven months in prison incommunicado, since my association with the ambassador of Prussia to London brought danger upon me in addition to those to which I was exposed on account of my opinions.

"When M. de Redern returned to France in 1794, I gave him what he could expect of the most affectionate, loyal and generous friend. At that moment my brothers and sisters were living with me, he became part of our family and was treated as an elder brother. I handed to him on the day of his arrival a written statement to the effect that all the properties acquired by me belonged to him. . . . I made him the principal associate when he should have been considered anything but a secondary associate.

"M. de Redern abused my excessive trust in him. He deducted in favor of one of his sisters, from the total of the properties which I had acquired, a share bringing an income of from thirty to forty thousand livres and he declared that the rest of the properties would remain in common between him and me. . . . His share should have been one third and mine two thirds. . . .

"On the return of M. de Redern almost all the properties which I had acquired were deeded to various persons who merely lent their names. Thus I could have appropriated exclusively for myself any part of the fortune I desired without the knowledge of M. de Redern. . .

"M. de Redern had been in Paris about three months when he proposed that I sign a contract. Each day our mutual affection grew stronger and stronger; our usual conversations dealt with the desire to spend our lives together. M. de Redern entered into details for carrying out this plan. 'We shall spend,' he would say, 'the winter in Paris; you will manage the household; I only want for my personal service the valet de chambre I brought with me, a coachman, a cabriolet and a horse. We shall buy a beautiful estate with fine buildings and we shall spend the summers in the country. If there should be a wing, a separate summer house, that's where I shall stay.' Happy time of my life! I loved, I was loved. . . .

"Reasons which M. de Redern put forward as an excuse for breaking his friendly relations with me and for having robbed me.

"M. de Redern said: 'M. de Saint-Simon was spending too much.'

"Let me remind M. de Redern that the time of my life when I had spent the most was the year 1794. . . .

"It is after being a participant in those expenses, after having fully enjoyed their advantages that M. de Redern left. I accompanied him to Basle where we separated, he assuring me that he wanted to come back and live with me as soon as possible. Before his departure he did not make any remarks about my expenditures. . . .

"When M. de Redern after having realized his plan to rob me became estranged from me, I decided to launch myself on a new career, the scientific career. I went to live opposite the Ecole Polytechnique with the 144,000 livres which I had saved from his hands, and I employed my money in acquiring a scientific education. Good cheer, good wine, assiduous attention to the professors to whom my purse was open gave me all the facilities needed for my purpose. . . .

"M. de Redern tells you: 'M. de Saint-Simon asked me for a sum to be paid in cash; I gave him that sum. He gave me a receipt in full. Therefore I have a document bearing proof that I owe him nothing; therefore I am justified in rejecting without examination all claims on his part.'

123

"Monsieur le Sénateur, I did ask M. de Redern a sum paid in cash, because I desired to devote myself to the work in which I am engaged to-day and as this work required the exercise of all my faculties, it was essential to assure myself of the means of existence and the necessary funds in order to perform experiments.

"I only asked for 150,000 livres for the reason that I thought that sum would be sufficient to carry out my project. I would have asked for more if it had seemed to me necessary for the execution of my plan of work.

"I gave a full receipt to M. de Redern as I did not believe that he intended to break our association. . . ."

Saint-Simon ended his letter with this remark:

"I shall give you an account, M. le Sénateur, of the discussion which took place between M. de Redern and me in a second letter. I will end this one with a comparison of M. de Redern's behavior and my own, which has been drawn by my secretary, M. Demoigny."[1]

If Saint-Simon were as poor as he tried to make every one believe how could he afford the services of a secretary? And how did he manage to occupy living quarters at such high rental as 4,600 francs a year? One may conclude that he lived mostly on gifts and loans if one may judge from a note to his landlord whose claims were becoming urgent. Asking for more delay in paying his debt, he wrote:

"There is an indispensable condition, which is that I must live, and I could certainly not live if you did not leave me the 575 francs which represent half of my quarterly rent."[2]

We also find in the Charavay collection of letters at the *Bibliothèque Nationale,* a promissory note dated Alençon, May 1812, for the sum of 19,700 francs received from M. Coutte. From this it would appear that although Saint-Simon had exhausted his revenues, he was still able to obtain substantial sums from some of his wealthy friends.

In his *Mémoire Introductif* Saint-Simon compared his behavior with that of Redern. Whereas the latter was occupied mainly with acquisition of wealth, Saint-Simon was planning the reorganization of the educational system. He proceeded to outline the history of education from medieval times until the reign of Napoleon, and proposed that the study of physiology be added to that of other sciences. With the proffered help of Doctors Burdin and Bougon and Professor Duméril, he was in a position to found an educational establishment where physiology as well as physics, ancient and modern literature, would be taught.

Physiology, according to Saint-Simon, gives us the knowledge of man and his place in the animal kingdom. "Positive knowledge of man will thus rid humanity of all sorts of errors and superstitions." Then he added this startling remark: "The studies will naturally end by a course in positive philosophy."

The above lines were written in 1812, eighteen years before the publication of the *Cours de philosophie positive* by Auguste Comte, who became Saint-Simon's secretary. To what extent the exponent of positivism was indebted to his one time employer will be discussed in a subsequent chapter. The fact is that by announcing a course in positive philosophy at this early date, Saint-Simon anticipated the foundation of a philosophical system which attracted world wide interest during the second half of the nineteenth century.

Again reviewing his life, Saint-Simon emphasized the dominant motive for his thoughts and actions:

"The desire for glory possessed me from the moment of my entrance into this world; it has dominated all my life; it still exerts upon me the most absolute command."

His passive attitude during the Revolution was rationalized with the self-righteousness of a man at ease with his conscience:

"I did not regard it honorable to take part in demolition. Consequently I resolved not to solicit nor accept any post. I was true to my determination. I remained a spectator during the period between the last dynasty and the brilliant advent of the one under whose laws we live to-day. During those dozen years (1792-1804) I had been solely occupied with financial and scientific measures for founding a great establishment of public usefulness as soon as the demolishers would have upset the theological notions which oppose the introduction of a desirable course of studies."

125

After recounting his past life to his own credit, Saint-Simon revealed his aims for the future in the most hopeful terms:

"I am working on a plan of studies to be used in the educational institution which I mentioned in this discourse. The advanced age I have reached, the abolition of the advantages of my birth, the ruin of the work I did in my youth, the defection of M. de Redern, the trying circumstances in which I find myself, have not extinguished the desire for glory which possesses my soul; I am consumed more than ever with the urge to distinguish myself by means of honorable works, works useful to humanity. I have two aims which I hope to attain, first, to improve the general system of education, second, to prove that financial power is greatly inferior to scientific greatness."

Thus ends the *Mémoire Introductif* of Saint-Simon. His biographers have drawn heavily on this document, taking it literally, and giving credence to every statement found in it. Rarely is Redern's answer quoted. Yet Redern's presentation of the case is just as available at the *Bibliothèque Nationale* in the Henri Fournel collection under the title of *Mémoire de M. de Redern*. Saint-Simon's apologists have made no use of it, although it is of primary importance in forming an impartial estimate of the situation.

Jean-Sigismond Ehrenreich de Redern (1755-1835) former minister to Spain and ambassador of Prussia to London, was a man of liberal ideas and humanitarian tendencies. In 1790 he abolished serfdom on his domains in Saxony and abrogated feudal dues and services. This action was evidently taken in sympathy with the French Revolution which had decreed the abolition of serfdom and proclaimed the Rights of Man. Did his admiration for revolutionary France induce him to come to Paris where he met again Saint-Simon, the former companion of his stay in Madrid? From a document in the archives of Péronne, dated December 22, 1793, we learn from his declaration that Redern was attached to France by love of liberty. Here he also stated he had renounced the diplomatic career because he did not desire to take part in any maneuvers of the royal courts against the establishment of freedom. For that reason he had retired to Florence, in the neutral state of Tuscany. He denied that the decree against foreigners applied to him since he was born in Saxony. That state had not joined the coalition against France and therefore he could not be considered an enemy alien.

In 1811 Redern acquired French citizenship and settled on his magnificent estate, the château de Flers in Normandy. He put back into operation the iron works he had bought with the property, and developed them with considerable skill and intelligence. In recognition of his industrial capacities he was elected member of the General Council of Manufacturers.

Apart from his achievements in the world of affairs, Redern wrote several books, two of which deserve mention. In the one entitled *Modes accidentels de nos perceptions,* the author treated metaphysical problems from the spiritualistic approach and his comments on somnambulism attracted much attention at the time. The other work, in two volumes, was called *Considérations sur la nature de l'homme en soi-même et dans ses rapports avec l'ordre social.* The philosophical and social views developed in this treatise are quite conservative compared to those of Saint-Simon. Nevertheless, granting the differences in their temperament and ideology, there existed between the two men a bond of understanding which explains their mutual attraction since the day of their first encounter in Spain. Redern, like Saint-Simon, married late in life a woman of literary ability, Henriette de Montperat, who achieved distinction with her sentimental poems and moral tales.

In answer to Saint-Simon's statements giving the story of their business relations, Redern published his version of the dispute from which we quote the main passages:

"When the question of the contract came up, M. de Saint-Simon declared that he would never consent to strike a bargain on profits to be derived from such a friend as I was, adding that he positively wanted me to be free to give him a share in the benefits as I thought proper at the termination of the business."

The agreement was signed on that basis. Saint-Simon was to receive 12,000 francs a year salary for managing affairs. After reviewing the details of various transactions, Redern wrote:

"I returned to Paris at the end of September 1797. . . . M. de Saint-Simon had associated himself without any discretion with a number of people in founding a service of stage coaches, a drayage business, a commission agency, and a wine shop. . . . M. de Saint-Simon had sold properties bearing over 80,000 francs of income from our joint-tenancy and had mortgaged the greater part of the rest of our holdings. The loans amounted to over 400,000 francs. The interest, in most cases, was five or six percent a month. . . .

"An income of from 35 to 40,000 livres had disappeared in the hands of M. de Saint-Simon. The value of the capital had diminished even more, since the new holdings consisted chiefly of city property. There remained an income of about 81,000 livres. . . .

"I divided the property so as to leave an income of 35,000 livres to M. de Saint-Simon and I kept 45,000 for myself. . . . M. de Saint-Simon wanted half of the property assigned to him to be placed in the name of his friend M. de Béhague and the other half in mine. . . .

"M. de Saint-Simon's interest in scientific learning dates from this period. He wished to promote himself *Captain of the guards of the great Newton* by means of a subscription in his behalf by all the inhabitants of France, at 30 sous each. . . .

"An audit of my half interest in the joint business was most embarrassing. It was a matter of fraudulent sales. On his demand and with my consent, the case was referred to arbiters.

"On my return to Paris in 1796, not only were new acquisitions bought in the name of dummies, but by a notarized act, November 26, 1795, two months before my arrival, Saint-Simon had placed all the rest of the properties, which were under my name, under the name of a straw man. This action was very singular, to say the least."

When it was agreed to terminate the partnership, Saint-Simon asked Redern to assume the payment of an annuity of 1,800 francs to a woman by whom he had a child. Redern promised to pay the annuity although, he remarked drily, it was rather a bizarre business.

"One can hardly imagine that M. de Saint-Simon whose possessions were his debts when I first met him, to whom I lent a substantial sum for the sake of friendship, who for a long time drew all his means of livelihood from the money I put at his disposal, who wasted a considerable fortune in the business under his care, a man with whom I made five successive contracts of which the last two have been authentically notarized after long discussion and mature examination, one can hardly imagine, I repeat, that M. de Saint-Simon has not ceased saying and printing for several years that I abused his confidence and robbed him of a fortune he had won by his own work and industry, while exposing himself to great danger, and that my invested capital was of no use whatever for *his business,* as he calls it. . . .

"I have some definite ideas concerning M. de Saint-Simon's work and industry. He has done little himself, but acted through others, giving or promising benefits to many, several of whom became rich, most of whom made profits. Purchases were made without reason or purpose. No repairs were done to the buildings he held. In his hands all properties were only packs of wares for resale to the first comer.

"The income from the original purchases kept diminishing in spite of the considerable profits made on the resales by the depreciation of the assignats. The causes are to be found in the complete lack of capacity of M. de Saint-Simon, his culpable prodigality, his disorderly conduct, his wrong choice of agents. . . .

"His behavior and his statements about me make it absolutely impossible for me to continue any aid. . . .

" I never participated in M. de Saint-Simon's scientific projects, and for a simple reason. I had broken relations with him at the time of his ignorance. It was only after our separation that he began considering himself a scientist."

The above memorandum was signed: "J. E. de Redern, at the château de Flers, July 8, 1812."

In studying the documents relating to the Redern-Saint-Simon transactions, one is oppressed by the turbid atmosphere in which the business was carried on. In the maze of devious and insidious manipulations it becomes impossible to discern justice from injustice, right from wrong. But in these documents the personalities of the two men stand out in bold and revealing contrast. Both were aristocrats and scions of distinguished families.

Like many other members of nobility, in their youth, they leaned toward liberal ideas and welcomed social reforms. However the temperaments of the two men were fundamentally different. Saint-Simon, profligate, impulsive, irrational, a plaything of his sensuous whims, victim of his delusions, kept wandering and faltering in the pursuit of fame. Redern, a cautious diplomat, an astute business man, a realist tinged with a streak of mysticism, did not permit his idealistic concepts to interfere with his material interests. He, too, believed in progress and social reforms, but he remained a staunch supporter of the church and the established order for the sake of safeguarding his wealth, if not for more elevated reasons.

Saint-Simon belonged to the class of eccentric, unbalanced, unstable individuals from whom are recruited poets, reformers, founders of religion. The world entrusts its safety to the Rederns, but its salvation comes from the Saint-Simons. Count de Redern, wealthy châtelain of Flers, became an influential and honored member of his community. Count Henri de Saint-Simon went on struggling against poverty and want, confident that in the near future he would be enthroned in the temple of glory.

CHAPTER NINE

Saint-Simon, abandoning all hope of getting Redern to revise the legal agreement concluded in 1797, left Alençon at the end of the year 1812. He arrived in Péronne, exhausted in body and depressed in spirit. Mr. Coutte, his former agent, offered him the hospitality of his home and nursed him back to health. Writing to his sister Adélaïde, February 8, 1813, Saint-Simon gave this account of his condition:

"I was delirious for a month without interruption. When the fever left me I found myself in such moral debility that I could not put two ideas together. I would inevitably have lost my sanity if I had not been taken care of by a capable and wise physician, and if Madame de Folville, M. Coutte and M. Danicourt had not given me abundant consolation and hope. . . .

"The friendship of M. Coutte was the first help in my recovery. This man possesses not an ordinary soul; he has great energy and he always succeeds in having his advice adopted. These are his words: 'A great moral revolution cannot be accomplished in a person without going through a great physical crisis. The illness through which you have just passed will be your salvation if you know how to profit by the circumstance.' I won't tell you more because I would have too much to say if I were to give a full account of the sensible ideas he presented." [1]

To complete the cure, Saint-Simon spent some time in a *"maison de santé"* at Charonne, near Paris, under the care of Doctor Belhomme. Pierre Leroux paid him a visit at this private hospital devoted to the treatment of mental diseases. Among other things, Saint-Simon complained to his visitor that he was not able to sleep. [2]

His fear of insanity was evidently well grounded, judging by the symptoms he pointed out to his sister and to Leroux: prolonged delirium, mental debility, inability to coordinate his thoughts, lack of sleep. The strain under which he had been living for the past months was enough to try the fortitude of even a well balanced mind.

His host at Péronne was an intelligent psychiatrist who realized that his guest's recovery could be effected only by restoring his self-confidence and hope. M. Coutte succeeded also in obtaining some financial aid for Saint-Simon from his family. His brothers and sisters consented in 1813 to grant him a small pension. They even obtained for him an apartment in Paris.

On recovering his strength, Saint-Simon established himself in his new quarters in Paris. With renewed hope, he made another attempt to convince Napoleon of his superior capacities. As a sequence to his *Mémoire sur la science de l'homme,* he wrote *Mémoire sur la gravitation,* which he subtitled: *A way of compelling the English to recognize the freedom of the seas.* Obviously the choice of this subtitle was a subterfuge to attract the attention of the Emperor. The blockade of the continent by the English fleet had created a dangerous situation for the countries under the Corsican's rule. It was reasonable to hope that any suggestion for the removal of this formidable obstacle would engage Napoleon's interest.

Copies of the manuscript were distributed as usual to a small group of scientists, among whom were Cuvier and Geoffrey Saint-Hilaire, and to influential government officials: Cambacérès, grand chancellor, Lebrun, minister of the interior, baron de Gérando, counsellor of state. The brochures were accompanied by three types of letters, worded according to the rank and function of the recipient. To those who held important positions or were distinguished for their wealth, Saint-Simon asked for financial aid in the most piteous terms:

"Monsieur,

Be my savior, I am dying of hunger; my present situation has deprived me of the means of presenting my ideas in an appropriate manner, but the value of my discovery is independent of the manner of presentation which circumstances compelled me to adopt in order to attract attention more immediately. Have I succeeded in discovering a new philosophical process? That is the question. If you take the trouble to read my essay, I shall be saved.

"Having devoted myself for many years to the finding of a new philosophical method, I was necessarily obliged to withdraw from society and I find myself at present, after making the most important discovery, in a state of absolute destitution.

"Solely occupied with the general welfare, I have neglected my personal affairs to such a point that this is exactly my situation: for two weeks I have been living on bread and water; I work without a fire, and I have sold everything, even my clothes, to cover the expenses of the copies of my work. The passion for science and public welfare, the desire to find a means of terminating peacefully the frightful crisis in which all European society is engaged, are the causes of my present distress. Therefore I am not ashamed to reveal my poverty and to ask the necessary aid in order to be in condition to continue my work.

"I am waiting for help with the impatience of a man clinging to a branch suspended above the deepest abyss." [3]

Of the minister of the interior, Saint-Simon requested employment in a library or the grant of some sort of endowment. He wrote on December 22, 1813:

"Monseigneur, I beg of you to grant me a post in a library or such a pension as is given to men of letters, in my case a subsistence pension, which I request of your kindness in consideration of my name, age and writings."

On the margin of this letter, M. Hallé wrote this recommendation:

"I believe that M. de St.-Simon, for his zeal in the advancement of science and progress of liberal ideas, for his writings and the talent he has shown, for his perseverance and the prestige of his name, deserves the consideration of the government."

Cuvier was also in favor of a grant to Saint-Simon and he added this marginal comment:

"I am glad to join my colleague M. Hallé, in calling His Excellency's attention in favor of M. de St.-Simon, whose present condition is due in part to his desire to advance and promote science. Cuvier." [4]

The Grand Chancellor minister of the interior, instead of

acting on the recommendation signed by the two eminent scientists, played the traditional game of shifting responsibility by advising the petitioner to address himself directly to the Emperor. Whereupon Saint-Simon composed the following letter:
"Sire,

I am the cousin of the duke of Saint-Simon, author of the *Mémoires de la Régence*. I was colonel of the Aquitaine regiment at the time of the Revolution. I am dying of hunger. Political events have ruined me, my enthusiasm for science has reduced me to penury. For fifteen years I have been working on a manuscript which would soon be finished if I had the means of livelihood.

"Cuvier and Hallé, knights of the Legion of Honor, are acquainted with the beginning of my work, they find it contains new and most important ideas. I beg Your Majesty to grant me aid. The prince Grand Chancellor gave me enough confidence to apply directly to the kindness of Your Majesty.

"I am, with deepest respects, Sire, of Your Majesty, the most devoted, the most obedient and faithful subject." [5]

It is reported, without confirmation, that Napoleon, when the essay on gravitation was presented to him under the title "A Way to make the English recognize the freedom of the seas," sought at first to understand the relation between the title and the subject matter. Unable to perceive any connection, he asked the courtiers around him what it was all about. All agreed that the essay must be the work of a madman, but a harmless one. Consequently the Emperor paid no further attention to the pamphlet nor to the author.

Had Napoleon read the brochure, he might not have been pleased with the advice to forsake his conquests for the sake of peace. As for Saint-Simon, it was not the most tactful way of securing imperial favors with an approach such as this:

"All the people of the continent will undoubtedly concur in bringing the English to recognize the freedom of the seas. But they will concur even more certainly on this point, namely, that Your Majesty give up the protectorate of the Rhineland Confederation, that you must evacuate Italy, restore liberty to Holland, and cease to interfere in the affairs of Spain.

"By renouncing the plans of conquest, Your Majesty will force the English to reestablish the freedom of the seas. If you desire to continue adding to the immense quantity of laurels you already have gathered, you will crush France and find yourself in direct opposition to your subjects."

The warning remained futile. The blockade which closed all the ports of the continent to British commerce, caused great hardship, not only to England, but to all Europe. It was one of the main causes of the European coalition against Napoleon and of his downfall.

In spite of reverses, of physical and moral afflictions, Saint-Simon kept a stout heart, an unalterable faith in his destiny, a mental exaltation which impressed all those he approached. However, he was not blind to his shortcomings. He knew his incapacity to organize his thoughts, and the inability to express them in clear writing. His mind in constant ebullition could not pause long enough to formulate a plan, to prove a demonstration by logical processes. He lacked the elementary qualities of a writer: sense of form, discipline, and order. In short, he needed a collaborator. We have had occasion to mention one amanuensis, who made some interesting comments on the life and thoughts of Saint-Simon and who preferred to remain anonymous. Two of his secretaries later acquired recognition and fame far beyond their master's: Augustin Thierry and Auguste Comte.

At the time when Saint-Simon frequented the leading institutes of science, he was attracted by a student who impressed him as having a remarkable intelligence and a keen sense of history. This was Augustin Thierry. Born at Blois in 1795, he had completed at the age of eighteen the two year term of studies at the Ecole Normale, after which he was appointed to teach at the college of Compiègne. Saint-Simon corresponded with the youthful instructor. He sent him a copy of his *Mémoire sur la science de l'homme,* requesting his advice and criticism. He then proposed to make the young scholar his secretary. To this offer Thierry answered on January 13, 1814:

"You write for scientists, while I must write for the public, therefore our manner cannot be the same. You can be as bold as you please, but I must be more cautious. . . . I am grateful to you for your kindness in asking me to be your secretary and for giving me the occasion of presenting my first writing under the auspices of your brilliant ideas. I shall respond, as much as I am capable, to your generous intentions. If you are kind enough to speak of me to newspaper editors, please do not mention my name, because in my profession reputations are frail and my fate depends on people who possess everything except common sense. You understand what I mean." [6]

Augustin Thierry had scarcely embarked on his teaching career when detachments of the Austrian army reached the outskirts of Compiègne. State functionaries, including teachers, were ordered to leave the city. Thus in early February 1814 the young man found himself again in Paris, but this time penniless, without a home and without a job. He applied to Saint-Simon who engaged him as secretary at a salary of two hundred francs a month.

How could Saint-Simon pay for the services of a secretary when at the same time he was complaining about his destitution? We found a letter, dated March 26, 1814, addressed to M. Rihouet, asking for a small pension. Appended to the letter was this significant disavowal: "It is absolutely false that I was seen riding horseback." In another letter dated the same month and year, he begged a friend to act as an intermediary and secure for him an advance of five hundred francs from either Redern or Béhague.

It is possible that Saint-Simon's soliciting letters netted him some money. Copies of *Mémoire sur la science de l'homme*, sent to a number of persons, also brought a few contributions. Whatever the source and amount of his income, his financial resources must have been sufficient to enable him to pay a secretary's salary of two hundred francs a month.

When Saint-Simon warned Napoleon of a threatened downfall, he had correctly read the signs of the time. The lucky star of the Emperor was beginning to wane. Year after year the dazzling memories of Austerlitz, Jena, Eylau, Friedland, Wagram had drugged the French nation with dreams of grandeur and glory, and conjured in the minds of the enemy the image of a formidable and invincible conqueror. But after the catastrophic Russian campaign, the heroic stature of Napoleon was reduced to the proportions of a mere mortal. The allied powers, emboldened by their victory at Leipzig, thrust their combined forces toward the French frontier which they began crossing by the end of 1813.

The invasion of France was swift and disastrous. On March 31, 1814, the allies entered Paris. Napoleon was deposed by the same Senate that had crawled at his feet during the glorious days of the Empire. The little Corsican who had shaken the thrones of the European monarchs was consigned to the island of Elba.

The allied potentates feared Napoleon, but they feared even more the Revolution. Their first thought therefore was to restore the ancient régime, not only in France, but in all the countries contaminated by the revolutionary ferment. A body of inept diplomats gathered at Vienna, intent on disposing of peoples like herds of cattle, and territories like pieces of real estate.

This manner of statesmanship represented the age preceding the fall of the Bastille and the proclamation of the Rights of Man. The members of the Congress of Vienna belonged to that previous age. They were the debris of an ancient world that should have vanished in the great cataclysm.

A new world had come into existence. New organizations and new directing powers were needed to establish the commonwealth of free men. These were the thoughts that agitated the minds of many French people. Books, pamphlets, newspapers multiplied, each proposing some plan, some scheme for a better social system.

Saint-Simon, too, had a project for the reorganization of the troubled world. His theories were borrowed in part from the writings of the abbé de Saint-Pierre, whose *Projet de paix perpétuelle,* published in 1713, exerted a deep influence on the eighteenth century philosophers. Saint-Simon outlined his views to Thierry, discussed the essential points with him and left to the young secretary the task of developing the theme.

In October 1814 a brochure appeared under the title: *De la réorganisation de la société européenne, ou de la nécessité des moyens de rassembler les peuples de l'Europe en un seul corps politique.* The purpose was fully defined by the cumbersome title: *The reorganization of European society or the necessity of uniting the peoples of Europe into a single political body,* by M. le comte de Saint-Simon and A. Thierry, his pupil.

137

Saint-Simon's project foreshadowed the conception of our recent League of Nations:

"All nations of Europe to be governed by a National Parliament, . . . which would decide the common interests of Europe. . . . Europe would have the best organization possible, if all the nations, each governed by its own parliament, would recognize the supremacy of a Continental Parliament placed over all the national governments and invested with the power of judging their disputes." [7]

This legislative body would also undertake to foster the material and intellectual welfare of the peoples by facilitating commercial intercourse and by offering educational advantages.

"The Parliament will join the Danube to the Rhine and the Rhine to the Baltic by canals, . . . will occupy the people with great internal projects, . . . will render it possible to travel and live everywhere in Europe, . . . will provide public instruction all over Europe." [8]

Thus selfish and narrow patriotism would give place to a collaboration of all the European peoples for their greatest advantage:

"The time will come when all the peoples of Europe will feel that points of general interest must be regulated before arriving at national interests; then misfortunes will diminish, disputes will be allayed, wars will be done away with."

In conclusion the authors expressed, with a striking image, their firm confidence in the progress of humanity:

"The imagination of poets has placed the golden age at the cradle of the human race, amidst the ignorance and grossness of primitive times. It would be more appropriate to consign the iron age to that period. The golden age of humanity is not behind us; it is before us and will be found in the perfection of the social order. Our fathers have not seen it; our children will one day behold it. It is our duty to prepare the way for them." [9]

The brochure of 112 pages attracted much attention and a second edition was offered to the public in November. Its publication was made possible during the short period of freedom the press enjoyed at the time. But the government felt uneasy about the subversive influence this pamphlet might have on the people.

138

It might reawaken in them dreams of world freedom. Accordingly an order was sent to the *Journal de la librairie* forbidding the announcement of the new issue:

"If it is not too late, you are requested not to announce in the *Journal de la librairie* the brochure entitled: *De la réorganisation de la société européenne,* by Saint-Simon. Pagès."

When the first edition of this booklet appeared in October 1814, Napoleon was on the island of Elba. The Bourbons were again in power and the émigrés had returned like a swarm of locusts. The nobility as well as the clergy wanted the return of their estates which had been confiscated and sold during the Revolution.

The owners of national properties represented a fairly large and influential group of bourgeois and peasants who had acquired considerable wealth through these transactions. Their interests were now seriously threatened by strong pressure upon the government from the church and the aristocracy. Saint-Simon saw an opportunity to come to their aid. It was natural that he who had made and lost a fortune in this speculative field should feel qualified to formulate a plan in favor of the new proprietors. For their benefit he published a series of pamphlets and newspaper articles in support of their cause.

Saint-Simon proposed the creation of a special credit bank in Paris, with branches throughout the country, from which the owners of national lands could get loans to meet their payments. And since this plan would bring untold benefits to the imperiled party, it was legitimate that the promoter receive a commensurate reward for his services. This plan was presented in February 1815 in a prospectus with the title: *Le Défenseur des propriétaires de domaines nationaux* par le Comte de Saint-Simon et d'autres gens de lettres. It was also announced that:

"The first volume will appear in March; and by the beginning of October six volumes will have appeared. The work will end when the value of national domains reaches the level of prices of patrimonial properties. The subscription price for 6 volumes is 12 francs, for a single volume 3 francs."

This was another financial promotion by Saint-Simon, but like many other projects of his it was never carried through. In this case fate intervened brusquely. Before the writing had fairly started, Napoleon had escaped from the island of Elba and landed on French soil.

In the days of victories, Saint-Simon had extolled to the skies the conquering Corsican whose favors he sought in vain. But when the restored Bourbons offered better prospects not only for peace but for the return of the privileges of the aristocracy, comte Henri de Saint-Simon, the prosperous sans-culotte in the time of the Revolution, had promptly taken back his title of nobility. In the return of Bonaparte, he would lose again whatever benefit he hoped to derive from his noble birth and social rank. His violent resentment was at once given expression in a pamphlet published on March 15, 1815, entitled *"Declaration of principles by the authors of the work announced under the title of Defender of the owners of national domains, of the Charter and liberal ideas, on the occasion of the invasion of French territory by Napoleon Bonaparte."*

Augustin Thierry lent an able hand in the writing of the pamphlet to which he imparted the eloquence and polished style characteristic of all his works.

"There appears on our frontiers a man who for ten years has devastated France by all the excesses of military despotism; this man was overthrown by our unanimous will, and he dares claim to rule again over us. . . . Does he really think that a people who have recovered their liberty will risk losing it a second time?" [10]

Meanwhile Napoleon reached Paris, the Bourbons fled, and the Emperor was once more the master of France's destiny. A new coalition was formed against him. But who could tell whether Napoleon's lucky star might shine again, and the imperial crown might be consolidated by fresh victories? Saint-Simon's attitude toward the abhorred "tyrant" changed suddenly to a conciliatory tone. On May 18, 1815, a fourteen page pamphlet made its appearance with the title: *Opinions concerning measures to be taken against the coalition of 1815,* by H. Saint-Simon and A. Thierry.

It is rather amusing to note how quickly the title of Comte de Saint-Simon which adorned the pamphlet of March 15th vanished with the flight of the Bourbons. In this last publication the

authors advised an alliance with England as the means for preventing the dreaded coalition and assuring peace in Europe. They
suggested that, in the new constitution which the Emperor
promised to the French nation, there should be included a special
clause regarding new conquests:

"Each time the government should deem useful and possible
to join to the French territory, by treaties or other arrangement,
part of a country the population of which exceeds one hundred
thousand inhabitants the will of the French people is that . . .
the people to be incorporated to France, on the one hand, and
the French people on the other hand, must be consulted in
advance and the union will not be considered legal until an
absolute majority has voted in its favor on both sides; otherwise
it will not take place." [11]

In other words the pamphlet advocated the right of a people
to decide on the choice of its nationality by means of a plebiscite.
At Vienna a handful of diplomats had been busy assigning the
peoples of Europe among the ruling potentates as so many heads
of cattle among land owners. This lamentable spectacle moved
the authors to protest for the sake of peace, if not for the sake
of humanity. Whether it originated with Saint-Simon or with
his secretary, the idea of a plebiscite to decide the fate of a people
introduced a new principle in European policy.

The *Opinions Concerning Measures To Be Taken Against The
Coalition* was favorably received by the imperial entourage. The
appeal for help previously addressed to the Emperor was at last
granted. The great naturalist Cuvier, elevated to the rank of
Minister of the Interior, recommended Saint-Simon for a post.
The physicist Halévy and the naturalist Lacépède joined their
recommendations to that of Cuvier. Comte Henri de Montesquieu added his approval in a letter to Cuvier:

"I join M. le comte de Lacépède to beg Your Eminence to do
all that is possible in favor of M. de Saint-Simon. This is not
an ordinary recommendation; it is dictated by the deepest interest, after an acquaintance of thirty years, for a man with an
illustrious name, formerly a colonel and wealthy, now in direst
need." [12]

During the Hundred Days Saint-Simon was appointed on April

15, 1815, assistant librarian at the *Bibliothèque de l'Arsenal*. This was a most desirable post since Saint-Simon would have time to devote himself to writing in the company of inspiring books. It was the sort of sinecure that every impecunious French writer had wanted since the death of Richelieu, whose collection of books was turned into a state library known as the Bibliothèque de l'Arsenal. Unfortunately the fall of Napoleon after the battle of Waterloo terminated this gratifying employment.

When Louis XVIII came back to the throne, Saint-Simon's loyalty veered again in the direction of the powers that be. He addressed himself to the king, November 1815:

"The philosophical and political studies to which I devoted my life, which in the past could only follow a vague direction, are now aimed uniquely at consolidating the sceptre in the hands of the Bourbons and strengthening the monarchy which Your Majesty has restored.

"I beg Your Majesty to grant me a moment of audience so that I may communicate to you the outline of a project of mine; I believe it will be of interest to Your Majesty to become personally acquainted with it.

Comte de Saint-Simon, rue des Fossés-St. Germain-des-Prés, no. 16." [13]

Needless to say the request was not granted.

Napoleon's continental blockade had practically destroyed commerce, but had given a strong impetus toward the development of manufactures since France had to become self sufficient. Food, clothing, war material had to be supplied to the imperial armies. New industries had been introduced, such as the cultivation of sugar beet and the preservation and canning of food.

Discussion of economic problems was much to the fore, and such able men as Jean Baptiste Say and Jean Charles de Sismondi were recognized as authorities in the field. The *Censeur Européen,* a liberal periodical, edited by Charles Comte and Dunoyer, opened its columns to those willing to participate in the controversial issues of the moment. From 1817 until 1820, Thierry contributed a series of articles, giving voice for the first time to historical theories which he elaborated in later years.

The collaboration of Thierry with Saint-Simon became even

closer after 1816, and Saint-Simon no longer called him "his pupil" but his "adopted son." A warm intellectual kinship had grown between them so that the master could confide his most ambitious projects to his young associate. His incoherent dreams now assumed orderly precision under the keen analysis of this young genius who was to become the great historian of France.

In imitation of the *Censeur Européen,* Saint-Simon decided to found a periodical that would be devoted exclusively to financial and economic matters. He sent the following prospectus, December 1816, to prominent men in finance, government, commerce, industry:

"Henri Saint-Simon to the gentlemen farmers, manufacturers, merchants and bankers,

"I propose to free you from the domination of courtiers, idlers, nobles and speech makers.

"I promise to employ only legal, loyal and peaceful means. I also promise to elevate you within a short time to the first degree of social distinction and to make you the principal leaders in the direction of public affairs.

"I am opening a subscription in order to secure the means for increasing the output of my writings and of disseminating them in profusion." [14]

As a result of this appeal, many imposing names (about 140) joined the list of subscribers with generous contributions of money. Heading the list was the Duc de la Rochefoucault, peer of France. There followed the Pereire brothers and Perrégaux, prominent bankers; Chaptal junior, manufacturer; Comte Antoine Roy, minister of finance; the Duc de Broglie, peer of France; Cuvier and Arago, of the Academy of Science; Lanjuinais, peer of France and member of the Institut; J. B. Say, professor of political economy; Talma, actor at the Théâtre Français; Lafayette, Casimir Périer, and Ternaux, deputies. The total amount of money subscribed was some twenty-five thousand francs, and this sum was deposited in the bank of Laffite. With such financial backing Saint-Simon's plan seemed assured of success.

The periodical was founded under the name of *L'Industrie.* A number of contributors promised to help fill its pages. Among these one may notice the following names: the distinguished

143

painter Ary Scheffer and his younger brother Henry; Saint-Aubin, who wrote articles on finance; Dr. Bougon, who had guided Saint-Simon's studies in physiology; A. Firmin-Didot, the learned hellenist and well known publisher.

To carry on this ambitious work, the services of Thierry did not suffice, and Saint-Simon engaged another secretary. This second aide has remained anonymous, but he has left a journal which contains interesting details on the life and habits of his employer at this period. Here is an extract from the journal:

"M. de Saint-Simon rented an apartment, rue Ancienne-Comédie, in the large residential building, number 18. It was then that he appointed me his secretary. I had known him in 1814, as well as M. Augustin Thierry, his adopted son, and I had worked for them on several occasions. I accepted the employment offered to me, and I was pleased to become their habitual guest, because I have always felt the highest esteem for both of them.

"M. de Saint-Simon had already chosen his collaborators. Every Thursday he gathered them at his table together with some friends. At these reunions of writers and artists, they discussed the matters to be treated in the next monthly issue. M. de Saint-Simon listened rather than talked during the discussions, which he took care to keep within the subject matter at hand. Then he would make a summary of the discussion with remarkable justness and precision."

The anonymous secretary furnished curious details about Saint-Simon's habits of work:

"While our contributors were busy writing the monthly volume, M. de Saint-Simon did not remain inactive. Ordinarily he spent the whole morning at work, and rarely prolonged the session beyond the noon hour. The remainder of the day was devoted to errands, visits, amusements. However, the morning work began rather early, and not infrequently soon after midnight. As soon as the peace and quiet of night allowed M. de Saint-Simon to seize upon an idea which he did not wish to lose, the bell rang to rouse me out of sleep and take dictation. He would dictate for a while, and then send me back to bed, only to call me again as often as his inspiration required.

"His plan was never outlined; his ideas were so vague, so

confused that it was impossible for him to expound them clearly and to convey what he perceived but dimly. Consequently we had almost invariably to do the work over again after I had read to him what he had dictated at a previous session; he would tear it up or throw it into the fire and ask me to take another sheet of paper.

¯ "The confusion of thought in Saint-Simon was principally due to his education which had not been bad, but undisciplined and desultory. This loose thinking was aggravated by a violent, unrestrained and unruly temperament. He had had too many eminent teachers who neglected the foundation indispensable to the development of his mind." [15]

In the spring of 1817, Saint-Simon issued the first volume of the announced publication under the title *L'Industrie, ou Discussions Politiques, morales et philosophiques dans l'intérêt de tous les hommes livrés à des travaux utiles et indépendants* (Industry, or political, moral and philosophical discussions in the interest of all men engaged in useful and free occupations). The volume of 464 pages bore the motto: *"Tout par l'industrie, tout pour elle."* (Everything by means of industry, everything for it.)

The contributors were Augustin Thierry who wrote on *L'Industrie Littéraire et Scientifique liguée avec l'Industrie Commerciale et Manufacturière* (Literary and Scientific Industry allied with Commercial and Manufacturing Industry) 136 pages. Saint-Aubin's article dealt with *Finances*, 224 pages. Another article on finance, 104 pages, bore no signature.

The thesis expounded was that society depended entirely on industry.

"Industry is the foundation upon which rests the very existence of society." [16]

Industry is the source of all wealth and prosperity, and whatever favors its development also aids the prosperity and happiness of the community. The importance of the producers is thus stressed:

"The single class in society in which we desire to see ambition and political courage increase, the single class in which this ambition can be useful or this courage necessary is the class of producers; for their individual interest is perfectly in accord with

145

the common interest, by the very nature of things. It is in the realization of this truth that we have warmly embraced the cause of the producers, regarding it as the real center and focus of civilization." [17]

The term "industriel", as used by Saint-Simon and which we translate by the word producer, included "the civil servant, the scientist, the artist, the manufacturer and the agriculturist." [18] The definition therefore comprised all those who are engaged in producing spiritual as well as material means for the satisfaction of the different members of society.

In the industrial state political government must logically give place to a new conception: "Politics is the science of production." It followed that financiers and industrialists should govern. Theirs is the power and theirs also is the responsibility of deciding what are the most efficacious methods of improving the welfare of the state.

The extolling of the men of finance and industry found favor among Saint-Simon's wealthy subscribers. Jacques Laffitte, governor of the *Banque de France,* guaranteed a monthly stipend of ten thousand francs to defray the expenses of printing the remainder of the volumes of *L'Industrie.*

Soon after the publication of the first volume in March 1817, serious dissension arose between Saint-Simon and his secretary. Thierry did not approve the conclusions of Saint-Simon's theories which led to a materialist determinism of history. "The adopted son" was shocked by these bold and radical doctrines, for at heart Thierry was a romanticist and sentimental idealist.

"I cannot conceive," Saint-Simon is supposed to have said, "a society without a government by some one."

"And I," answered Thierry, "cannot conceive a society without liberty." [19]

The three year association between the two men came to an end.

The second volume of *L'Industrie* published in May 1817 contained the *Lettres de Saint-Simon à un Américain.* In a fictitious correspondence with an American, Saint-Simon expressed admiration for the country which he had helped gain its independence, and which had achieved the industrial state he proposed for

146

France. We need quote but a paragraph to illustrate Saint-Simon's attitude toward the United States:

"What had been considered until now as mere dreams, what had been classed among utopias, has at last become a reality. We have seen the founders of your independence make use of the powers vested in them to establish individual liberty on solid and well measured foundation. We have seen public and personal liberty constituted together; we have seen national prosperity develop together with the amelioration of the state of each member of the new society; we have seen, in a word, in that society wealth and enlightenment growing with the population with a continuous and unparalleled rapidity."

Not content with the task of editing the various issues of *L'Industrie,* Saint-Simon found time to study a problem closely related to the development of industrial progress. Modern industry, with its perfected tools and complex machinery, requires the use of skilled hands with a certain degree of intellectual development. For the first time in history, education of the masses was recognized as a social necessity. To train the industrial workers one must begin with the child and adapt him to the requirements of his future trade. The need of schools for the children of the poorer classes was keenly felt in industrial circles. An organization was formed under the name of *Société d'instruction primaire* with the purpose of influencing the government in this direction.

The *Société* founded a model school in one of the workingmen's districts in Paris. Saint-Simon took an active part in founding and supervising this private establishment. Under the date of August 1816 there is a detailed report given by him before the *Société d'instruction primaire.* He was critical of the teachers who were badly paid, of the crowded classes, of the surroundings which were the worst slums in the city. In conclusion Saint-Simon submitted the following recommendations:

"I wish, gentlemen, that our school were located in a central, rich and populous district. I wish the halls in which classes are held be made pleasant and kept clean; I wish the children to be neatly dressed and properly brought up, I mean that they should not come from the poorest class but from among the workers who enjoy a certain amount of comfort. . . . I wish the teachers would present, besides excellent educational qualifications, polite and engaging manners, not to mention pleasing appearances."

A favorable impression should be made on the people who can best serve the cause of public education. The recommended changes "would encourage rich people to visit our schools and thus gain their attention to our aims and methods."

The aim of the *Société* was to establish similar schools throughout the country, but Saint-Simon advised that they confine their efforts to Paris. If they made a success of their educational institution in Paris, the provinces would, as is their custom, follow the example of the capital. Saint-Simon offered an argument which should have impressed the industrialists engaged in international competition. The founding of elementary schools, he claimed, would be "a means of giving to France the advantage of having a class of workers superior to that of other countries."

He did not belittle the humanitarian and philanthropic aims of education, but his main thought turned toward the rebuilding of France. To regain leadership among nations, France must acquire riches through work and industry. "Its primary object is the development of industry." All education therefore must tend toward that aim. However, elementary education was not sufficient. Industry required specialists for whom higher instruction was necessary.

Saint-Simon invited the *Société* to offer a prize to any one who would present the best essay on that subject.

CHAPTER TEN

Saint-Simon, unable to carry on the task of editing *L'Industrie* without the aid of a collaborator, was fortunate in meeting during the summer of 1817 Auguste Comte, a young mathematician, graduate of the Ecole Polytechnique.

Isidore Auguste Marie François Xavier Comte, born at Montpelier, January 19, 1798, entered the Ecole Polytechnique in 1814 and had just graduated from that distinguished school. He was then nineteen years old, idling about town, anxiously looking for a means of livelihood. He had received an offer to go to the United States as a surveyor, but for some reason the proposition fell through. Now came the invitation to become Saint-Simon's secretary at a stipend of 300 francs a month. This was sufficient to engage the young man's interest, the more so as he felt strongly inclined toward philosophical speculations. Because of his lucid intelligence and liberal tendencies he was just the person to fill the place of the former "adopted son."

The third volume of *L'Industrie* was carefully planned by Saint-Simon and his new secretary, but the actual writing was done by Comte. A number of chapters were printed during September and October 1817. Although emphasis was placed on the advantages of the industrial régime, the main thought was that "theological morality" was to be replaced by a "positive, industrial morality" and that "no one shall be ordained priest unless he has proven, after a preliminary examination, that he has sufficient knowledge of the principal positive sciences." In other words, the clergy shall be composed of philosophers and scientists, rather than of theologians.[1]

The criticism of Christian theology and institutions was considered highly subversive, and many of the subscribers withdrew their patronage. In a letter which appeared in the *Journal des*

Débats they publicly declared their disavowal of the opinions expressed in *L'Industrie*:

"Paris, October 30, 1817.

"To His Excellency Monseigneur the Minister Secretary of State, department of General Police:

"Monseigneur,

There has been distributed a publication entitled *L'Industrie,* or *Political, Moral and Philosophical Discussions* by M. Henri Saint-Simon, in which we noticed to our surprise a list of supposed subscribers. From this it might be assumed that the persons whose names figure on the list share the opinion published by the author and gave encouragement to their publication.

"We wish to declare emphatically to Your Excellency that none of us had any knowledge of these writings before their publication; that there was on our part no subscription for the purpose of encouraging some writings the ideas of which we are far from sharing.

"M. Saint-Simon came to see each one of us about a year ago, with the announcement that he intended to publish some observations about the progress of commerce and industry, such as he had published at that time. Since he was not able to cover the publishing expenses on account of his financial situation, we yielded to his incessant solicitations by an act of mere generosity in his favor.

"We beg Your Excellency to demand that our formal disavowal be recorded in the newspapers." [2]

Among the signatories of the letter were the financiers André, Cottier, de Foncin, Hottinguer, Périer, and Roux. Banker Laffitte, however, defended Saint-Simon's advocacy of an industrial society, and manufacturer Ternaux said that Saint-Simon was his friend and he did not wish to offend him.

With the publication of the fourth volume in 1818, the series of *L'Industrie* came to an end. Financial difficulties again harassed the versatile promoter. There was no money for the secretary. Yet Auguste Comte remained faithful to his employer for whom he had a deep admiration and to whom he owed the discovery of a new vocation. The letters he wrote to his schoolmate and friend Valat, during the period of his collaboration with Saint-Simon, contain impressions and details of unusual interest. For this reason some of the letters are quoted here at length: "Paris, May 15, 1818.

"To monsieur Valat, professor at the Communal College at Béziers.

". . . For three months I worked with an excellent man of whom I shall tell you more in my next letters. . . . The work was interesting and fairly well remunerated: 300 francs a month paid every ten days. I had taken an interest in it, but unfortunately it did not last, and père Simon, notwithstanding his good will and the fact that he was very well pleased with me, has fallen into misfortune, so that our financial relations had to end after a period of three months. I have kept friendly relations with this excellent man and I even keep working with him. I am still writing on political science for him, and although I do this without pay, I am quite certain that if he manages to get out of this terrible financial difficulty, which is not impossible, I shall not lose anything by the delay. He is over fifty years of age; well, I can assure you that I have never known any young man as energetic and vivacious as he is. In every respect he is different from other men. . . . Through my association in work and friendship with one of the men who sees farther than any one else in political philosophy, I learned a lot of things I would have vainly sought in books, and I have mentally progressed more in six months since our relationship started than I would have done in three years if I had been by myself. This work has formed my judgment on political science and, as a result, it has broadened my ideas on all other matters, so that I have acquired a more philosophical attitude, a keener and higher capacity of perception. Besides, this writing revealed to myself a political aptitude which I never would have thought I possessed. . . . Père Simon and several publicists I have met at his home were often amazed at my high capacity for social and philosophical sciences, and they tell me that my talent would be lost elsewhere." [3]

Here is another letter to Valat, even more dithyrambic in its praise of his patron: "Paris, May 15, 118.

"You want me to tell you more about Saint-Simon? I shall be

151

glad to do so. He is the most excellent man I have known, a man whose life, writings and sentiments are most in harmony and most steady. Born of one of the most noble families of France, raised early in life to a high rank in the army, had he been willing to play the courtier he could play a great part at the court of France and in the Chamber of Peers. But he voluntarily renounced the title of nobility. . . .

"If some people do not do justice to his ideas, it is because his views rise so high above the commonly accepted ideas that they cannot be appreciated yet; but that will come sooner or later. . . . There would be no end of what I could tell you of the generous deeds he has done and which are well known all over Paris. This time I shall only tell you that he is the most estimable man and the most amiable I have ever known in my life, the one among all people with whom I find it the most agreeable to have relationship. Consequently I have sworn eternal friendship for him, and in return, he loves me as if I were his son (he is not married). I forgot to point out to you a trait, an extraordinary aspect of his astonishing character, it is this. At the age of almost sixty [actually he was fifty-seven] he still has all the fire of youth; he has much more ardor and energy than I have, and yet you know that I am not cold. Oh! I could tell you some piquant things about him." [4]

Referring to the work at hand, Comte wrote to his friend:

"We have just launched a very important work[5] which, I believe, will create a sensation in the political world. I think I am really bound to a fine enterprise which will be, not only famous, but lucrative as well, I hope. It is the sort of work that can be carried on during a lifetime, a continuous activity of great interest, something in the manner of *Le Censeur,* only with more advanced ideas. Just think, my friend, *Le Censeur* in the first three years of its publication brought in 200,000 francs net to its owners, and now, although that periodical has lost a great deal of its splendor, it still brings in from 10 to 15,000 livres income to each of the two editors. Oh! you have no idea what resources there are in a political career."

Both dreaming of a fortune, Saint-Simon and Comte decided

on issuing a periodical which they named *Le Politique*. Instead of being paid a salary, Comte became a partner in the new enterprise. An agreement dated February 22, 1819, provided for ownership of *Le Politique* to be divided into twenty-four shares of which ten were assigned to Saint-Simon, two to Comte, and the other twelve shares were bought by M. Coutte and M. La Chevardière at the cost of one thousand francs a share.

The announcement of *Le Politique* made it clear that, while there would be numerous issues of the periodical during the year, no regular date of publication would be adhered to. This was a precaution to avoid payment of stamps required of journals appearing at stated intervals. The editors however promised that thirty-six issues would be presented to subscribers during the year 1819. The price was seven francs for six numbers, twelve francs a dozen.

Le Politique came out at the moment when a liberal minority had obtained power with the support of Decazes, the minister who made Louis XVIII dissolve a most reactionary parliament. As a result the press enjoyed greater liberty. Newspapers, of which there was an insufficient number, were eagerly read by the public and journalism thrived. The launching of a new periodical seemed therefore most opportune.

The policy of *Le Politique* was directed in particular against financial waste by the government. It favored reduction of taxes, and on this point it was likely to gain the support of the *industriels* or producers. The journal also advocated freedom of the press which, it declared, was the best substitute for universal suffrage. To give all citizens a "deliberative voice" in the government was an absurdity, but through the press they could have a "consultative voice" and thereby equal rights would be achieved for all.

Contrary to their expectations, *Le Politique* did not bring fame and fortune to its promoters. The twelfth and last copy appeared on May 15, 1819. Undaunted, three months later, we find Saint-Simon launching a new journal, *L'Organisateur*, of which the first number appeared November 1819. It began with a letter signed "Henri Saint-Simon, French citizen, member of

153

the European Society and of the American Society." The letter predicted a dire future for Europe unless measures were adopted for an immediate reconstruction.

"France, England, Germany, Italy and Spain are threatened with great misfortunes; at any moment civil war may break out in any one of those countries while a general war may set Europe on fire; therefore it is my duty to communicate to you the results of my research."

The first article contained the famous parable of the drones. In order to impress on his readers the idea that productive workers alone are of use in society, Saint-Simon asked this question:

"Suppose that France should suddenly lose her fifty foremost physicists, her fifty foremost chemists, her fifty foremost physiologists, her fifty foremost mathematicians, her fifty foremost poets, her fifty foremost painters, her fifty foremost sculptors, her fifty foremost musicians, her fifty foremost writers;

"Her fifty foremost mechanical engineers, her fifty foremost civil and military engineers, her fifty foremost artillery men, her fifty foremost naval officers, her fifty foremost architects, her fifty foremost physicians, her fifty foremost surgeons, her fifty foremost pharmacists, her fifty foremost clockmakers, . . ."

The enumeration went on through the list of all the occupations by deducting from each fifty or more casualties, according to the number of people engaged in it. What would happen should France lose three thousand of her most useful citizens?

"Since these men, of all Frenchmen, are the most essentially productive ones, whose activities are the most important, who direct the works most useful to the nation and promote progress in science, the fine and commercial arts and the trades, they really are the flower of French society; of all Frenchmen they are the most useful to their country, those who procure for it the most glory, who most contribute to the progress of its civilization and to its prosperity. The nation would become a body without a soul the moment it would lose them."

On the other hand, let us consider what would happen in another case:

"Suppose that France keeps all the men of genius she possesses in science, fine arts, commercial arts and trades, but that she

154

has the misfortune of losing, on the same day, Monsieur the King's brother, Monseigneur the Duc d'Angoulême, Monseigneur the Duc de Berry, Monseigneur the Duc d'Orléans, Monseigneur the Duc de Bourbon, Madame the Duchesse d'Angoulême, Madame the Duchesse de Berry, Madame the Duchesse d'Orléans, Madame the Duchesse de Bourbon, and Mademoiselle de Condé...."

To the highest members of the royal family, Saint-Simon added all the State ministers, the State counselors, marshals, cardinals and all the high ecclesiastic authorities, the prefects, judges, and clerks of the ministries, plus the ten thousand landed proprietors living on their income. If thirty thousand of these persons who are considered the most important in the nation were to disappear all at once, what would become of France? There would be great mourning, but the prosperity of the country would remain unimpaired. Plenty of Frenchmen could take the place of the King's brother, and many French women would make as good princesses as Madame the Duchesse d'Angoulême. Many priests are worthy of becoming bishops, plenty of soldiers are capable of being marshals, plenty of lawyers could act as judges, plenty of administrators are qualified to manage the affairs of a department better than the actual prefects.

"As for the ten thousand proprietors living on their income, their heirs will need no apprenticeship to do the honours of their salons as well as they do." [6]

These suppositions prove how badly organised society is, how men "allow themselves to be governed by ruse and violence, how the human species, politically speaking, is still plunged in immorality." The present social system is indeed highly immoral "since ignorance, superstition, idleness and profligacy are the natural attributes of the highest leaders, while men capable, thrifty, laborious are used only as subalterns and tools. In all the fields, incapable men are in charge of directing the capable ones; ... the most immoral men are entrusted with the care of forming virtuous citizens; ... the great criminals are appointed to punish the faults of petty offenders."

It is not surprising that the first issue of *L'Organisateur* was seized by the authorities as it came off the press in the early days of January 1820. A few days later Saint-Simon was called to appear before the police magistrate. He ignored the summons. The case was brought before the assize court on February 3rd, and a judgment by default was pronounced. The author of the article was condemned to three months' imprisonment and a fine of five hundred francs for "offense to the members of the royal family."

Saint-Simon decided to appeal the sentence.

A sudden event gave to his case a tragic aspect. On February 13, Charles Ferdinand, duc de Berry, son of the king's brother and heir to the throne, was stabbed to death as he was coming out of the opera house. Asked what induced him to commit the crime, the assassin Louvel replied:

"The desire to free France from one of its most cruel enemies. The Bourbons are tyrants and the most cruel enemies of France."

Had he any accomplices? "None," was the answer.

The ultra-royalists seized the occasion to get rid of Decazes, whose liberal policy they accused of being responsible for the assassination. Officers of the royal guard called Saint-Simon an accomplice of the crime. Since minister Decazes was incriminated, the author of the bold parable could hardly escape the same accusation. In an attempt to check the wave of anti-liberal reaction, Saint-Simon and Auguste Comte made haste to bring out the second issue of *L'Organisateur*. After a few words condemning the horrible deed, the authors attacked the government for pretending to protect the royal family, while taking advantage of the fatal incident to infringe upon the rights of the individual and to destroy the freedom of the press.

Saint-Simon's appeal against the judgment by default was referred to a trial by jury. To win the attention of the jurymen he addressed to them a series of four letters, explaining his political attitude and attesting his innocence:

"If I am guilty of lack of respect," he wrote in the first letter, "it is certainly not towards the princes of the royal family, it is towards the whole political system now existing. If I have committed any offense, it is for having proved that the mode of administration of public affairs is far behind the present state

156

of knowledge, and for having indicated the direction towards a better social order.

"You are aware, gentlemen, that innovators have always been persecuted. . . . Galileo was condemned for having demonstrated a new important truth, because that truth led to the destruction of certain doctrines considered unshaken in those days." [7]

In his second letter Saint-Simon, professing attachment to the Bourbons, claimed that by advocating changes in the social order he was only attempting to save the royal family from the danger of further revolutions. In the same letter, under the title *History of my Political life,* the writer gave a brief outline of his activities since his American campaign to the time of the publication of *L'Organisateur.* It is diverting to note how he changed his view point in regard to the place of the artist in society:

"I had explained in this work [*L'Industrie*] that the industrialists, the artists and the scientists should be considered the true leaders of the nation. . . .

"Thinking the matter over I have come to the conclusion that at the head of the new order the artists should be first, the scientists next, and the industrialists only after these two first classes. That is the order in which I present my ideas in *L'Organisateur.*"

The fourth letter is a historical résumé of the relations between the royal crown and the communes. Saint-Simon blamed the decline of royal power on Louis XIV for allying himself with the feudal aristocracy, instead of relying on the communes as did his predecessors. From then on the Bourbons followed a wrong path, "a path that will inevitably lead them to their final perdition, if they do not forsake it at once. Royalty must ally itself again with the communes in order to entirely destroy the political influence of the aristocratic class."

The trial was set for March 20. Saint-Simon came to the courtroom wearing the decoration of the Order of the Cincinnati. [8] The Solicitor-General stressed the connection between the murder of the Duc de Berry and the incriminating comment on the royal family in the parable of the drones. The attorney for the defense attempted to show his client's loyalty to the reigning house. As for the jury, they had been favorably impressed by Saint-Simon's letters. He was declared "not guilty."

The notoriety of the trial served at least one purpose. The political conflict between the liberals and the "ultras" was shown to be in reality an economic struggle, and its social implication could not escape the attention of the thinking public. This was good publicity which should have assured the success of the third issue of *L'Organisateur*. Subscribers however failed to materialize. Saint-Simon's funds became exhausted again and the periodical ceased to appear.

Saint-Simon had the alert mind of a publicist prompt to seize opportunities of the moment. The year 1820 being an election year, he lent his pen to the support of the party he favored. This was the newly created *parti industriel* of which his friend Ternaux was the head.

Guillaume-Louis Ternaux born at Sedan in 1763 became at the age of sixteen manager of the textile factory founded by his father. In the days of the Empire he had a whole string of factories spread throughout France. For his services in furnishing clothing material for the armies he received from Napoleon the cross of the Legion of Honor. However when the Bourbons returned to power Ternaux, as so many men of wealth welcomed the new régime, took part in politics and in 1818 was elected deputy to parliament.

The *Biographie pittoresque des députés* of the year 1820 furnishes some interesting details about the man:

"Monsieur Ternaux had come to Paris with his brother. Both are convinced that industry is about to make great progress. The Ternaux establishments which include twenty-one factories and 12,000 workers are scarcely enough to keep them busy. The brothers Ternaux are getting rich while giving work and subsistence to a whole population. . . . M. Ternaux is what the aristocrats may call a *parvenu*. But many a nobleman would be glad to exchange his unsubstantial nobility for the tangible assets of the industrialist and his real popularity. All comforts and luxuries are assembled in his house at Saint-Ouen. There Monsieur Ternaux is pleased to welcome a few friends and a large number of scientists and writers.

158

"What the devil could have tempted him to leave his woolen goods to become head of a political party?"

Ternaux found favor with the liberal minister Decazes, who conferred upon him the title of baron. But after the fall of Decazes, as a consequence of the assassination of the duc de Berry, the coming into power of an ultra-reactionary government led to a bitter struggle between the independent left and the royalist right, a struggle that was to end in the July revolution of 1830.

Ternaux thought there was room between the two irreconcilable extremes for a moderate faction. With this in view he founded the *parti industriel,* which proposed to bring the attention of the government to the study of economic problems instead of wasting its efforts in acrimonious strife.

Saint-Simon championed the cause of the *parti industriel* and became its ardent propagandist. To stir up interest in the electoral campaign he thought an appropriate song would be most useful. For some time he had known the composer Rouget de Lisle, who was one of his admirers and who shared his views on social reconstruction. The creator of the *Marseillaise* had more than once suggested the use of music as a powerful means of action for establishing the projected world order. Had not the *Marseillaise* helped the cause of the Republic as much as cannon fire? Saint-Simon, remembering the friendly suggestion, asked Rouget de Lisle to write a piece that might arouse enthusiasm in favor of Ternaux's political party.

De Lisle rose to the occasion and wrote the words and music of the *Chant des Industriels,* of which we translate the first verse and the chorus:

> "The times prepared by our fathers,
> The times at last have arrived,
> All obstacles have been removed,
> Prosperous days are here.
> Already yielding before us
> Force and error have been dethroned,
> A few more efforts, a few more days
> And they will collapse at our feet.

Glory to us, the sons of industry!
Glory, glory to our happy labors!
In all the arts we surpass our rivals,
We are the hope, the pride of our country."

A rendering of the *Chant des Industriels* was given at Ternaux's textile mill in Saint-Ouen with the workers participating. It is not related whether the composition was sung anywhere else. Several manufacturers manifested their displeasure because Rouget de Lisle bestowed such exclusive honor on Ternaux. Saint-Simon explained that the homage was not directed to the man, but to the principles he represented. Copies of the song were distributed gratis from his apartment at 34 rue Richelieu. Judging from the hostile attitude just mentioned, it is doubtful that the *Chant des Industriels* gained popular success.

Saint-Simon gave evidence of an extraordinary activity during the electoral campaign. He traveled through the northern provinces calling on influential manufacturers who had been on the list of subscribers to his *Organisateur*. But his main effort, as might be expected, was through his writings. In June 1820, in collaboration with Comte, he produced a series of tracts under the title: *Considérations sur les mesures à prendre pour terminer la Révolution.* These proposed means to terminate the Revolution included the principles advocated by the *parti industriel* with a generous addition of the authors' favorite themes. The tracts were in the form of letters, six in all, addressed to "gentlemen farmers, manufacturers, traders and other producers." The second *Letter,* in a postscript, gave explicit directions on how to vote:

"I advise you, gentlemen, to choose as deputies none but farmers, manufacturers, merchants, and bankers; the interests of industry cannot be effectively protected except by professional producers."

At the elections which took place in December, the *parti industriel* won only half a dozen seats. In the struggle for the control of power the aristocracy of birth was not ready to give way to the aristocracy of money before another decade.

160

It was to Saint-Simon's advantage to maintain contact with the people who had backed the defeated party, not only for the sake of propagating his theories, but in the hope of financial support as well. His meagre revenues were derived mostly from his pen, and there was a chance that the wealthy men to whom his *Letters* were addressed would pay for the essays dealing with the establishment of an industrial society.

The following year, 1821, appeared a large volume entitled *Système Industriel,* part first, by Henri Saint-Simon. Published in three parts, the book, in the main was a reprint of the six preceding *Letters.* It bore the epigraph: "God said: Love and aid one another." The third part which did not come out before January 1822, was named *Philosophical, scientific and poetic studies intended to facilitate the reorganisation of European society,* by Henri Saint-Simon.

The author came to the conclusion that the social order he wished to establish must be founded not only on material but also on spiritual principles. Addressing himself to Louis XVIII, he wrote:

"Sire, the fundamental principle laid down by the founder of Christianity commands all men to regard themselves as brothers and to cooperate as completely as possible for their mutual welfare. The temporal power must belong to men useful, laborious and pacific; the spiritual power must belong to men possessing the knowledge useful to the human species; in a word, the industrial and scientific system must be constituted."

This new system would create a social organization devoted to the greatest good of the greatest number:

"The direct purpose of my undertaking is to ameliorate as much as possible the condition of the class which has no other means of existence except the work of its hands. My purpose is to better the condition of this class not only in France, but in England, Belgium, Portugal, Spain, Italy, in the rest of Europe, and in the entire world. This class, despite the immense progress of civilization, is still the largest in most civilized countries . . . The governments should be concerned with this class primarily, but on the contrary they care the least for its interests; they re-

161

gard it essentially as governable and taxable, and they only care to maintain it in the most passive obedience."

As to the means for improving the condition of the working class, Saint-Simon presented the following suggestions:

"The common people, just as the rich, have two kinds of needs: they have physical needs and moral needs; they need to make a living, they also need education.

"What is the means of securing for the generality of the common people, as immediately as possible, the best possible living?

"One must first consider that the general means of securing a living for the people is to secure work for them. The question therefore reduces itself to this: what is the means of securing the greatest quantity of work possible?

"The best means is to entrust the leaders of industrial enterprises with the care of making the national budget, and consequently of directing public administration. By the very nature of things, the leaders of industrial enterprises (who are the real leaders of the people, since it is they who command the people in their daily tasks) will always be inclined, in their own interest, to expand their production as much as possible and from these efforts there will result the greatest amount possible of work done by the common people.

"The education most needed by the common people is the kind that can render them most capable of performing the work confided to them. Therefore, some elements of geometry, physics, chemistry and hygiene are incontestably the kind of knowledge most useful to the people in order to govern their lives, and it is evident that the scientists specializing in physics and mathematics alone are qualified to give them a good educational system.

"The educational system for the primary schools must therefore be organized by the scientists who specialize in positive science."

It is interesting to watch Saint-Simon's growing concern for the working classes. His philanthropic attitude derived logically enough from his concept of industrial society. But a new element was introduced by the epigraph to the *Système Industriel:* "God said: Love and aid one another." This religious note seems difficult to reconcile with the reformer's insistence on pos-

162

itive science as the spiritual guidance for the people. Was the use of the evangelical precept a mere literary figure, a catch phrase to attract the attention of religious minded readers? Whatever the intention, the insertion of the Christian motto indicated a new direction in Saint-Simon's thoughts. This new trend, as will be seen in a subsequent chapter, will lead the philosopher in search of glory to his final goal.

CHAPTER ELEVEN

Saint-Simon's residence on rue Richelieu consisted of a small apartment four flights up, which he shared with his secretary Julie Juliand. The living room, overlooking the street, served as bedroom, dining room, and study. The furnishings were most simple: a table, a bed, and a few walnut chairs. A kitchen, a small room for Julie, and an entrance hall completed the lodgings.

We owe to Léon Halévy's *Souvenirs de Saint-Simon* a detailed account of this period in Saint-Simon's life. The portrait of Julie is sketched with telling impressionistic touches:

"A woman, 38 years old, fresh and plump, with a frank and cheerful air, a graceful but somewhat common expression, Julie had for Saint-Simon the respect of a daughter and the affection of a sister. She had been in his service for many years and exerted herself to the utmost to please him and anticipate his every wish. She had no education at all, but was endowed with a natural intelligence, and a sense of propriety which often lent her an air of social distinction, resulting either from a fortunate instinct or the companionship of the distinguished man for whom she was caring in his old age and whose fate she was sharing. Her cheerful temperament kept sadness, if not poverty, away from the philosopher's abode. When Saint-Simon thought he had reason to complain and got angry with her (which happened occasionally as any one is apt to be unjust at times), she would laugh and make him feel how wrong he was to reproach her, in a tone of respectful familiarity that cannot be described, a mingling of independence and subservience."[1]

Julie was indeed a most devoted and serviceable helpmate. She prepared meals for her aged companion, took care of his linen, cleaned the apartment, wrote under his dictation, copied his manuscripts, and even stitched the printed pages. No wonder she earned Halévy's admiration and perhaps his envy.

"Of all the bachelors I have known," Halévy commented, "Saint-Simon is the only one whose fate I have not pitied, so much did this excellent and devoted woman compensate him for the misfortune of being alone and without a family at the age of sixty."

Halévy was not altogether correct in asserting that Saint-Simon was without a family in his old age. He had a daughter, an illegitimate child, Caroline-Charlotte Thillays. Saint-Simon, it may be recalled, had asked Redern to give a life income of one thousand eight hundred francs to madame Thillays, who had sued him for the maintenance of the child. Caroline, by this time, was married to a Parisian merchant, monsieur Bouraiche, and had children of her own.

Saint-Simon maintained an affectionate correspondence with his daughter. One letter was written during his visit to a number of manufacturing centers in a vain attempt to interest industrialists to give financial support for the publication of his writings. It was dated from Rouen, February 16, 1822:

"I did not write to you sooner, my beloved Caroline, because I thought I could announce to you to-day my return to Paris. My affairs are doing well, but not as fast as I hoped. I think it will take me another week or so. This town is much better than Saint-Quentin, I have found here several very intelligent business men who take a keen interest in my works.

"I think you'll do well to sell out your stock before the new business opens on your street. I shall have to come several times to this town; our plan of going together to the seashore will be postponed to a little later. I kiss you with all my heart, as well as my dear grandchildren. I shall not write any more, because my mind is so occupied. As for my heart, it is entirely yours.

"This Friday. Henri Saint-Simon"[2]

A few weeks later, still at Rouen, Saint-Simon corresponded again with his daughter who had her share of financial worries, which the kind father tried to assuage.

"Rouen, March 9, 1822.

"We will succeed, my dear Caroline. How glad I shall be to dispel your anxieties, for yourself and our dear children! The letter you wrote me was charming, I read it twenty times; you have a loving, generous and courageous soul, your affection is the greatest reward I could hope for.

"Have you sold your stock? What are you doing now? I won't give you any details of my affairs, but I can assure you that a great and happy result is not more than two months ahead.

"I shall soon be happy to press you against my heart, I cannot tell you the exact date. Let me hear from you, I shall certainly be here when your letter comes." [3]

His optimism was misplaced, for appeals to his former friends both in Paris and in the provinces were of little avail. Saint-Simon had offered to Dupuytren a purse of a thousand francs, when the latter was a young medical student having a difficult time financially. Dupuytren had rejected the offer, but now in his days of prosperity he might remember the man who made it, and be inclined to return the proffered generosity. Pierre Leroux related the following incident repeated to him by Dupuytren himself, who was now the surgeon to king Louis XVIII:

"One day my servant told me that a gentleman who had already presented himself several times wished to speak to me. I gave the order to let him in. 'Don't you recognize me?' said the stranger. 'Once I saw you when you were young. Of course time has changed our features, as it has changed also our position in the world.'

"I did not understand what he meant. I made it clear to him that I was busy.

"'Always busy!' Then in a serious tone he said: 'Do to-day for me what I tried one day to do for you.' Can you understand such a queer fellow? Because he once tried to give me a thousand francs, which I refused, he wanted me to give him a similar sum. . . . He said to me: 'You were young, not everybody could guess how you would turn out, what services you might render to society. I foresaw those services, I had money, I offered you some. It was not my fault if you did not avail yourself of it. Many other scientists made use of my purse. Well, to-day I am old and poor. You are rich. I am still interested in science, and I believe something will come out of my works.'

"While speaking thus, he handed me a brochure. I still have it. You can see it there in my library. He handed me this bro-

166

chure, as I said, or rather he placed it on my desk. I did not extend my hand to take it. He then came out with it: 'It is fitting that you do for me what I once tried to do for you.'

"I looked at the brochure. I saw it might be worth thirty sous. I drew from my pocket a five franc piece and offered it to him.

"He turned his back on me and made toward the door. I urged him to take back his book, since he did not wish to accept the price I offered him for it. He did not say a word and went out.

"I rang for my servant and told him to return the book to the man. The fool came back and left it."[4]

Blainville, the eminent naturalist, one of Saint-Simon's friends, told a no less poignant anecdote. One day Saint-Simon came to see him at the moment when he and his guests were finishing dinner. Blainville invited him to sit down and have something to eat. At first Saint-Simon refused, then suddenly he seized the chunk of cheese on the table and started to eat like a starving man.

During his lifetime Saint-Simon had known many a set-back, experienced many a downfall, but had always managed to rise again. Now he was sixty-two years old and facing starvation. Did the voice of Charlemagne lead him in quest of a fleeting shadow? Had the flame that beckoned him to the temple of glory died out in the wind? For the first time he lost his self confidence and gave way to despair. He penned a farewell note to his friend Ternaux:

"Sir,

After deliberation I am convinced you were right in telling me that it would take more time than I thought before the public shows any interest in the works which have been engaging all my attention for so long. Consequently I have decided to bid you adieu. My feelings are those of profound regard for you and great affection for your noble and philanthropic character. Permit me to offer to you my heart for the last time. I am grieved to leave the woman who was with me in this frightful situation. This woman has given me the greatest evidence of unselfish devotion. I beseech you as earnestly as I can to grant her your protection. She is not a servant, she is a worker whose great intelligence and scrupulous conscience render her capable of filling a position of trust. I end, and I wish you live a long time for the happiness of those who have had relations with you.

Saint-Simon."

Saint-Simon's solicitude for his mistress was no less touching than his paternal devotion to his daughter. We do not need other proofs of his fundamental good heartedness.

When he wrote his letter to Ternaux on the night of March 9, 1823, Saint-Simon was alone in his apartment on rue Richelieu. He had sent Julie away for the day. Hubbard relates how, having signed the letter, he calmly loaded a pistol with seven buckshot, and placed it on the table which served as his writing desk. With an eye on his watch lying near the pistol, he continued writing until the hand pointed to the hour he had decided on. At that moment he raised the firearm to his temple and pulled the trigger. The shot blew out one eye, but did not reach the brain.

A neighbor, attracted by the gun report, entered the room where he saw Saint-Simon sitting on the bed, watching the blood flow into a basin. He called Dr. Sarlandière, the physician who lived in the same building. On seeing the doctor, Saint-Simon asked:

"Tell me, my dear Sarlandière, how a man with seven bullets in his head can still live and think."

The physician's first care, after examining the wound, was to verify if any of the shots had lodged in the brain. None could be detected in the wound, six were found in the room but the seventh could not be located. Dr. Sarlandière concluded that one shot had entered the brain and therefore the wounded man was lost. He told him so, explaining that with the progress of inflammation a violent hemorrhage would set in and death would follow. Auguste Comte just then entered the room. Addressing himself to his pupil, Saint-Simon said:

"Now then, let us make good use of the moments left and discuss our work."[5]

Night came and Saint-Simon was in agonizing pain. He begged those present to release him from his torment and open his jugular vein. Neither the doctor, nor Comte, nor Julie would accede to his request, but believed death would soon end his suffering.

The night went by and at daybreak Julie started to kindle the fire and prepare breakfast. In stirring the ashes, the seventh bullet was found. There was now hope for recovery. In fact, the pain had already abated and merciful sleep had overtaken the injured man. By the end of two weeks, Saint-Simon was out of danger.

The report of the superintendent of police of the district, made on March 13, stated that Saint-Simon would survive the wounds. An attempt was made to disguise the fact that suicide had been contemplated and it was explained that the wound was caused accidentally. But the police officer was not deceived.

Auguste Comte wrote to M. de Blainville to kindly call on Saint-Simon and try to comfort him. Messrs. Ternaux, Laffitte, Ardoin, and other friends, shocked by Saint-Simon's attempt to commit suicide, rallied to his aid, with the result that the last years of his life were spent in comfort. He was now surrounded by a group of admirers who not only gave financial assistance but spiritual encouragement as well. He was deprived of one eye, but completely cured of his despair, and he resumed his work with as much gusto as ever.

In May, two months after his attempt at suicide, while visiting M. Ardoin, Saint-Simon met a young man who became his first and most devoted disciple. He was Olinde Rodrigues. Born at Bordeaux in 1794, Rodrigues belonged to a wealthy Jewish family engaged in banking. Because of his racial origin he was denied entrance to the *Ecole Normale,* where he had hoped to qualify for a professorship. Instead, he devoted himself to a financial career and became director of a bank in Paris. Attracted to Saint-Simon, he catered to his needs and helped to finance his publications.

Soon after, Rodrigues introduced to Saint-Simon the young poet Léon Halévy, who became deeply attached to the master and later wrote the *Souvenirs de Saint-Simon.* These *Souvenirs* contain interesting details referring to the last years of the aging philosopher. The devoted care he received from Rodrigues was related with touching admiration:

"Here I must say it with the pleasure one always feels in telling the truth: Saint-Simon, since Olinde Rodrigues came to him, was no longer exposed to those painful and humiliating trials which can move the strongest soul to despair and even to the contempt of life. Olinde Rodrigues became a real providence for Saint-Simon. By his warm, enthusiastic and spontaneous approval of the ideas of the abandoned old man, who up to now had encountered nothing but scorn, he raised his fallen morale and encouraged his high mission. By his activity, zeal and truly filial devotion he gave him the means for continuing and publishing his works.

"He tried to have everybody share with him the profound admiration he had for the ideas of a man who, he believed, was called to lead humanity in a new direction. It was no mediocre joy for Saint-Simon, after so many illusions cheated and many hopes vanished, to welcome a man who devoted himself entirely to him, sympathised with his theories, a man who believed in him, and who possessed a methodical and philosophical mind, a lively imagination and an inspiring voice. Saint-Simon felt his strength doubled, his courage revived, and he owed to Olinde Rodrigues the happiness of his last years."[6]

Another source of contentment came from his correspondence with his daughter who, either divorced or widowed, had contracted a second marriage. She was now madame Charon and resided in Beaumont, in the department of Seine-et-Marne. A letter to her dated November 15, 1823, reads:

"Heaven has granted me the sweetest of all rewards in giving me my Caroline. My greatest pleasure, after my long efforts, will be to press her in my arms. My affairs are doing very well. I hope to give you positive good news within a month. I kiss with all my heart my Caroline, her little children and her husband, if he makes her happy.

"I now turn over my pen to my secretary Julie.

H. Saint-Simon."

And Julie put in a word:

"I add my hope to that of your good father, my dear friend, that he will soon have good news for you. I hope also that we won't always be as far as now from each other. How happy we all shall be then! I really think that, before the end of this unfortunate year, we shall be assured of great success.

"Adieu, my dear friend, my best regards to your husband, and kiss your little 'devils' for me.

Your friend,   Julie Juliand.

Paris, November 15."

Halévy, in his delightful narration, added to the picture of the philosopher's ménage a few more details worth quoting:

"A second personage completed the household with Julie. This was Turc, the admirable poodle, a super-intelligent animal, the constant companion of Saint-Simon. The dog was well known in the gardens of the Palais-Royal, the favorite haunt of our philosopher, and at the Café de la Régence, where Saint-Simon would go at times to watch the Caesars and Alexanders of the chess-board engage in memorable combats. Turc was indeed a superior animal, and of rare intelligence, even for a species noted for its mental capacities. Saint-Simon told me one day how man can fascinate animals by his gaze. He believed, and related to me to prove his point, that one day he had stopped short and subdued by his gaze a bear which had escaped from a travelling circus. When I knew Saint-Simon, he had but one eye and the penetrating force of that eye was extraordinary. Saint-Simon's dog obeyed the merest glance of his master and knew its meaning."

Adding more touches to the portrait of Saint-Simon, Halévy wrote:

"In spite of the wound which disfigured him, Saint-Simon had a handsome head, a strong and imposing physiognomy. His conversation, at times slow and difficult, was at other times charming and lively. But whether his speech was more or less abundant, more or less happy, his thought was always new, bold and paradoxical. He had an admirable way of judging a philosophical or literary book, he went to the bottom, to the heart of the work and dissected it with a prodigious dexterity. He did not have a thorough knowledge of history in detail, but he knew it in the whole and divided it according to philosophical lines with a superior intelligence. Often his talk would sparkle with clever flashes of witticism, and, whenever he wanted to, conversation could become gay and vivacious. With women in a salon, he no longer was the profound and abstract thinker, but a frivolous and

171

gallant man of the world jesting with polished cleverness. His long and adventurous life was full of strange and exciting memories. I have never known a better raconteur."[7]

Saint-Simon's reading preferences during moments of relaxation are related by Halévy with a complacent smile of amusement:

"When I was taken to his room, Saint-Simon was seated in one corner reading with rapt attention. Since I have said that Saint-Simon was reading, I must mention the kind of books he read. Saint-Simon read nothing but novels, and his taste in this regard was peculiar since he read anything at random. 'Get me a novel,' he would say to Julie and she would bring him one. No matter what it was, he devoured it. Madame de Senlis or madame Barthélemy-Hadot, Auguste Lafontaine or Ducray-Dumesnil, Pigault-Lebrun or Victor Ducange, Paul de Kock or monsieur Paccard, it did not matter. Whether it was Amanda or Theresa, Georgina or Evelina, provided there was a heroine, a forest, a post-chaise, a cottage, and two or three torrents, that was all he cared for. He read for relaxation, and he wanted a novel, that was all. One day he told me confidentially that, in regard to novels, he preferred the most stupid ones. And I must say he got what he wished from his bookseller."

We need not reproach Saint-Simon for his choice of melodramatic and sentimental novels any more than accuse of bad taste our contemporary business and political leaders for indulging in detective stories. Sentimental and melodramatic literature was the vogue at the time of the Restoration, and the aging man gratified his romantic bent by reading popular fiction as a means of relaxation. His mind was more active than ever and he was about to begin the most important phase of his intellectual life.

CHAPTER TWELVE

The collaboration between Saint-Simon and Auguste Comte continued unfailingly in spite of constant financial disillusionments. Their new undertaking, *Catéchisme des Industriels,* came out in December 1823. The so-called catechism was an attempt to popularize the theories of the industrial system. Under the form of questions and answers, it presented in a clear and systematic order the points to be emphasized for the readers, as one may judge from this extract:

Q.–What is an *industriel?*

A.–An *industriel* is a man who works to produce or to provide for the different members of society one or several material means of satisfying their physical needs or tastes. Thus, a farmer who sows wheat, raises chickens or cattle is an *industriel;* a manufacturer of shoes, hats, textiles, cloth, cashmere, is also an *industriel;* a merchant, a carter, a sailor employed on merchant vessels, are *industriels. . . .*

Q.–What rank should *industriels* (producers) occupy in society?

A.—The producing class should occupy the first rank because it is the most important of all.

Q.–What rank do the producers occupy in society?

A.–In the present social organisation they occupy the lowest rank.

Q.–What is the scope of the study you have undertaken? In other words, what is your purpose in writing this Catechism?

A.—We propose to show the producers' ways of increasing their welfare to the utmost; we propose to reveal to them the methods they should employ in order to improve their social importance.

Q.–How will you do that?

A.—First, . . . we shall show the producers that their social rank is very much below what it should be, since they form the most capable and most useful class of society. Then, we shall point out to them the steps they must take in order to put themselves in the first rank in regard to social recognition and power.

Q.—So, in this Catechism, you preach insurrection and revolt?

A.—Far from preaching insurrection and revolt we present the only way to prevent acts of violence which would threaten society if the industrial power remained passive among factions wrangling for power. Public order cannot be stable as long as the most important producers are not in charge of directing and administering the public welfare. . . .

Q.—What means will the producers employ in order to bring about the radical changes you propose?

A.—The producers compose more than twenty-four percent of the nation; thus they have superiority in regard to physical power. It is they who produce all the wealth, and therefore they possess the financial power. They have superiority in regard to intelligence, because they contrive the most to produce national prosperity. Furthermore, since they are the most capable, they are designated by human as well as divine laws to take charge of the financial interests of the nation. The producers are thus invested with all the necessary means for bringing about the changes which will uplift them from the rank of the governed to that of the rulers."

The above quotation will help to define, better than any comment, the saint-simonian conception of an industrial order. One might possibly compare it, in substance, with the tenets of technocracy or, in more than one aspect, with the present American industrial system.

The second part of the *Catéchisme des Industriels* was published in March 1824, and in the following month appeared the third part, or *cahier* as each issue was called. This third *cahier* bore the title: "*Système de politique positive* by Auguste Comte, pupil of Saint-Simon."

Up to now Comte had refrained from signing his name for fear of causing displeasure to his family. His parents, royalists and catholics, who resided in Montpelier, would not approve their son's advocacy of new ideas. Furthermore, since the father held a government post, that of receiver-general of taxes for the district, it was not wise to stir up trouble which might bring disaster to the family.

In the spring of 1824, Auguste Comte thought the time had come to declare his independence from both Saint-Simon and his parents, as he explained in this letter to Valat:

"I did not sign my name to what I wrote, partly so as not to displease my parents, partly for the sake of my collaborator who . . . preferred the whole credit to the half credit which at most he would have received otherwise. I am not sorry it was thus, because my previous writings did not deserve my name to be signed to them. I now consider them as exercises which were very helpful to me, but only preliminary. I would much rather make my entry in public with a capital work all my own and entirely free from the influence Saint-Simon had previously had over me, an influence, I must say, which has mightily contributed to my philosophical education. As I said, until this essay my writings did not bear my name and only a very few people in whom I had confided knew that I was dealing with ideas of that sort. But in composing this work, I felt the moment had come to shake off the tutelage of both my parents and of Saint-Simon. Through a sort of instinct that guided me, I understood that work was too important for me to overlook this occasion. And, in fact, had I been foolish to do so, I would have done myself an almost irreparable wrong, and Saint-Simon would have definitely set his foot on my throat. You will understand this readily if you consider that all my subsequent writings are to be strictly the continuation of this one, and it would be very difficult to set my name to them if I allowed the first part to appear under some one else's name. The public could not make out the disparity, and besides Saint-Simon would turn opinion against me. So I let him know that I was determined to sign all my writings from now on, beginning with this one. Evidently he realized as much as I did the importance of my decision, because he appeared deeply annoyed by it. Nevertheless, as he could not help it, he had to let me do as I said. But from that time on he felt a strong aversion to publishing my work and he tried to postpone the publication as long as possible, using all the means he could imagine for doing so and taking particular advantage of the fact that he was the administrative director of our association."

Toward the end of the letter, Comte again mentioned his indebtedness to Saint-Simon in these words:

"Intellectually I do owe a great deal to Saint-Simon, which is to say that he had helped me mightily to direct my steps toward the philosophical career I am determined to follow from now on for the rest of my life."

With confident pride, therefore, Comte signed his name to the manuscript of the *Système de politique positive*. It was in reference to this writing that differences of opinion arose between the two men. Saint-Simon prefaced the third volume of the *Catéchisme* with a warning to the reader that his pupil had treated only the scientific side of the social problem. By neglecting to deal with the sentimental and religious aspects, he was guilty of serious omission.

The foreword was, in turn, followed by a notice from Comte stating:

"Having meditated for a long time upon the leading ideas of monsieur Saint-Simon, I set for myself the task of developing and improving exclusively those ideas which refer to scientific organization. As a result of this work I have originated the *Système de politique positive* which I now submit to the judgment of the thinking public.

"I thought it was my duty to render the above declaration, so that, if my writings deserve any approbation, the credit for it be attributed to the founder of the Philosophical School to which I have the honor to belong."

It is difficult to evaluate to what extent Comte's positivism is due to Saint-Simon's influence, and it is no less difficult to establish who originated the main thesis of the *Système Industriel*, the master or the pupil. Most of the ideas developed by Comte in his *Système de politique positive* had already been enunciated by Saint-Simon in a more or less desultory way. Comte presented his thesis in a precise and orderly manner, shaping his thought and building it into an architectonic body.

By dividing history into three successive stages, theological, metaphysical, and scientific or positive, Comte drew his rational conclusions from the past. Granted that human society has reached the positive stage, the art of governing must become a science in the same way as astronomy or physics are subject to the laws that govern science. All sciences have undergone successively the above three stages, biology being the latest to make its appearance. Government, being the science of complex phenomena, was for this reason the last one to reach the positive stage. But now that government has attained a degree of scientific development, it must be treated as such and not as a theological matter dealing with the divine right of kings, nor as a metaphysical abstraction such as Rousseau's *Social Contract*.

The greatest hindrance to the progress of society, argued the author, was the continued ascendancy of the revolutionary spirit among the people. The only means of assuring order was to create a social system on a positive or scientific basis, in regard to ethics as well as politics and economics.

A new power must be substituted for the medieval hierarchy in church and state. This power will reside in the hands of men who will govern in accordance with positive principles. From the scientific point of view, declared Comte, it is evident that freedom of thought and the sovereignty of the people are wrong principles, since both of them were "born for destruction, and unfit for construction."

"There is no freedom of thought in astronomy, physics, chemistry, physiology, in the sense that every one would think it absurd not to believe implicitly the principles established in those sciences by competent men.

"Freedom of thought is merely individual infallibility taking the place of papal infallibility. The sovereignty of the people replaces the arbitrary power of the kings by the arbitrary power of the masses. It entrusts the most ignorant among men with the right of absolute control of ideas and principles discovered by superior minds, it tends to disrupt the body politic by giving power to the least educated classes."

The industrial system, as may be seen from the above quotation, was far from favoring the democratic regime. Instead of a dictatorship of the proletariat, which later exponents of socialism conceived, we have here what appears to be a claim for the dictatorship of the industrialists. But the author anticipated the objection by stating that under the industrial system men will no longer be subjects, but members of the corporate body:

"The human species was destined to live first under a governmental régime; it is due to pass from the governmental or military régime to the administrative or industrial régime."

This could mean that the political government would be replaced by an economic administration, a theory with which Friedrich Engels fully concurred. Comte had full confidence in the blessings of a social order founded on the principles of his positive philosophy:

"When we look toward the past we see the masses of people struggling against each other by force of arms; if we look toward the future we see these masses in friendly rivalry competing with one another in civic virtues, science and industry."

While sharing most of his pupil's views, Saint-Simon reproached Comte for his excessive positivism which excluded religious sentiment as one of the fundamental factors of social order. The differences between the two collaborators, which now reached the breaking point, had been widening from year to year. They were due to several causes, the primary one being that of temperaments. Both were animated by exaggerated pride, each of them eager to impose his thought and compel recognition of his genius. That was the only trait they possessed in common. The capricious, imaginative and sensual nature of Saint-Simon contrasted sharply with the cold, scientific, logical mind of his pupil.

Saint-Simon publicly admitted the superior intellect of his collaborator, when the latter wrote *Contrat Social* (1822), which was a succinct summary of the tenets of the industrial system. In the introduction to that brochure, Saint-Simon stated:

"One of my friends and collaborators has taken charge of this important essay. Here is his work, which corresponds to the preliminary discourse of D'Alembert to the Encyclopedia."

That was indeed high praise. But Saint-Simon was careful not to mention the name of his collaborator who might thereby share the glory. There were also financial difficulties between the two in regard to author's rights. On Rodrigues' advice they entered into a new contract. Saint-Simon promised to pay to Comte a sum of two thousand four hundred francs in twelve monthly instalments for the latter's *Tableau Historique,* which had previously appeared in *L'Organisateur* and for his *Politique positive.*

The publication of the *Politique positive* was a further cause of disappointment for Comte. He had expected this important work to appear in a separate edition, but instead Saint-Simon included it as part of his *Catéchisme.* As a result Comte felt that he was deprived of the full credit for his authorship, since his *Politique* was buried, as it were in the issues of the *Catéchisme.* To his friend Valat he complained that Saint-Simon's "moral standard is made of the Machiavellism of a man who has a very determined aim, which is to create a sensation in the world."

Thus was broken the bond that held the two men together for a period of seven years. Comte had passed the most receptive years, from the age of twenty to twenty-six, in intimate association with one of the most active minds of the time. The master's influence upon the sensitive and intelligent pupil is beyond doubt.

While Comte was working as a young secretary under the direction of Saint-Simon, he did not spare eulogious comments on the man to whom he owed his vocation. But later, pride and vanity connived to turn praise into bitter denunciation and even base vituperation. It is indeed inconceivable that a man who founded a philosophical system of universal import should condemn his relations with his former teacher, counselor, and friend as "a baneful association with a depraved clown." The most rational mind swayed by conceit and vainglory can become subject to strange incongruous distortions.

Years afterwards, when he was claimed by the Saint-Simonians as one of their sect, Comte protested and gave the reason for his rupture with Saint-Simon:

"I began to perceive in him religious tendencies utterly incompatible with my philosophical views."

By a singular irony of fate the originator of positive philosophy fell victim to the very weakness of which he accused Saint-Simon. Following the example of the master he disowned, Comte founded the Religion of Humanity, reserving for himself the title of high priest.

In May 1824 the two men parted and each went his own way, Comte to found a new philosophy, Saint-Simon to establish a new religion.

CHAPTER THIRTEEN

The defection of Auguste Comte did not seem to dampen the effervescence of Saint-Simon's thoughts, nor did the aged philosopher lack collaborators in preparing the next publication, *Opinions littéraires, philosophiques et industrielles,* which appeared early in 1825. Four of his disciples, the financier Olinde Rodrigues, the poet Léon Halévy, the jurist Jean-Baptiste Duvergier, the physiologist Dr. Bailly, contributed to the contents of the new volume.

Besides the chapter on industry and finance by Saint-Simon, it contained various essays on banking, legislation, philosophy, literature, economic and physiological sciences. The social implications of the volume were contained in this epigraph:

"The golden age, which blind people placed in the past, belongs to the future."

By now, however, the religious sentiments to which Comte objected began to absorb Saint-Simon's interest. He was then sixty-four years old. Time was pressing, and the approach to the temple of glory must be quickened. The moment was opportune, for religious problems were much to the fore. Under the restored monarchy, fear of revolution was the uppermost concern of the wealthy and ruling classes. They realized the necessity of strong spiritual forces to stem the mounting discontent of the masses ruthlessly exploited by the development of industrial production. Writers and philosophers advocated the return to religion as the best safeguard against disorder. Some favored strengthening the authority of the established church, others desired a liberalized catholicism in accord with changes in the modern world. It was not even infrequent among intellectuals to propound the establishment of a new creed in conformity with present scientific knowledge and social conditions.

The first two volumes of Lamennais' monumental work *Essai sur l'indifférence en matière de religion* had stirred up interest in religious matters to the highest point. His attempts to liberalize the Catholic Church ended in failure, but he had voiced with force and eloquence the wishes of the youth of his generation.

Joseph de Maistre, the ultramontanist thinker, did not hesitate to remark:

"It seems to me that every true philosopher must choose between these two hypotheses, that either a new religion is to be founded or Christianity must be renewed in some extraordinary way."[1]

A renewal of Christianity was also preconised by Chateaubriand the great writer whose works played such an important part in reawakening religious sentiment in the early days of the nineteenth century. He echoed the thought of de Maistre when he remarked:

"The degenerated world calls for a new promulgation of the Gospel; a new Christianity is to come."[2]

Saint-Simon promulgated the new Christianity in 1825 when he published his last and most notable book *Le Nouveau Christianisme*. This was in fact an ambitious effort to establish a universal religion which the author intended to be adopted by all the nations of the world. His mission was to reshape the world according to the plan God had revealed to him:

"It is God who has spoken to me; could a man have invented a religion superior to all those that have existed?"[3]

The social aspect of the new creed was introduced by the epigraph borrowed from Paul's Epistle to the Romans:

"He that loveth his neighbor hath fulfilled the law. Thou shall love thy neighbor as thyself."

The author enunciated the fundamental principle of his New Christianity in these words:

"Religion must direct society toward the aim of improving as speedily as possible the welfare of the poorer class."

Catholicism as well as Protestantism had failed in the performance of this duty. The new religion will bring Christianity to its original purpose. God said but one thing, that men must

182

act as brothers toward one another. All the rest was invented by man and consequently is susceptible to change. The Church did admirable work until the time of the Reformation. The spirit of Christianity is one of love, kindness, and charity, of tolerance and persuasion. But the spirit of the Church since the middle ages has been one of violence and cruelty, of avidity and despotism. The apostles were the protectors of the poor, whereas their successors became the protectors of the rich and mighty. This great heresy at last ended, for God has entrusted Saint-Simon with the mission of renovating Christianity:

"Last night I heard these words: Rome will renounce the claim to the see of my church; pope, cardinals, bishops and priests will cease speaking in my name."[4]

In conclusion, Saint-Simon addressed himself to the rulers, admonishing them in these terms:

"Princes, listen to the voice of God who speaks through my mouth. Become good Christians, cease to consider the soldiers in your pay, the nobles, the heretical priests and perverted judges as your main supports. Be united in the name of Christianity and accomplish the duties it imposes on the rulers. Remember that it commands you to make use of your power to increase as promptly as possible the social happiness of the poor."

One may wonder why Saint-Simon, who in his previous writings openly manifested a materialistic philosophy, now directed his attention toward religion. Is this the eighteenth century aristocrat who declared himself the continuator of the Encyclopedists, the amoralist who tried all sensuous experiments, the epicurean who fared sumptuously, the land speculator, merchant and manufacturer who recklessly strove for riches? The only plausible explanation is that at this moment Saint-Simon pursued fame in a new way. He would become the new Messiah, the saviour of mankind.

"There are no two orders of things, there is only one, the physical order." This quotation from the *Introduction aux travaux scientifiques* typified Saint-Simon's attitude in regard to spiritual matters. It is true that he frequently invoked the

Supreme Being, or claimed to have direct communion with God, but it was primarily as a literary fiction or as a means of propaganda for his theories.

In the *Lettres d'un habitant de Genève,* he claimed that God spoke directly through his mouth. In the letter to his nephew Victor, it was Charlemagne who entrusted him with a message. In the *Mémoire sur la gravitation,* Socrates spoke in his name and Saint-Simon presented himself as the reincarnation of the Greek philosopher. Evidently the voices that spoke to him did not all come from the beyond but from his own imagination.

Among those voices there was one call that rang loud and persistent and would not be downed. In his adolescence he heard it when his valet awoke him with the words: "Arise, monsieur le comte, for you have great things to do." It became insistent when he wrote in the *Mémoire sur la science*: "The aim of my writings, the object of my hopes, is to obtain the favors of a living glory." Its clamor was heard again in *Ma Vie*: "I kept ascending the arid and steep mountain which bears on its summit the temple of glory." And in another passage: "I have lost the titles and fortune of the duc de Saint-Simon, but I have inherited his passion for glory."

When Saint-Simon was ruined, the possibility of playing the rôle of patron of letters and science vanished with his wealth. But the desire for glory never abandoned him. In 1798 he started a new life, and it was with the hope that fame awaited him in the rôle of philosopher and social reformer. While pursuing this path, he retained all the attributes of the former aristocrat: conceit, arrogance, boldness, and independence of mind. But this road to fame was becoming more and more tortuous and strewn with many pitfalls. There must be found a safer, a shorter way, for his life was on the ebb.

In 1821, while evolving his industrial system, Saint-Simon perceived the right direction. The road to glory was traced by the footsteps of the founders of religion. What fame could surpass that of Christ and Mohammed, Luther and Calvin? His real mission was at last revealed. The destiny of Henri de Saint-Simon was to destroy the old theology and to initiate a new spiritual power. Of this power he would be the founder, the high priest, the pope.

The writing of the *Nouveau Christianisme* occupied Saint-Simon's remaining days. Halévy described his life at this time. The detailed account of his habits and the comments on his manner of work are of sufficient interest to warrant quoting at length:

"Saint-Simon led a very retired and regular life. He would spend one hour a day writing or dictating to Julie. What he dictated or wrote was unwieldy, heavy, but full of substance. Saint-Simon knew absolutely nothing about style. A man trained to write for the newspapers could easily have made ten columns out of one of his pages. Julie wrote in formal round hand, like a laundress' bill. The orthography was deplorable, but the handwriting was even and legible. . . . After an hour of work, Saint-Simon read his novels. About three o'clock he went out, took a walk in the garden of the Palais-Royal whenever the weather permitted, or went to the Café de la Régence. He dined at five o'clock. Almost every evening, Olinde and I came to spend an hour with him. He received very few people. Saint-Simon enjoyed seeing people who shared his ideas or his writings. He preferred the company of a plain workingman to that of the most intellectual idler. . . .

"Every Friday, Olinde Rodrigues and I dined with Saint-Simon. Sometimes monsieur Duvergier joined us at those dinners, after which we stayed together until a rather late hour in the evening. During those intimate reunions Saint-Simon abandoned himself fully to his philosophical flights of fancy. Sundays we also held a dinner for the purpose of discussing plans for our new publication."

Saint-Simon was interested in founding another periodical in collaboration with his young disciples. This was to be *Le Producteur,* the contents of which were considered at those Sunday dinners.

Halévy terminated his *Souvenirs* with the narration of Saint-Simon's last moments:

"It was after one of those Sunday reunions that, having left him in perfect health the day before, we found him struck with the lingering illness which within six weeks led him to his grave.

"It was towards the end of March 1825. Saint-Simon had moved from the apartment he occupied on the third floor to smaller but more pleasant and better situated rooms on the first floor. He had just finished *Le Nouveau Christianisme,* his most remarkable work. The last Sunday of March, when Olinde and I came to see him at the accustomed hour, we found him taken with a dry and violent cough and a disquieting heavy breathing. Although he was obviously in pain, he would not stay in bed; but he was not able to sit at the table and have dinner with us. I can still see him on that day, standing in front of the fireplace, trying to appear gay and to take part in our conversation in spite of his shivering all over with fever and the chattering of his teeth. Dr. Bailly most opportunely called that morning. He put Saint-Simon to bed, had leeches applied to him and left orders to have him bleed as long as possible. Unfortunately this prescription was but too faithfully followed; for in the evening when Saint-Simon, weakened by the flow of blood, wished that it be stopped, one of the wounds made by the leeches would not close. At midnight the blood was still flowing freely, the old man's bed was covered with it. At last they were able to stop it. I left Saint-Simon with a sad foreboding which was only too well founded.

"However he seemingly recuperated, but this was more of a truce of death than a cure. His voice scarcely audible, his eyes dimmed, his emaciation left me without hope. A change of lodging was found advisable. At the end of April, Saint-Simon went to live at number 9 rue du Faubourg-Montmartre."

Among those who stood by the deathbed, Olinde Rodrigues gathered the last words of the master. It was he who described the death scene to Hubbard, Saint-Simon's first biographer. We must bear in mind that by this time Saint-Simon had become for all of his disciples, and particularly for Rodrigues, an object of reverent worship and pious veneration. With these reserves, we give Hubbard's account:

"The morning of the 19th of May, when M. Rodrigues came to see Saint-Simon, he had had a high fever all night, even

186

delirium, but his pulse was not bad; he was fully conscious and even in good spirits. He was asked by Dr. Bailly if he would give authorization to have doctors Gall[5] and Broussais come to see him. He did not object. Gall came first about half past twelve. "Good day, doctor," said Saint-Simon. "I am glad to see you." Gall examined the chest, thought that the lungs were congested and gave him only three days to live.

"After Gall left, the disease grew much worse during the next two hours. . . . Speech became difficult. At three o'clock arrived Broussais, Burdin and other doctors who came to assist Doctor Bailly. 'The consultation is quickly over,' said one of them, 'the patient is dying.' However they came near the bed, and after having examined the lungs and tongue of the dying man, they asked him several questions. Saint-Simon answered distinctly and then added: 'Gentlemen, I am happy to offer to you a new subject for observation: you see a man who has experienced such terrible crises as no man could withstand, a man who has been so engrossed with his life work that he cannot talk with you about his illness. Do anything you see fit, I am entirely confident and ready to second you.' According to the doctors' consultation, he had no more than ten hours to live and the prediction was correct. 'What a brain!' said Broussais as he left, 'what a vigorous mind!'"

Some one among those who surrounded Saint-Simon asked him if he wanted any member of his family to come, for example his nephew Victor, now General Saint-Simon, for whom he had a special affection and whose early education he had supervised. He insisted that he wished to consecrate his last moments exclusively to the elaboration of the ideas which engrossed him, and this he did without the least sign of weakness.

"Death approached rapidly. At six o'clock, Dr. Bailly asked Saint-Simon if he suffered. 'No,' he answered. The doctor said: 'In no part?' 'It would be an exaggeration to say that I do not suffer,' said Saint-Simon, 'but it does not matter, let us talk about something else.' He asked those present to sit near him. Messrs. Rodrigues, Bailly and Halévy who were in the room hastened to obey him. Then in a broken voice, Saint-Simon collected his last strength and said:

" 'For the last twelve days, my friends, I have been occupied with plans designed to assure the success of our enterprise (the projected journal called *Le Producteur*) ; for three hours, despite my sufferings I have been endeavoring to present to you a résumé of my thoughts. You have arrived at a period where by your combined efforts you will achieve great success. . . . The fruit is ripe; you can gather it. My last work, the *New Christianity,* will not be immediately understood. It has been thought that every religious system ought to disappear because men have succeeded in proving the weakness and insufficiency of Catholicism. People are deceived in this. Religion cannot disappear from the world; it can only change.' Addressing his favorite pupil: 'Rodrigues, do not forget that to accomplish great things you must have enthusiasm. All my life is comprised in this one thought: to guarantee to all men the freest development of their faculties.'"[6]

He spoke with difficulty. *"Nous tenons notre affaire,"* (We are sure of success) he whispered. He fell into a coma, and three hours later he died. This was on May 19, 1825, at ten o'clock in the evening. He had reached the age of sixty-four years, seven months, and two days.

He drew his last breath surrounded by friends and disciples of whose devotion and understanding he was fully confident. After so many vicissitudes, so many trials and downfalls in the pursuit of glory, he had at last reached the end of the road. And before his peaceful and contented gaze, there stood in the twilight, shining on the sacred hill, in a haze of molten gold, the high temple of fame. Did Charlemagne appear to him in a last vision, throwing open the gates and beckoning to him to enter? He died with a happy and peaceful countenance, in the firm belief that the goal was attained.

An autopsy was performed by Dr. Gall, who found the brain of large size and made up of a great number of circumvolutions, in which he recognized, among other faculties, perseverance and improvidence. The judgment of the phrenologist only confirmed Saint-Simon's two predominating moral attributes as evidenced by his thoughts and actions.

The funeral took place the day after the autopsy. It was a

civil affair with no religious ceremony. Augustin Thierry and Auguste Comte joined in the group that followed the cortège to the cemetery.

The liberal newspaper *Le Constitutionnel,* in its issue of May 22, 1825, described the funeral in these words:

"To-day at noon a funeral cortège, fairly numerous, proceeded from Montmartre to the Père-Lachaise cemetery. The superintendent of the cemetery asked who were the relatives. No one answered.[7] Then he asked who were the friends. Everybody wanted to answer. They had to search for a grave, as none had been prepared. Soon a crowd assembled, attracted by curiosity on learning that the defunct was Henri Saint-Simon, one of the most ardent philanthropists of our time.

"Whatever opinion one might have about the bold and frequently new ideas he promulgated in his writings, one cannot deny the late Saint-Simon the credit of having raised a great number of questions related to the highest interests of society. He had another merit, rather rare in our vainglorious France. People he had known for a long time were not aware of the fact that he was the Comte de Saint-Simon, a Spanish grandee, a descendant of the famous author of the *Mémoires,* and related to the illustrious family of Lorraine. What would the Duc de Saint-Simon, the scornful enemy of the bourgeois and men of letters, have said if he had heard his grandson expound his ideas on scientists, artists and industrialists?"

Two orations were pronounced at his grave, one by Léon Halévy, the other by Dr. Bailly. From Halévy's eulogy, we quote:

"A spectacle worthy of the gods, said an ancient sage, is that of virtue grappling with misfortune. There is another spectacle, no less worthy of the admiration of man and the approbation of the gods, and that is a mind grappling with death. I have witnessed this struggle, both terrible and sublime. I have witnessed the thoughts of this man, whose life had been entirely intellectual, rising clear and strong from the writhing of death agony. I have heard words full of philanthropy and of lofty exaltation rising from a chest already heaving with the death rattle. . . . Others, in this supreme moment, think of their friends, of their relatives, of themselves. As for him, he gave his last thoughts to those who work, to those who suffer, to that great family whose cause he had espoused and his heart had adopted. While he was discoursing with a depth of judgment, a sagacity of viewpoint, a choice of expressions of which any man in good health would have been proud, he was asked whether he was in pain and he answered: 'It would be an exaggeration on my part to say I have no pain; I feel such anguish as few persons in my place could endure. But I am not thinking of myself.' And he went on speaking until death, which came two hours afterward. Heaven spared him from that terrible state which disfigures the fairest of God's creatures at death's portals. He was not in a state of delirium, unless we designate by that word his unbounded confidence in the future happiness of mankind."[8]

Dr. Bailly, the young physiologist, who contributed to *Opinions littéraires, philosophiques et industrielles,* also pronounced a funeral oration from which we quote:

"You, gentlemen, who have shared with me the honor of listening to discourses in which he gave us the result of his research and meditations, were you not astounded at his ability to treat the highest and the most varied philosophical problems with a knowledge that might be expected only from experts on those subjects?

"You heard him, gentlemen, speak to each of us the language of our special studies, sum up the general principles of the different branches of our knowledge, and draw new conceptions which we so often admired.

"Those who have contributed to the progress of civilization owe their success to the improvement of some determined branch of science. Monsieur Saint-Simon, with his transcendent genius, viewing all human knowledge from above, was able to assemble the data of science into a philosophical whole. . . .

"To Saint-Simon was reserved the task of laying the foundations of a new science, of calling attention to the real nature of the organic forces of society, in a word, of being the founder of the *physiology of the human species.* In saying that Henri Saint-Simon was the first to conceive the human species as an organic whole we state the most characteristic trait of this genius, the friend we mourn, the man who was understood only by the very few with whom he shared his thoughts. . . .

"The publication of *Le Nouveau Christianisme* which completed the series of his writings, marked the highest and final point in a career devoted to social reform. When this great work was finished, we saw him seek eternal sleep with the satisfaction and contentment of having been useful and having sowed the seed of social improvement to which all his life had been devoted. . . .

"The highest tribute of gratitude we can offer him will be for us to continue his works for the development of human progress."

Saint-Simon's grave is located at the remote end of the Père-Lachaise cemetery, among numerous monuments dedicated to the generals of Napoleon Bonaparte. Surrounded by green foliage, the place of burial is indicated by a modest stone slab. But instead of resting flat on the ground, the slab is held in an inclined position over the half open grave "so that the spirit of the dead master may communicate with the living disciples." The partial opening by the tilting of the stone, as well as the inscription, was done later by the Saint-Simonians. On one side of the stone was carved one of the philosopher's celebrated maxims:

"The golden age is not in the past, it is in the future."

Saint-Simon, 1824

And on the other side:

"Henri Saint-Simon

"Died in Paris, May 19, 1825, at the age of 65 years."

A touching letter from Julie Juliand to Caroline announced the death of her father. The letter was dated May 20, 1825:

"My dear Caroline,

With my heart full of the deepest grief I come to announce to you the loss we have just suffered, yesterday, Thursday, at 10 in the evening, of our excellent father who died without being in the least conscious of his condition. He received all the care and attention possible, but there was no remedy. Like all others interested in him, I was kept, as much as himself, ignorant of the gravity of his illness. He expired without

191

suffering, and he was made happy by the devotion of the persons who surrounded him. This morning a drawing was made of him and it is a striking likeness. They intend also to have a bust of him modeled, and that will be at least a consolation for us, my dear Caroline. If he could speak to you, he would tell you to have courage. That was one of his virtues; you must act according to his ideals and prove yourself the worthy daughter of such a great man. His disciples and friends have a religious, reverential attitude towards him. His life will be written, his acts will lose nothing by being brought into full light.

"Adieu, my friend, or rather au revoir. He would be happy to have us living together.

Your devoted friend,

Julie Juliand."

Another letter to Caroline, written two months later, furnished intimate details of Julie's life immediately after the death of her beloved master.

"My dear Caroline, my good, my excellent friend,

"If I have not written to you sooner, please do not blame me. For the last two months I have had nothing but grief and trouble. I think I told you I had to affix the seals to the private belongings of your good father. They were not removed until Saturday. It was extremely annoying for me because I had to give up the apartment. You cannot imagine all the red tape I had to go through to have the seals removed. Then I had to find another place to live; which was not easy, since the time of the quarter's rent was past. Besides, I was obliged to look for work, and it is only to-day that I can count on getting some. It is not easy to get along and I worried so much on that account. It would have been a pleasure to go and join your sorrows with mine, but you realise, my dear friend, that when one is asking for work one must be on the spot. For that reason I shall be unable, at least for the present, to spend some time with you. I must first be well settled, and then may be it will be possible. How sweet it will be to recall with you all the qualities and kindnesses of the dear friend, who up to his last breath, kept thinking of and busying himself with the happiness of mankind.

"My good Caroline, I did not forget I promised to send you a little parcel. The delay is due to the portrait. The lady friend who has undertaken to make it has not finished it yet and cannot promise it before next week. Yesterday I saw your sister-in-law. I decided to entrust to her the other objects I intended to send to you: your shawl and parasol which will be quite appropriate at this time when the weather is extremely hot. Speaking of hot weather, do you know I had all sorts of difficulties trying to keep poor Presto from the horrible grip of the poundman. For three days they committed atrocities on the poor dogs, even on those who were muzzled. They even killed them while with their masters. But a few of the dog catchers paid for the others. They say some were wounded and even killed by the dog owners. They carried their orders much too far. Now they are forbidden to bring dead dogs to the pound under penalty of not getting their pay. They were being paid 30 francs for each dog. In one day 2,500 animals were caught. You can realize how worried I was about my Presto, to whom I am still more attached since that fatal 19th of May. If you only knew how he misses his master, you would love him as much as I do.

"I have now with me the modeled bust. I wish you could have seen his surprise on seeing his master's likeness, which is very good indeed, although it was done twenty hours after his death. I must tell you also that I went to the Père-Lachaise cemetery to deposit a wreath in your name and mine. No praise, no title is engraved on the stone, only this: Henri Saint-Simon, died May 19, 1825, aged 65 years. This does not prevent him from being recognized as a great man. And it seems to be the usual thing, since the graves of Molière, La Fontaine and other men of genius have no other inscription. Those are, my dear friend, some details for you. Adieu. My love to you and your husband.

                              Your devoted friend,

Rue Saint-André-des-Arts, 18."   Julie Juliand.

This pathetic letter revealed Julie's deep affection for her master. Her touching solicitude for his dog, when dogs were being destroyed in great numbers for fear of rabies, was another mark of kindness and devotion.

Saint-Simon's daughter, Caroline-Charlotte, did not survive him for many years. She died at the age of thirty-nine, October 10, 1834, at Chatelet-en-Brie, Seine et Marne.

Besides the portrait of Saint-Simon painted by Mme Labille-Guiard of which a number of lithographic copies were made, a sketch was drawn of his face immediately upon his death, as mentioned by Julie, and a bust was modeled. At the *Bibliothèque de l'Arsenal* there is a painting representing the philosopher on his deathbed as he is giving final instructions to his disciples. It is conceived in the manner of Raphael's *Death of Socrates*, of which it is a labored imitation.

The sculptor Raymond Bonheur, father of the famous animal painter, Rosa Bonheur, modeled the bust of the philosopher. A number of plaster plaques were also distributed among the disciples. In the *Bibliothèque de l'Arsenal* a special room is devoted to a collection of Saint-Simonian relics.

Saint-Simon found in death that which he ardently pursued all his life. To him came at last honor, praise, and glory, far beyond the expectations of common mortals.

CHAPTER FOURTEEN

Saint-Simon said to the small group of friends surrounding his deathbed: "People are mistaken, religion cannot disappear from the world, it only keeps changing." And turning to his beloved disciple, he added: "Rodrigues, do not forget that."

Rodrigues did not forget. Neither did the fervent disciples who consecrated themselves to the service of the master. Within two years of his death, a new cult was founded in his name.

In his last moments Saint-Simon told the disciples gathered around him:

"The last part of our work will be ill understood. By attacking the medieval religious system we have proved one thing, that it was no longer in harmony with the progress of positive science, but people were wrong in concluding that religion had to disappear entirely: it must only conform to scientific progress."[1]

These words referred to the *Nouveau Christianisme,* which was the holy writ Saint-Simon bequeathed to his followers. And a sacred fire was kindled in their hearts, and they set forth on their mission with the passionate zeal of the first Christians.

Immediately after the funeral, a small group of friends met in Rodrigues' home. They statred putting into execution the periodical Saint-Simon had been planning for them. A capital of fifty thousand francs was raised for the purpose of financing the project. The first issue appeared in October 1825 with the title: *Le Producteur, Journal de l'Industrie, des sciences et des Arts.* It dealt with philosophical, scientific, and economic subjects, but steered away from political discussions to avoid a clash with the reactionary government. Even the name of Saint-Simon was kept discreetly in the background, but his economic theories were expounded with skill and conviction. Among the contributors were Armand Carrell, Adolphe Blanqui, and Hippolyte Carnot, staunch liberals destined to play important parts in the political history of France.

Deriding the doctrines expounded in the new periodical, Stendhal published a brochure entitled: *D'un nouveau complot contre les industriels*. What the author called "A new conspiracy against the producers" was a clever attack against the economic order advocated by Saint-Simon and his followers.

"I too have read Mill, McCulloch, Malthus and Ricardo," boasted Stendhal. But he would not admit that industrialists or producers be entrusted with the leadership of nations. When did they perform a single act of disinterested heroism? he asked. Could they be compared to Lafayette, who sacrificed a fortune for the cause of American independence? To Lazare Carnot, who raised fourteen armies for the defense of the republic? To Lord Byron, who had a year ago given up his life for the freedom of Greece? Where was the industrialist who would sacrifice his entire fortune for a noble cause?

Stendhal illustrated his point with this imaginary dialogue:

"Industrialist—My dear friend, I ate an excellent dinner.

Neighbor—So much the better for you, my dear friend.

Industrialist—Not only is it so much better for me. Public opinion should confer on me a high reward for having given myself the pleasure of eating a good dinner.

Neighbor—I say, that is rather extravagant.

Industrialist—Are you by any chance one of those aristocrats? This is a very clear summary of the *Catéchisme* by M. de Saint-Simon and of six or seven first numbers of a journal written in an obscure style, and which claims to defend the cause of industry."

Stendhal's satirical pamphlet was immediately refuted by the editors of *Le Producteur*, which now came out openly as the organ of saint-simonism. It stated in the May 1, 1826, issue:

"Its purpose is to unite the scientists, artists and producers by philosophic doctrines consistent with the present state of civilization and favorable to the progress of humanity in scientific, moral and industrial spheres."

The readers of the journal, limited in number, belonged to a cultured minority interested in social problems and attracted by

196

the emotional appeal of a humanitarian religion. Young liberals, such as Carnot and Michel Chevalier, disillusioned by the reactionary political régime and eager to serve the cause of humanity, found in saint-simonism the needed spiritual incentive for action.

However, the publishing of *Le Producteur* was a costly undertaking. Neither the limited capital nor the few subscriptions and private donations sufficed to defray expenses. The last issue of the journal was brought out December 1826; it had lasted a little longer than one year.

In his monograph *On Saint-Simonism,* Carnot told about the beginning of the Saint-Simonian school. In his home on rue des Saint-Pères, once a week he entertained a number of friends, and at these gatherings they discussed the doctrines of Saint-Simon. Before long the small apartment could not accommodate all the people who were attracted by these talks. A hall was hired at 12 rue Taranne where Bazard, one of the leaders of the group, gave a series of lectures. They were a great success and drew large and distinguished audiences, in which students from the *Ecole Polytechnique* and the *Ecole des Mines* figured in conspicuous numbers.

An amazing number of men of talent joined the Saint-Simonian group: economists as Michel Chevalier and Gustave D'Eichthal; financiers as the Péreire brothers; philosophical writers as Pierre Leroux and P. B. Buchez; Charles Duveyrier, an able journalist, Henri Fournel, a capable engineer, besides Blanqui, Carnot, and Carrel, already mentioned.

Almost from the start Bazard and Enfantin put themselves at the head of the movement. Barthélémy Prosper Enfantin, a banker's son, was born in Paris, February 8, 1796. He distinguished himself as a brilliant pupil at the *Ecole Polytechnique.* In 1814, he organized his classmates into a company of artillery to defend Paris against the invasion, and was decorated with the cross of the Legion of Honor for bravery on that occasion. After the fall of Napoleon he left the army to become the business agent for one of his relatives. In that capacity he travelled through Switzerland, Germany, Holland, "making more friends than customers."

In 1821 he was employed by a French banking house newly established in St. Petersburg. Two years later, on his return to

Paris, he was appointed cashier in another financial establishment, the *Caisse hypothécaire*. It was at this time that he renewed acquaintance with Olinde Rodrigues, who interested him in Saint-Simon's ideas. He was introduced by Rodrigues to the master on the occasion of the first reading of the *Nouveau Christianisme* to a group of sympathisers. Present at that reading, besides Rodrigues and Enfantin, were Léon Halévy, M. Martin, the French consul in America, J. Azevedo, chief secretary to the minister of commerce, the lawyer Duvergier, and Dr. Bailly. Enfantin was so impressed by Saint-Simon's religious philosophy that he resolved to devote his life to bring about its complete fulfillment.

Next to Enfantin, and sharing with him supreme power over the sect was Saint-Amand Bazard (1791-1832). A man of will and action, a fiery republican opposed to the restored monarchy, he founded, in 1820, the French branch of the Carbonari under the name of *Amis de la vérité*. Liberals, including LaFayette, joined the revolutionary movement in considerable numbers. Encouraged by the uprisings in Italy and Spain, the *Amis de la vérité* fomented rebellions in several French cities, notably in Belfort. The outbreaks ended in bloody reprisals from which Bazard and LaFayette had a narrow escape. The unsuccessful attempts to overthrow the government led to the dissolution of the organization. The leaders were obliged to conceal their identity under assumed names. Bazard went by the name of Saint-Amand.

Brief mention should be made of a few other prominent members. Philippe Benjamin Buchez, a distinguished historian, was the author of *Histoire parlementaire de la Révolution française,* which served as the main source for Carlyle's *French Revolution*. After the fall of Louis-Philippe in 1848, he became president of the Constituent Assembly. Lazare-Hippolyte Carnot, the notable statesman, became minister of education in 1840, and his son Sadi Carnot was later elected to the presidency of the Third Republic. Of the eminent writers who fell under the spell of Saint-Simonism, the critic Sainte-Beuve, the poets Alfred de Vigny and Heinrich Heine, were most profoundly affected.

The weekly periodical, *L'Organisateur,* was started August 15, 1829, bearing as motto the words of Saint-Simon:

"All social institutions must aim at the amelioration of the moral, physical and intellectual condition of the most numerous and poorest class." Below this appeared the celebrated maxim:

"From each according to his ability, to each according to his work."

By the beginning of 1830 the Saint-Simonian group was definitely established into a church with appropriate hierarchy. The adherents were classified into three degrees. The highest degree comprised the Supreme Fathers, Enfantin and Bazard. Next in importance were the members of the College who presided over the various departments. The third degree was made up of novices. The departments included oral propaganda in charge of Barrault, written propaganda under Chevalier, instruction under Carnot. Missions were confined to the care of Duveyrier, conversions to Talabot. Fournel supervised teaching, and D'Eichthal had the responsibility of industrial enterprises. Mesdames Bazard and Fournel were entrusted with the conversion of women.

The Saint-Simonians took advantage of the political freedom granted during the July revolution of 1830, and began to propagandize their creed in earnest. Numerous placards were posted in the streets of Paris, as well as in the provinces. Copies of a pamphlet *Manifeste aux Français,* explaining the tenets of the new religion, were widely distributed. But at one of the sessions of the Chamber of Deputies, the Saint-Simonians were denounced as a subversive organisation which advocated the nationalisation of women and the abolition of private property.

In answer to this accusation, Bazard and Enfantin addressed to the president of the Chamber of Deputies, October 1, 1830, a remarkable letter in which they confessed the principles of their faith:

"The Saint-Simonians reject the equal sharing of property, which would constitute for them a greater violence, a more revolting injustice than the unequal sharing which first originated by force of arms and conquest.

"The Saint-Simonians believe in the natural inequality of men and consider this inequality as the very basis of association, as the indispensable condition of social order. . . .

"The Saint-Simonians demand the abolition of all privileges of birth, without exception, consequently the abolition of inheritance, the greatest of these privileges, the one that includes all the others nowadays, because it leaves to hazard the distribution of social privileges among the few and condemns the most numerous class to depravity, ignorance, poverty.

"The Saint-Simonians demand that all tools of production, land and capital, which to-day constitute the foundation of private property, be exploited in common so that the community receive from each according to his capacity and give to each according to his work. . . .

"Christianity rescued women from bondage, but condemned them to an inferior position, and throughout Christian Europe they are still deprived of religious, political and civil rights. The Saint-Simonians proclaim the final emancipation of women, their complete independence, but do not for this reason want to abolish the holy institution of marriage; on the contrary, they work towards the complete fulfillment of this institution. . . . They demand that a single man be united to a single woman, but they proclaim that the wife must be the husband's equal, and that she must be the husband's associate in the functions of the church, the state and the family; so that the social individual who up to now was man alone will in the future be man and woman." [2]

Needless to remark that the alleged nationalization of women, and the abolition of private property have been the usual and traditional accusations against proposed changes in the social order. As for the social and economic reforms advocated by the Saint-Simonians, most of them have by now become common practice in various countries of the world.

The membership of the church grew to such proportions that a building was leased on rue Monsigny to accommodate its activities. It not only served for lectures, recitals, and receptions, but also became the home of some thirty members. On Thursday evenings the salon was open to visitors, and many distinguished guests were often present. Among these could be seen the renowned composers Berlioz, Liszt, and Félicien David, the singer Nourrit, the poet Heinrich Heine, the critic Sainte-Beuve, the artist Raymond Bonheur, the novelist Emile Souvestre. Liszt would sit at the piano and abandon himself to improvisations.

Adolph Nourrit would sing operatic arias. Félicien David would render his compositions. At other times the evening would be devoted to dancing.

The members who lived in the house called each other "brother," but in addressing the higher rank, they would say "father." They took their meals in common. Life was intense in the community and religious exaltation reached the highest pitch. The converts reminded one of the early Christians who sacrificed all earthly interests to the practice of their faith. Jean Reynaud, for instance, held an important post as engineer in Corsica. When Enfantin called on him in October 1830 to join the ranks of the disciples, Reynaud gave up his position and hastened to Paris.

"My Fathers call me," wrote Reynaud, "to aid in organising the Saint-Simonian family. My soul is filled with happiness and love beyond expression."

Henri Fournel likewise abandoned the career of director of the metallurgical works of *Le Creusot,* and joined the congregation of rue Monsigny. He turned over his not inconsiderable fortune of 89,000 francs to the propagation of the doctrine. Michel Chevalier, engineer and superintendent of the coal mines in the department of Le Nord, also gave up his career for this religious and humanitarian cause.

Barrault's emotional outpouring might be considered typical of many young intellectuals in search of religion:

"In the midst of the darkest gloom, overwhelmed with sadness, repeating in sorrowful tones the songs of despair of the poet, I grumble, I doubt, I blaspheme, I exclaim: God I have sought for, God of love, God of hope, where art thou? Priests, scientists, industrialists, none answers, and all is silence. Then, oh God, like an unexpected illumination there shines before my eyes Saint-Simon's revelation, then I love, then I hope and live again." [3]

In his *Histoire de dix ans* Louis Blanc described the religious fervor of the dwellers of rue Monsigny in these words:

"Giving up their occupations, their dreams of fortune, their life friends, engineers, artists, physicians, lawyers, poets had come together and united their unselfish lives. Some brought with them their books, others their furniture, others their wealth. Meals were taken in common. They practiced the religion of fraternity."

Commenting on this extraordinary phenomenon, Auguste Comte wrote to Gustave D'Eichthal, December 6, 1828:

"Their heads have become progressively exalted to such a point that they have actually instituted a new religion, a sort of incarnation of the divinity of Saint-Simon."

Pierre Leroux and Sainte-Beuve, editors of *Le Globe*, turned their paper over to Enfantin on January 18, 1831. From then on the title of their daily journal read: *Le Globe, journal de la doctrine de Saint-Simon*, with this maxim inscribed below: *"A chacun selon sa capacité, à chaque capacité selon ses oeuvres."*

It may be of interest to note that this aphorism is incorporated in the Constitution of the Union of Soviet Socialist Republics. Article 12 of the Constitution reads:

"The principle applied in the U.S.S.R. is that of socialism: 'From each according to his ability, to each according to his work.' "

The Globe, founded as an organ for disseminating liberal ideas, served also as a vehicle for the works of writers of the romantic school. After the conversion of the journal to Saint-Simonism, the same writers were for the most part prepared to adopt or at least to sympathise with the new gospel. For this reason the influence of Saint-Simonism on French romanticism cannot be overestimated. Yet it is only of late, because of a growing interest in social sciences, that such influence has received due credit from scholars and students of literature.

Le Globe laid stress on the Saint-Simonian theories in the field of economics. Besides Enfantin who contributed a treatise on political science, there were remarkable articles by Stéphane Mony, the engineer who built the first railroad in France, on modernization of industry, and by Emile Péreire on the science of statistics. Michel Chevalier described the new order to come in the most glowing colors. Moral and philosophical questions were propounded by Leroux, Jean Reynaud, Charles Duveyrier.

The journal launched a lively campaign in favor of building railroads, canals, and other types of public works. It even appealed to Louis-Philippe and asked the citizen-king to transform the army into an industrial institution, a professional trade school for the masses. Work was to be considered a sacred duty, an act of religious significance. Work was the modern form of religion from which humanity would derive the same spiritual benefits as it did from the metaphysical creeds of the past.

In Paris, under the direction of Hippolyte Carnot, instruction in the Saint-Simonian doctrine was given in four separate halls, at the salle Taitbout, the Athénée, in rue Taranne and rue Monsigny. The daily lectures were skillfully adapted to varying classes of auditors, popular and simple when addressed to workingmen, poetic and sentimental for writers and artists, precise and austere for scientists and industrialists. Henri Fournel established centers of propaganda in each ward of the capital. In the provinces, churches were founded at Toulouse, Montpelier, Lyons, Metz, and Dijon.

It was also in the course of the year 1831 that the members of the church reached the highest pitch of exaltation in their religious fervor. Like all revealed creeds the new cult did not hesitate to offer miraculous proofs of its divine origin. How could the apostles be known as God's messengers, as the propagandists of the revealed truth? Here was the answer. The real miracle of Christianity consisted in the fact that it instilled spiritual values in a materialistic and corrupt world. The miracle of Saint-Simonism was no less transcendent. It propagated religious faith in a time of unbelief, founded a society on love and brotherhood in an era of selfishness, established order and discipline in a world of anarchy.

Saint-Simonism was of divine inspiration and Saint-Simon was the new Messiah. "After Moses and Jesus came Saint-Simon. This man whose word has given us life is in truth more than a prophet, since he has come to fulfill all prophecies, to accomplish all God's promises." [4] The fiery apostles proclaimed the glory of their master and urged mankind to listen to the revealed word:

"Come and hear the apostles of a new Evangel, of the eternal Evangel, of which the Gospel of Jesus was but the sublime preface." [5]

The parallel between Jesus and Saint-Simon furnished the text for more than one edifying sermon.

> "Recognize the sign of the times!
> Jesus was born poor and obscure in a stable of
>   Bethlehem;
> Saint-Simon was born in wealth and splendor at the
>   foot of the most glorious throne in the world.
> Jesus hides part of his life; he appears only at his birth
>   and at his death.
> Saint-Simon exposes in full view each step of his career
>   and each step is a progress.
> Jesus, when about to die, asks his father to take away
>   from him the cup of bitterness.
> Saint-Simon also said once: "Take away from my life
>   this cup of bitterness."
> But while Jesus dying cries out from the cross: "My
>   God! my God, why hast thou abandoned me?"
> Saint-Simon on his deathbed turned to the one who
>   understood his word and said to him: "My son,
>   glorify me, the world is ours." [6]

Its adherents based the superiority of Saint-Simonism over Christianity on the fact that their religion promoted the material as well as the spiritual interests of man, and removed all taint of sin from the enjoyment of life.

"Let the Prophet of the religion of suffering and mortification disappear before the Revealer of the true God, who washes matter clean of opprobrium, who classifies all men according to their capacities, does away with humility, rewards human efforts, suppresses abnegation, conciliates duty with interest.

"Earth rejoice! Saint-Simon has come! Cross that saved the world, to-day you weigh down upon it, disappear!" [7]

There was however opposition to the deification of Saint-Simon on the part of some of the disciples. Léon Halévy composed an ode in protest against what he considered an absurd procedure:

> "He who flayed with his words all sham and false belief,
> Behold they made him god and put the new idol on their
>   absurd altar.
> He built on solid rock a school and not a church!

He was a man of truth,
To seek it and spread it was his true ministry
And for its sake he lived in want and poverty
Higher than king or pope. . . ."[8]

The question arose as to whether the Saint-Simonians should put their theories into practice at once and thus hasten the advent of the new society. They decided in favor of immediate application of their hopes. Workshops were established in two buildings rented for that purpose: one on rue de la Tour d'Auvergne, another on rue Popinancourt, where workmen were also lodged and boarded. The children were given instruction and training in some trade.

Divine institutions are subject to human frailties and passions, and the Saint-Simonian church could not escape a similar fate. Differences of opinion soon arose between the two fathers, Enfantin and Bazard. The latter was a realist, experienced in political action and fully aware of the danger of applying in real life principles contrary to the established order of things. Enfantin was of an imaginative and emotional temperament. His appeals found response among artists, poets, idealists, whereas Bazard's support came from men of science and practical experience.

Enfantin held extreme views on marriage, divorce, and the equality of women. Bazard did not agree with him. Saint-Simon was no guide in this matter, since he had made no mention of woman's part in the future society. The only reference to woman in his writings was to be found in *Lettres d'un habitant de Genève:* "Women should be permitted to subscribe and also they could be named to positions." From that single remark Enfantin jumped to the conclusion that the emancipation of women meant more than the equality of the sexes; it implied also that the couple, man and woman, constituted the social unit.

It was logical to apply the social unit principle to the church leaders, and consequently a Supreme Mother should be adjoined to each of the Supreme Fathers. Enfantin also stressed the doctrine of the rehabilitation of the flesh according to which flesh and spirit, mind and matter, both emanate from God, both participate of the divine and both should be regarded as holy. This concept led inevitably to heated discussions on matters of love, marriage, and traditional morality. Bazard would not follow Enfantin to extremes, even on theoretical grounds, being fully aware of the risk of misinterpretation by hostile outsiders.

Long and violent debates took place between the two men. The controversy was taken up by individual members with such vehemence that it resulted in public confessions, delirious prophecies, ecstasies, catalepsies.

"We have been through a furnace," exclaimed Duveyrier. "What sighs and tears and anguish! What days without repose, nights without sleep!"

It was at one of these tumultuous meetings that the final break came between the two high priests. Bazard rose from his seat, stalked out of the hall, never to return. He was followed by a small group of dissidents, among them Pierre Leroux, the brothers Péreire, and Reynaud. Enfantin, now the only Father, promptly attributed a symbolic meaning to the vacated seat. God had manifested that the place of Bazard was to be filled by the Woman.

Among the orthodox members, waiting for the woman Messiah became an obsession. She was invoked and prayed to every day. Where was she to be found? Women from all classes of society were invited to dinners and parties. The winter of 1832 presented a succession of festivities at the headquarters on rue Monsigny. Wine, music, and dancing attracted many representatives of the fair sex, not a few of them young, elegant, and charming. But they came for the sake of amusement and mundane purposes, with little regard for the religious motive.

The elaborate receptions were costly and the financial resources of the church were soon exhausted. The workers' cooperative shops ended in failure. Four thousand workers had been given employment, but their material condition was not greatly improved. And now they were left to shift for themselves.

How to replenish the treasury became a problem. Olinde Rodrigues conceived the plan of *"le crédit Saint-Simonien."* A joint stock company was founded, shares were issued at par value of one thousand francs with an annual interest of five percent. From July 1830 to July 1831, some 250,000 francs were collected, of which 100,000 were spent on *Le Globe*. Collections however did not keep pace with expenditures and the joint stock company was declared bankrupt. The family of rue Monsigny was broken up.

Enfantin owned a large estate at Ménilmontant, a suburb northeast of Paris. This he turned over to the church and the property became a pious retreat. In April 1832, forty of the faithful retired to this place to lead a communal life. The spacious building was surrounded by five acres of landscaped grounds. An alley over three hundred feet long, bordered with lime trees, led from the entrance gate to the main building.

The interior was composed of several salons, a dining room, a reception hall twenty by forty feet long, a billiard room, a number of bedrooms accommodating seventeen beds and twenty-three hammocks, two bathrooms to which water was pumped from the outside. A small building was used as a chapel. The barn, which could accommodate twelve horses, contained various implements.

The forty anchorites withdrew to this peaceful hermitage and consecrated themselves to a conventual life of abnegation, obedience, and chastity. Interdiction of sex intercourse was imposed on all members in answer to the accusation of moral laxity by enemies of the church. The recluses divided their time between manual labor and spiritual exercises. Life was regulated hour by hour as in a well ordered monastery. The rising time was at five in the morning, breakfast at seven, dinner at one, supper at seven, and retirement at ten in the evening.

Each member was assigned his special task, and engineers, lawyers, physicians, musicians, writers, painters, bankers, army officers attended to the humblest menial duties. A physician was head cook and his aides were a college professor and a lawyer. A newspaper editor was in charge of washing dishes. A lawyer was responsible for the garbage disposal. A general staff army officer attended to the laundry. An engineer, a bank director, and a physician waited on tables.

The care of the park was under the direction of two artists. Refined and cultured men could be seen handling the shovel or the wheelbarrow, pruning trees, spading, tilling, sowing, watering. All work was considered holy and was accompanied by appropriate hymns composed by Félicien David and other musicians. The public was admitted at certain hours to watch the disciples at work or to listen to their choral singing.

Enfantin intended to build up, under rigid discipline, an elite battalion for the spiritual conquest of the world. Most of these men were under thirty years of age, resolute, courageous, fanatically devoted to their leader. Enfantin defined his purpose in no ambiguous terms:

"We must come out of this retreat a compact and unbreakable nucleus. We must form habits which distinguish and characterize us as much as a priest or a soldier is characterized even when in civilian clothes. . . . We must harden our body by work and exercise, train our voices by singing and our ears by harmony, nourish our minds with all knowledge, familiarize ourselves with music, astronomy, architecture, geography, poetry, geology." [9]

To approximate more closely a monastic order, the members wore a costume designed by Raymond Bonheur. A well known writer and sympathizer, Maxime du Camp, described the Saint-Simonian attire:

"The trousers were white, the waistcoat red and the tunic blue-violet. White is the color of love, red that of work, blue-violet that of faith. The name of each member was inscribed in capital letters on his chest. On Enfantin's chest was written 'The Father,' on Duveyrier's 'Charles, poet of God.' " [10]

The waistcoat was buttoned in the back, as a symbol of fraternity, as it could not be put on without the assistance of one of the brothers, so that each time the member was reminded of the spirit of mutual assistance.

In this retreat Enfantin collaborated with Michel Chevalier in the writing of a biblical epic, *Le Livre Nouveau*, designed to become the new Genesis.

"This is the new Genesis, historical and prophetic, announcing that which is to be destroyed and what is to be created, that which is to die and what is to be born."

The authors assumed the inspired tone of the Scripture and the visionary images of the Apocalypse.

"I saw in the darkness of ancient times most wondrous things.

"The earth said to God, in whose bosom it moved:

208

" 'Will the beloved come soon?'

"And God said the earth was not yet ready for the coming and must prepare for the advent. Christ came and there was rejoicing all over the world. But the time of Christ is past, and humanity has need of a new saviour.

"And to-day God deemed that the wedding of man with the earth was to be renewed and he sent again his Christ."

The new Christ was none other than Saint-Simon in whose message humanity would find salvation and happiness.

Life at Ménilmontant did not long remain undisturbed. In February 1832 an investigation was started of the leaders of the Saint-Simonian family. On August 27, Enfantin, Chevalier, Duveyrier, Barrault, and Rodrigues were summoned to appear befor the Assizes court. They came out of their retreat, and on their way to the Palais-de-Justice they marched down the street lined with curious spectators, in full uniform and in processional order.

The Saint-Simonians took up their defense individually and collectively. To the prosecuting attorney who accused them of imposture and speculation, Chevalier gave this proud answer:

"Men who have done what we have done to propagate their belief are men of deep conviction. In these days when official devotion to ephemeral governments that succeed each other is a most common quality, I doubt whether one could find many people who, having to choose between their convictions and their salary or rank, prefer resigning from their posts. In these days when many courageous men do not hesitate to risk their lives, I doubt whether there are many who consent to risk their wealth. Yet wealth and appointments most of us had to sacrifice and did so willingly. And this is not all. We had to give up the affection of people who were dear to us, we had to break up ties which were precious to us, we had to abandon the comforts of an honorable living for a troubled existence, we had to renounce public esteem and accept the insults of frivolous men, the scorn of the indifferent, the censure of the wise. I ask you, who besides ourselves has done as much nowadays for his convictions?"

But the defendants wearied and annoyed the jury with the interminable justification of their doctrines and display of religious ceremonial. They were found guilty, probably for no other reason. Enfantin and Chevalier, accused of forming an illegal association, were condemned to serve a year in prison. They were incarcerated at Sainte-Pélagie, inside the very walls where Saint-Simon had been confined during the Terror.

The mockeries of skeptics, the relentless attacks of the Catholic Church, the hostility of the government did not dampen the ardor of the Saint-Simonians.

"No, no! neither raillery nor calumny can cool off the ardor of any one whose heart once burned in the Saint-Simonian fire; far from it. We frankly admit we are ridiculous, quite ridiculous, we who come to preach love, faith, abnegation, obedience, order in a society which knows only doubt, distrust, jealousy, insubordination." [11]

Protests against the official persecution came from many sources, but perhaps the most courageous attitude was that of an army officer. Bruneau, a captain of the general staff, sent his resignation to the minister of war, with these remarks:

"I began my military career under the walls of Paris on the day when the allied European nations were threatening its gates. I was then a student at the *Ecole Polytechnique*. Since then I have served in the ranks of the army with honor, as evidenced by the decoration I wear on my chest. But now I have found another mission. I am a Saint-Simonian and I shall consecrate my life to the apostolate. To-day our religion is exposed to outrage and persecution, our Supreme Father has need of all his sons, honor commands me to remain by his side." [12]

Heinrich Heine, who at that time was living in Paris, expressed his sympathies for the persecuted cult. The celebrated German poet wrote more than once in favor of the Saint-Simonians, but the following article was particularly eloquent:

"Saint-Simonism is accomplishing all that which religion, philosophy, education and politics have been trying to do for centuries; it brings a remedy for our ills and presents to our vision a future such as we could not have dared to expect even in our most ambitious dreams. Its intellectual and moral conceptions transcend all that our sages, our scientists, our philanthropists,

210

our statesmen have been able to offer or establish. And the men who propagate those ideas combine the most ardent enthusiasm with the soundest judgment.

"I am writing this profession of faith the very day the news came that the French government is taking legal action against the Saint-Simonians. I am writing in the midst of mockeries and calumnies that are lavished unsparingly upon this religion which they imagine is about to die. Well, I shall declare it openly, the present form of Saint-Simonism may be broken, its leaders may prove unworthy of their task; one could even conceive there might be among them impostors, ambitious and selfish individuals; what of it? The ideas would nevertheless remain alive with all their power. I do declare myself the most enthusiastic admirer of the new doctrine; I wish tó devote my time and efforts to understand it better and better, and to elevate my soul to its sublime height." [13]

The condemnation of Enfantin was the signal for the dispersion of the Saint-Simonian family. Some returned to the world where they continued to spread a discreet propaganda while devoting themselves to their various professions. But the majority of the members who had undergone the rigorous training at Ménilmontant would not be released from their religious vows. Their fervor, far from waning under the new tribulations, was fanned to greater efforts at proselyting. Missionaries left for Marseilles, Toulon, Lyons, Rouen.

The apostles, who could have chosen a life of ease and comfort, accepted the most arduous tasks and performed the lowest manual labor. At Lyons they shared employment with the silk weavers; at Rouen they toiled in the cotton mills. Some became street porters, others farm hands and grape harvesters, and asked for no other reward but to share the journeyman's soup bowl. Besides physical hardships, the propagandists often had to endure the hostility of the people.

"On Saturday, March 9, 1833, under the leadership of father Hoart, a captain of artillery who had become a cobbler, nine Saint-Simonians made their entrance into Nîmes. Their costume —blue tunic, white trousers, leather belt, heavy beard, a sack car-

211

ried on the back and a walking stick—was indeed of the kind to arouse curiosity. In the Catholic quarter . . . there was hostility. Against this audacious sect the people yelled their threats.

"At Beaucaire, the same opposition as before. One of the disciples received a serious head injury."[14]

Hope in the coming of the Woman Messiah had not been abandoned. It became evident that she could not be found among the corrupt and skeptical populations of Europe. Yet somewhere she was living and waiting for the call. Where else could she be if not in the Orient, the land of mystery, the birthplace of all creeds, the cradle of mankind?

This conviction moved a group of members to call themselves the "Compagnons de la Femme," and they sailed from Marseilles bound on the holy quest. Their landing in Turkey was met with disapproval, and the disappointed missionaries decided to join their brothers in Egypt. A party of Saint-Simonians had previously gone to Egypt with the grandiose scheme of digging a canal establishing communication between the Mediterranean and the Red Sea. Great enterprises, particularly those facilitating commercial relations between people had been advocated by Saint-Simon as a practical step toward industrial progress. Works of this nature were considered by his disciples as most beneficial to mankind by securing an abundance of material blessings to all the people of the earth.

The Egyptian expedition was composed of several engineers, graduates of the Ecole Polytechnique under the leadership of Fournel. There were also chemists, mineralogists, physicians, writers, artists, musicians. The plan of the canal was chiefly the work of Fournel and Talabot, the latter having solved the difficult problem of overcoming the differences of water level.

Enfantin, released from prison within three months of his condemnation, embarked at Marseilles for Alexandria to join his fellow workers in Egypt, where he was welcomed by the French vice-consul, Ferdinand de Lesseps. His arrival brought encouragement to the men who were encountering difficulties of all sorts. The opposition of the sultan to the canal project was the main source of their disappointment. The Egyptian ruler was more interested in the building of the Nile barrage, which would be

212

of immediate service to his people, and he was not in favor of a water lane that would only profit some European nations.

Enfantin would say in answer to the opponents of the canal:

"We are not like the British engineers who ask for millions of pounds. We live like workers. This great enterprise, of a truly universal nature, must be the work of enthusiasm and devotion."

The Saint-Simonians had among them capable men of various skills who could direct the works of the barrage. "Let them take charge of that enterprise," said the sultan, and more so since these queer religious fanatics did not ask for pecuniary remuneration or other rewards.

The group of apostles, for lack of financial means, had to comply with the sultan's wishes. They worked on the barrage with heroic courage, exposed to a trying climate, eating the same food and living under the same conditions as the native laborers. It was not long before the plague broke out in their camp, and twelve of them died victims of the dread disease. Enfantin realized that the task of digging the Suez Canal had to be abandoned for the present. He and a number of the disciples returned to France, where each followed the profession for which he had been trained.

However, several Saint-Simonians remained in Egypt where they filled important functions. Lambert was commissioned by the sultan to found a Polytechnic School at Cairo. Bruneau was appointed director of the artillery School at Thora. Linant became chief engineer of highways. Perron was given the post of director of the School of Medicine.

The Saint-Simonians never became reunited after the Egyptian expedition, but they remained faithful to their principles and kept advocating many industrial projects. Three of the engineers who had been apostles of the church, Lamé, Clapeyron, and Flachat wrote a book on the subject of railroads: *Vues politiques et pratiques sur les chemins de fer.* Another disciple, the financier Emile Péreire, raised the five million francs needed to build the railway line from Paris to Saint-Germain. The entire engineering work of this undertaking was done by Saint-Simonians. Later, when several lines had been constructed, the multiplicity of small companies became an obstacle to the expansion of this new industry. In 1846 Enfantin was appointed administrator of the three railroad companies which ran parallel lines from Paris to Marseilles, and he was able to unify them into a single organization with joint ownership. Other lines followed this example, so that twenty-eight small railways, which barely managed to exist separately, became the six large companies of the modern network. As a consequence the cost of transportation was considerably lowered, and speed greatly accelerated. Such was the triumphal accomplishment of the Saint-Simonians in the domain of industry, in which they placed, in conformity with the teaching of the master, the ultimate salvation of mankind.

Enfantin, however, had never given up the project of the Suez Canal. This undertaking, if carried out, would be a worthy commemoration of the faith, the dreams, the hopes, the sacrifices of Saint-Simon's disciples. And on the day of the inauguration of the canal a monument would be unveiled bearing the inscription: "To Humanity, the sons of Saint-Simon."

Enfantin won the respect of the industrial and financial leaders. He was thus in a favorable situation for raising the money needed to put the plans into execution. In November 1846 he founded the *Société d'études pour le Canal de Suez.* But, because of the Revolution of 1848 and the stubborn opposition of England, the enterprise suffered considerable delay.

Ferdinand de Lesseps, the young diplomat the apostles had met in Alexandria, was finally able to conciliate the British as well as to obtain the support of the Egyptian government. Enfantin turned over to him all the documents of his *Société d'études,* which de Lesseps renamed *Compagnie universelle,* with himself as director and general concessionaire. The name of Enfantin was not even mentioned on the list of founders, and de Lesseps received all the honors and glory for a work conceived and started by the Saint-Simonians. Enfantin suffered the deception without other protest than the following comment:

"I had hoped that the Suez canal would be a Saint-Simonian enterprise and would bear our name. I thought that all our living members would find in it the reward for their sacrifices to the new faith."[15]

He consoled himself with the hope that some day the world

would realize that the initiative of the gigantic project had been taken by "the very people who were regarded as utopians, dreamers and insane."

In the official account of the opening of the canal a tribute was paid to the originator of the project by the *Journal officiel*. On October 9, 1869, the day of the inauguration, this official state organ declared:

"It was Enfantin who, in the name of civilization and progress, vigorously affirmed the possibility of the enterprise and who, so to speak, broke the ground twenty-three years ago. To a group of friends and disciples he inspired the noble desire to give a new highway to the world."

Other disciples developed banking facilities. The Péreire brothers established the *Crédit mobilier,* the *Compagnie immobilière,* and the *Compagnie maritime.* Duveyrier founded a land bank under the name of *Crédit foncier.* The prosperity of the Second Empire owed much to the activities of the Saint-Simonians who had placed industry in the forefront of their humanitarian creed.

The best summary of the practical achievements of the Saint-Simonians is to be found in the letter Enfantin addressed to Lamartine, on September 15, 1849. This letter, written in answer to some derogatory remarks the poet had made on Saint-Simonism, is given here in translation as a conclusion to this chapter:

"Dear Sir,

"I was prompted to thank you and congratulate you for what you wrote recently in your *Sixth Advice to the People.* To-day I feel obliged to make a complaint and, I am sorry to say, to reprimand you for several passages in your *Seventh Advice.*

"You say that you have been studying socialism for twenty years, and you classify under that name Saint-Simon and his school. Stupidity, perversity, imbecility, idiocy, divagations, ineptitude, old women's tales, etc., etc., such are the words you apply without discrimination, without exception, to all the men you include and wish to crush under your anathema.

"Is it your colleague Carnot, minister of education, together with his friends and counsellors Jean Reynaud and Charton, who are also your colleagues in the Constituent Assembly, and all three of whom are former members of the Saint-Simonian College, are these the men you intend to expose to the scorn of elementary school teachers and to the animosity of the people?

"Is it Michel Chevalier, as well as Xavier Raymond and Broet who run the *Journal des Débats;* Jourdan and Bernard, who run *Le Siècle;* Guéroult, who manages *La République;* Duveyrier and the small group of enlightened men who founded the *Crédit foncier,* the land bank which yesterday you praised so justly and so warmly; or is it Arlès and myself you wish to treat in like manner?

"Are those the flowers you throw on the twelve graves I dug in Egypt of dear friends who had come with me to study and plan the great industrial and political undertaking of this century, the junction of the two seas, and who found as reward for their sacrifices only privations, plague and death?

"Of these poor martyrs you know neither the life nor the works nor the death, and if you were asked what kind of men they were and what was accomplished by Bazard, Eugène Rodrigues, Edmund Talabot and many others who also died in harness, you would not know what to answer. Who then have you known in these twenty years you have been studying socialism, who inspired you with the insults you lavish on us?

"Is it Péreire and Flachat, because they were the first to endow France with railroads with the help of our engineer friends Clapeyron and Lamé? Is it all those first class engineers, Didion, Borrell, Bazaine, Chaperon, Parandier, Boucaumont, Boulanger, Job, Capella, and many others, who were also Saint-Simonians, and who lent a hand in and associated their names with all the great works undertaken in France in the last twenty years?

"Or is it your colleagues in the Constituent and Legislative Assemblies, Buchez, Renouvier, Laurent, Barrault, Bac, Allègre, and also Denjoy, Freslon, Barthe and Lamoncière? Or is it Pierre Leroux himself? But you must know this man is one of the kindest and most erudite men of our times; if at times his heart overflows with kindness and his head with knowledge to an abnormal degree, the errors of this socialist philosopher deserve our respect much more than those of the egoistic philosophers of the

216

last century, even though their names be Condillac and Helvé-tius, or even Locke and Voltaire.

"Is it especially our proletarian fellow members who were guided by our principles of work, order and peace, principles that comforted them in their poverty, that quieted their resentment by giving them hope and faith, none of whom shed his brother's blood in our days of rioting, several of whom sang of the future of mankind in excellent poetry, true followers of Béranger, such as Vinçard and Lachambeaudie, whose friend you ought to be, but perhaps those you believe to be your friends have not permitted their names to reach your ears?

"Or could it be Cazeaux, head of the Hydrography department; Lambert, director of the *Ecole Polytechnique* in Cairo; Bruneau, former director of the Artillery School in Egypt, and Perron, director of the School of Medicine also in Egypt? Could it be Transon, assistant master in our *Ecole Polytechnique* in France; d'Eichthal, author of several learned treatises and of a remarkable book on the Orient; Fournel, the engineer who is now completing a great study on the metallurgic richness of Algeria? Could it be that dear Raymond Bonheur to whom the *Moniteur,* so recently paid such a moving tribute and who left us in the person of his daughter one of the greatest artists of our time? And last, is it my favorite, my Félicien David, who is admired by everybody and loved by all who know him? . . .

"If you know a single one of us who lives a life contrary to the doctrine he taught, and which you said you studied, but of which you have no knowledge since you misinterpret it in this manner; if you know a single one deserving of your accusations at whom you have the right to cast a stone, you who have squandered so much wealth and enjoyed so many pleasures, cast it at him, he deserves it."[16]

CHAPTER FIFTEEN

As Georg Brandes pointed out, like his German prototype, the French Faust was drawn ever onward by his restless spirit and his craving for knowledge. One might carry the comparison still farther by noting that Goethe led his romantic hero to a point where at last he experienced the feeling of perfect happiness by devoting his intellectual faculties to the promotion of the welfare of mankind. Saint-Simon, at the end of his life, also attained a state of tranquil contentment in the belief that he had found the way to save the world from war, fear, and poverty. Moreover the German Faust and his French counterpart were bent on learning the secrets of nature. And both were led on by a dominant passion, the desire to convince the world of their superiority.

In the case of Saint-Simon this dominant passion took the form of vainglory and pride. It was a family trait, and a conspicuous motive in the *Mémoires* of the Duc de Saint-Simon, who had judged the court of Versailles in relation to his self-importance. His grand-nephew, Claude-Henri de Rouvroy, comte de Saint-Simon, also had an inordinate regard for his ancestry and a supreme confidence in his own preeminence.

He placed himself above Newton, regarded Laplace beneath contempt, treated Napoleon as an equal, dictated to pope and king, posed as an arbiter of war and peace. He justified his attitude by saying that he was commanded by Charlemagne and commissioned by the Almighty to change the world.

This delusion of grandeur lured him into every field of human endeavor. He sought distinction on the field of battle. He pursued wealth in commercial, industrial, and financial enterprises. He assumed authority in the domain of scientific and philosophic speculations. Every attempt ended in dismal failure until, on his deathbed, he discovered the secret of achieving greatness by promulgating a new creed. After his death, he was glorified, worshipped, and deified.

The inexorable quest spurred his mind to turn from one direction to another.

"From positivism to pacifism, from pacifism to industrialism, from industrialism to socialism, from socialism to new Christianity, such were the various steps in the development of the ideas of Saint-Simon."[1]

In these words does one capable scholar aptly summarize the intellectual evolution of our social philosopher.

To classify Saint-Simon as an exponent of socialism is a matter of controversy. He was in favor of private property and acknowledged the right to possess and inherit riches. In his industrial system no class struggle existed. On the contrary, there was identity of interests between workers and employers. Not that he advocated democracy, since the governing power was to be entrusted to the heads of enterprises, in other words, to the big capitalists.

On the other hand, the socialists themselves claim Saint-Simon as their own. Friedrich Engels found in him "the breadth of view of a genius, thanks to which almost all the ideas of later socialists, which are not strictly economic, are contained in his own works in embryo."[2] And he added: "We, German socialists, are proud to be descendants of Saint-Simon." One should note, however, that Engels placed Saint-Simon among the utopian socialists, together with Fourier and Owen. He is also given recognition by the Union of Soviet Socialist Republics. On an obelisk erected in one of the central parks in Moscow and dedicated to the pioneers of socialism, Saint-Simon's name is fourth on the list, after those of Marx, Engels, and Lassalle.

On the occasion of the centennial anniversary of the 1848 revolution, the following motion was made and adopted at a meeting of the City Council of Paris (1948):

"The house of the Saint-Simonians shall be transformed into a museum of French socialism."

In spite of the claims of the socialists, some commentators are inclined to regard Saint-Simon as an exponent of modern capitalism:

219

"It is not socialism which is the essence of Saint-Simon. Rather he was the prophet of the high state of capitalism which marks our day."[3]

"He must be described as a promoter of the bourgeois-capitalistic ideology."[4]

⸂The fact is that Saint-Simon referred to the nation as a business enterprise, a society of producers whose main object was the manufacture and distribution of goods. He might even be called the founder of technocracy. His most important contribution to social science was his contention that the problem created by modern industrialism could be solved only by a scientific concept of society,⸃ a theory which was further developed by Comte, his collaborator.

Whatever point of view we may take in judging Saint-Simon, we must admit that he and his school had a definite influence on the history of contemporary ideas, both economic and political. That he was far ahead of his times may be seen by his advocacy of One World of United Nations:

"The day when all humanity realizes that the only purpose of men united in a social organization is the greatest happiness of each member in particular, that day there will be but one nation: that nation will be entire humanity."[5]

It is no less interesting to note that Saint-Simon's proposal in 1814, of a fusion of France and England, was suggested again by Winston Churchill at the beginning of the Second World War.

By recognizing the necessity of religion to give support to his social reorganization and by advocating a return to primitive Christianity, he paved the way for the recent movement of Christian socialism.

In summarizing the significance of Saint-Simon's writings, J. F. Normano concluded:

"The influence of Saint-Simon is universal. He affected *philosophy* through Auguste Comte; *socialism* through his embryonic theory of the class struggle; *history* through Augustin Thierry; *politics* through his interpretation of it as a reflection of the modes of production, and his sketch in 1814 of a League of Nations; *theology* through his theories on the New Christianity;

and in *sociology* he may be represented as one of the chief founders."[6]

Saint-Simon's influence extended outside of France. In England, Thomas Carlyle acquired most of his constructive radicalism from Saint-Simon, particularly from *Le Nouveau Christianisme*. Gustave d'Eichthal wrote to Carlyle in July, 1830, congratulating him on his article the "Signs of the Times," and urging him to become a member of the Saint-Simonian church. At the same time he mailed to him a copy of *Le Nouveau Christianisme* and several issues of the periodical *l'Organisateur*. Carlyle noted in his journal:

"Received a strange letter from Saint-Simonians at Paris,[•] grounded on my little *Signs of the Times*. These people have strange notions, not without a large splicing of truth, and are themselves among the *Signs*. I shall feel curious to know what becomes of them. *La classe la plus pauvre* is evidently in the way of rising from its present deepest abasement. . . . A man with £200,000 a year eats the whole fruit of 6666 men's labor through the year; for you can get a stout spadesman to work and maintain himself for the sum of £30. Thus we have private individuals whose wages are equal to wages of seven or eight thousand other individuals. What do these highly beneficed individuals *do* to society for their wages? *Kill partridges! Can* this last? No, by the soul that is in man, it cannot, and will not, and shall not!"[7]

In a letter to his brother John he announced that he had completed a translation of *Le Nouveau Christianisme*, which he wanted to have published:

"To Dr. Carlyle, London,

Craigenputtock, 19 December 1830.

"I have translated Saint-Simon's *Nouveau Christianisme*, a heterodox Pamphlet (about forty Review pages), which I mean soon to send *you*. I have prefixed a very short introduction; and you may try whether any pamphlet-printing Bookseller (some Socinian or Anti-Church or quite indifferent character) will give you the matter of five pounds for the copyright thereof, or will give you nothing whatever, which also will be a decision. *Nouveau Christianisme* contains several strange ideas, not without a large splice of truth; is ill written, but easily read, and deserves a reading. T. Carlyle"[8]

The contents of *Sartor Resartus* was, in the words of one critic, "almost entirely a synthesis of the ideas of the German philosophers and the Saint-Simonians."[9]

John Stuart Mill also recognized the importance of Saint-Simon and the diffusion of his ideas into the domain of contemporary thought. In 1834, Mill wrote:

"There is scarcely a thinker of any importance in France, at the present moment, who is not largely indebted to St.-Simonism; and many have the candour to acknowledge the obligation. Nor would it be easy to find a parallel in history to the striking improvement which, aided no doubt by the circumstances of the times, the St.-Simonians have introduced into the whole character of public discussion in France."[10]

Across the Rhine Saint-Simonism gave a decided impulsion to the Young Germany movement. Writers and political leaders who represented the new liberal forces found in that doctrine a religious and humanitarian incentive which made a strong appeal to the young generation of 1848. The sociologist Friedrich Muckle devoted two volumes to the study of this influence.

In Russia, secret societies flourished in a characteristic way, namely as centers both for study and for conspiratorial actions. Among others "there was the Alexander Herzen's group whose members one by one ended in Siberia when the authorities discovered that they were engaged in spreading the teachings of Saint-Simon."[11]

The Saint-Simonian theories spread also to Latin America where they were espoused by the radical intellectuals. According to J. F. Normano:

"Not the economic program, but the nebulous socialism and religious and mystic enthusiasm of its content became the fashion, and developed cults of an intellectual movement in these countries. It is curious to note how the industrial program of Saint-Simon was neglected in Spanish America, while his social ideas, strangely distorted, became the passionate credo of the intelligentsia. Revolutionists and ruling government preached Saint-Simonism. . . .

"In the case of Brazil, Saint-Simon's influence was different. Not his theories, but the practical activity of his followers, especially of the brothers Péreire, found a worthy counterpart in the inter-American financier, statesman and diplomat Visconde de Maua. . . . Both the governments and their oppositions, were superficially infected by Saint-Simonian contagion, while the intelligentsia used and imitated its schemes for social reconstruction."[12]

Anglo-Saxon America did not need encouragement of Saint-Simon to realize the "American System," but one may agree with Normano that the United States fulfilled the industrial dreams and ambitions of the French philosopher:

"His main ideas and his formulated plan of industry were predestined for adoption in the U.S. in its railroads, banks, canals, and factories. But the soil of the United States was not propitious for the cultivation of theory. The industrial system became here a matter of fact, not of thought."[13]

In the field of literature, the Romantic school of the period extending from 1830 to 1848 was deeply affected by the Saint-Simonian conception of art. Artists and poets were pleased to be included with the scientists and industrialists among the potential rulers of the world. The gospel of love and universal brotherhood appealed also to their idealism and renewed the source of their inspiration. Alfred de Vigny turned his back on the allurements of nature to bestow his sympathies on suffering humanity. Victor Hugo freed himself from the witchery of rhyme to take up the cause of the victims of social injustice. George Sand came under the influence of Pierre Leroux, the prominent Saint-Simonian, whom she aided in establishing the *Revue indépendante*. In several of her novels, George Sand makes heroes of peasants and workers, whom she idealised and inspired with all the social virtues.

The close relation between Romanticism and Saint-Simonism was clearly envisaged by contemporary writers. "Romanticism and socialism are the same thing," declared Victor Hugo.[14] And Musset wrote in his satire of Romanticism: "From 1832 to 1833 we thought that Romanticism was a system of philosophy and political economy."[15]

In his youth Napoleon III manifested the liberal tendencies of the time, to the point that Sainte-Beuve was moved to call him on his becoming emperor, the "Saint-Simon on horseback." Napoleon III promoted extensive public works, including the completion of the Suez Canal, and favored general progress in the true Saint-Simonian fashion.

Victor Hugo in *Les Misérables* spoke of "Saint-Simon, unknown, elaborating his sublime dream." Many of his contemporaries attributed these dreams to the vagaries of a deranged mind. There may have been an element of madness in the philosopher's constitution. But perhaps madness is a necessary component of genius, and for that reason great men are apt to be misjudged by their contemporaries. Such was the thought of Béranger, when he wrote in praise of Saint-Simon and his disciples, a poem entitled *Les Fous* (The Madmen), part of which we translate as follows:

"We who behave like toy soldiers,
All neatly set by rank and file,
When some of us step out of line
We cry out: Down with the fools!
We harry them, and we kill them.
But years after we understand
And erect fine statues to them
For the glory of humankind.

I saw Saint-Simon the prophet,
At first wealthy and then in debt,
Who, from foundation to summit,
Was rebuilding society.
He lived for this unfinished task,
And though he was a mendicant,
He knew the findings of his mind
Would some day redeem humankind."

Béranger continued by evoking the memory of two other "madmen, who dreamt of a better world, Fourier and Enfantin." Instead of mocking them, said the poet, let us honor them, for all great things are done by madmen. And to sustain his assertion, he concluded with these examples:

"Who did discover a new world?
A madman whom they all laughed at.
A madman we nailed to the cross,
Whom we made God after his death.
And should to-morrow's daylight fail
Some madman would rise again
And hold a torch to humankind."

The torch Saint-Simon held up to guide humanity is not extinguished. There is in fact a renewal of interest in Saint-Simonism. The centenary of Saint-Simon's death was celebrated in May, 1925, at the *Bibliothèque Nationale* by an exposition of miscellaneous documents and souvenirs relating to the social reformer and his disciples. The *Revue d'Histoires Economique et Sociale* published a special number on this occasion. It contained a partial reprint of Léon Halévy's *Souvenirs de Saint-Simon,* and articles by some students of Saint-Simonism. Magazines of wide circulation, such as *L'Illustration,* devoted numerous articles to his memory.

There was, before the Second World War, a revival of the Saint-Simonian journal *Le Producteur,* and a movement started under the name of Néo-Saint-Simonisme. It was an attempt to adapt the early nineteenth century theories to the economic and social conditions of our days.

The problems that confronted Saint-Simon may forever remain insoluble. Yet he deserves credit for being among the first to awaken public interest to their importance and intricacy. For half a century he dominated French opinion in the field of sociology and economics, not so much through his own writings as through the interpretation and propagation of his ideas by his disciples. His influence spread also to the literary movement of the time, which he inspired with humanitarian ideals.

One may regret that, soon after his death, he was transformed by the excessive zeal of his followers into a prophetic Messiah and worshipped with the ritualistic pomp accorded to divinity. One may also reject as extravagant his claim to the highest rank in the temple of glory. But it is fitting that he be granted his due place and given at least a modest share of fame, in search of which he spent his adventurous life.

225

NOTES

Foreword

1. Brandes, Main Currents in Nineteenth Century Literature, V, p. 59.
2. Casson, Saint-Simon, the First American, The Arena, 1904, p. 514.

I.

1. Saint-Simon et Enfantin, Oeuvres, I, p. 101.
2. Ibid. (1868 edition) pp. 99-100.
3. Ibid. p. 71.
4. Michelet, Jules, Histoire du Dix-Neuvième Siècle, I, p. 38.
5. Archives of the Somme, Amiens, 1761.
6. Balde, J., A Propos d'un Centenaire. Le Comte Henri de Saint-Simon, La Revue Hebdomadaire, 1925, p. 174.
7. The pamphlet found in carton C 2744 was entitled: "Pétition aux membres de la Chambre des Députés pour demander un amendement à la Loi sur les Impôts."
8. Notice sur Saint-Simon et sa doctrine et sur quelques ouvrages qui en seraient le développement par son ancien secrétaire. Bibliothèque de la Ville de Paris.
9. Lavisse, Histoire de France, IX, chapter II.
10. Saint-Simon, Mémoire Introductif.
11. Chateaubriand, Mémoires d'outre-tombe, I, p. 102.
12. Genlis, Lettres sur l'Education.
13. Picard, Les Etudes classiques avant la Révolution, p. 191.
14. Saint-Simon et Enfantin, op. cit., I, p. 68.
15. Leroy, M., La Vie Véritable du Comte Henri de Saint-Simon, pp. 66-67.

II.

1. Ségur, Memoirs, p. 120.
2. Ibid., p. 117.
3. Ibid., p. 321.
4. Larrabee, Henri de Saint-Simon at Yorktown, pp. 102-103.
5. Washington, Correspondence of General Washington and Comte de Grasse, p. 27.
6. Thacher, Military Journal of the American Revolution, p. 279.
7. Larrabee, op. cit., p. 104.
8. Lafayette, Correspondance et Manuscrits, p. 446.
9. Contenson, Deux Documents sur la Guerre d'Amérique.
10. Pearson, Tom Paine, p. 143.
11. Santo Domingo.
12. Martinique.
13. Guadeloupe.
14. Count de Grasse.

15. Barbadoes.
16. Lieutenant-colonel.
17. Shirley.
18. The Vicomtesse (viscountess) referred to was his sister Adélaïde-Blanche.
19. Henri's brother, five years younger.
20. Charavay, Le Général LaFayette.
21. Hubbard, Saint-Simon, Sa Vie et Ses Travaux, pp. 12-13.
22. Santo Domingo.
23. The English influence may be noted by the way Henri signed his name.
24. The manuscripts containing the two letters to his father were found in the Bibliothèque de l'Arsenal in Paris.
25. Saint-Simon et Enfantin, op. cit., p. 64.
26. Heilbroner, The Worldly Philosophers, p. 109.
27. Saint-Simon, Mémoire Introductif. Aide-major-général might be translated as adjutant-general or assistant adjutant-general.
28. Casson, Saint-Simon: The First American, p. 514.

III.

1. In the December 28, 1953 issue of *Life* magazine appeared the photograph of the Society of the Cincinnati, with this caption: "Stag Dinner for the Society of Cincinnati—limited to the male descendants of Revolutionary War officers—is held each year in ornate dining room of society's Anderson House headquarters."
2. Saint-Simon et Enfantin, op. cit., p. 65.
3. Rodrigues, Oeuvres de Saint-Simon, pp. xvii-xviii.
4. Saint-Simon et Enfantin, op. cit., XV, p. 66.
5. Hubbard, op. cit., p. 22.
6. The commune of Falvy was included in the district of Marchélepot.
7. Hubbard, op. cit., pp. 23-24.
8. Archives of the district of Péronne, Amiens, fo. 2.
9. Ibid., fo. 79.
10. Ibid., fo. 82.
11. Ibid., fo. 87
12. Conseil Général de la Commune de Péronne, Séance du vendredi, 20 septembre 1793.
13. Archives of the district of Péronne, fo. 183.
14. Ibid., fo. 126.
15. November 19, 1793.
16. Mathiez, L'Arrestation de Saint-Simon, p. 572.
17. Saint-Simon, Mémoire Introductif.
18. Mathiez, op. cit., p. 573.
19. Michelet, op. cit., I, p. 42.
20. Saint-Simon, Mémoire Introductif.
21. Leroy, op. cit., p. 169.
22. Archives of the district of Péronne.

IV.

1. Coissin, Almanach des Prisons.
2. Leroy, op. cit., pp. 129-130.
3. Archives of Péronne.
4. The Letter was dated 14 frimaire year II (December 4, 1793) and was found among the documents at the Bibliothèque Nationale at Paris.
5. Mathiez, Saint-Simon et Ronsin.
6. Alméras, L'Amour Sous Les Verrous.

V.

1. Michelet, op. cit., I, I, p. 17.
2. Weill, Saint-Simon et Son Oeuvre, p. 12.
3. Allemagne, Les Cartes à Jouer.
4. Archives d'Amiens, district of Péronne.
5. Larrabee, Un chapitre peu connu de la vie d'Henri de Saint-Simon, pp. 201-210.
6. Alençon in Normandy.
7. Saint-Simon, Mémoire Introductif.
8. Document at the Bibliothèque Nationale.
9. Saint-Simon, Mémoire Introductif.
10. Leroy, op. cit., p. 141.
11. Saint-Simon, Mémoire Introductif.

VI.

1. Rodrigues, op. cit., pp. xx-xxi.
2. Saint-Simon, Mémoire Introductif.
3. Leroux, La Grève de Samarez, pp. 261-263.
4. Rodrigues, op. cit., p. xxi.
5. Gagne, Madame de Bawr, pp. 10-11.
6. Janin, Mme de Bawr.
7. Bawr, Mes Souvenirs, p. 254.
8. Rodrigues, op. cit., p. xx.
9. Halévy, Souvenirs de Saint-Simon, p. 528.
10. Ibid.
11. Gagne, op. cit., p. 22.
12. Ibid., pp. 22-23.
13. Rodrigues, op. cit., p. xxiv.
14. Vauthier, Le Premier Mariage de Mme de Bawr, p. 369.
15. Rodrigues, op. cit., p. xxii.
16. Ibid., pp. xxii-xxiii.
17. Ibid., p. xxii.
18. Quérard. La France Littéraire, p. 853.
19. Nouvelle Biographie Générale, p. 119.
20. Goncourt, La Société française pendant la Révolution, p. 6.
21. Ivray, Le Centenaire de Saint-Simon, p. 485.
22. Saint-Simon, Lettres d'un Habitant de Genève, p. 8.
23. Rodrigues, op. cit., p. xxii.

VII.

1. Catalogue of letters, Bibliothèque Nationale.
2. Rodrigues, op. cit., p. xxiii.
3. Saint-Simon et Enfantin, op. cit., p. 74.
4. Fonds Fournel, Correspondance entre M. de Saint-Simon et Redern.
5. Ibid.
6. Ibid., pp. 10-11.
7. Ibid., pp. 12-13.
8. Weill, op. cit., pp. 48-49.
9. Rodrigues, op. cit., pp. xxvi-xxvii.
10. Saint-Simon, Lettres au Bureau des Longitude: first part 75 pages; second part 23 pages.
11. Saint Simon et Enfantin, op. cit., p. 71.
12. Rodrigues, op. cit., p. xxxviii.
13. Catalogue of letters, Bibliothèque Nationale.
14. Rodrigues, op. cit., pp. xxv-xxxvii.

VIII.

1. Fonds Fournel, Collection of letters, Bibliothèque Nationale.
2. Charavay, Collection of letters, 142, 2-11, Bibliothèque Nationale.

IX.

1. Saint-Simon et Enfantin, op. cit., pp. 136-137.
2. Leroux, Le Livre de Job, p. 4.
3. Saint-Simon et Enfantin, op. cit., p. 142.
4. Collection of letters, Bibliothèque Nationale.
5. Saint-Simon et Enfantin, op. cit., pp. 143-144.
6. Ibid., IV, pp. 150-151.
7. Ibid., pp. 196-197.
8. Ibid., p. 204.
9. Ibid., p. 247. Ralph Waldo Emerson used the phrase: "The Golden Age is not behind but before you," as mentioned by A. T. Mason in his biography of Brandeis, p. 39.
10. Saint-Simon, Oeuvres Choisies, p. 332.
11. Saint-Simon et Thierry, Opinion Sur Les Mesures A Prendre Contre la Coalition de 1815, p. 360.
12. Leroy, M., op. cit., p. 250.
13. Saint-Simon, lettres, brochures, (Fournel), pp. 355-356.
14. Pereire, Autour de Saint-Simon, pp. 2-3.
15. Allemagne, Les Saint-Simoniens, p. 10.
16. Mason, E. S., Saint-Simonism and the Rationalisation of Industry, p. 655.
17. Saint-Simon et Enfantin, op. cit., III, p. 168.
18. Gide and Rist, A History of Economic Doctrines, p. 206.
19. Thierry, D'Après Sa Correspondance, p. vii.

X.

1. Halévy, Elie, La doctrine économique de Saint-Simon, pp. 654-655.
2. Fournel, Bibliographie Saint-Simonienne, pp. 18-19.
3. Comtes, Lettres d'Auguste Comte à M. Valat, pp. 36-38.
4. Ibid., pp. 51-53.
5. Saint-Simon, L'Industrie, fourth volume.
6.| Saint-Simon, Oeuvres Choisies, II, pp. 396-401.
7. Saint-Simon, Lettres à Messieurs les Jurés, mars 1820.
8. Gouhier, La Jeunesse d'Auguste Comte, II, p. 121.

XI.

1. Halévy, Léon, Souvenirs de Saint-Simon, pp. 533-534.
2. Saint-Simon et Enfantin, op. cit., I, p. 96.
3. Ibid.
4. Leroux, La Grève de Samarez, pp. 263-265.
5. Hubbard, op. cit., p. 95.
6. Halévy, Léon, op. cit., p. 537.
7. Ibid., p. 538.

XIII.

1. Maistre, Joseph de, Considérations sur la France, p. 84.
2. Brunet, Le Mysticisme Social, p. 102.
3. Saint-Simon, Le Nouveau Christianisme, p. 48.

4. Ibid., p. 47.
5. Franz Joseph Gall, 1758-1828, anatomist, physiologist, founder of phrenology.
6. Hubbard, op. cit., pp. 106-108.
7. His favorite nephew, Victor, was then in Denmark on a government mission. Victor, peer of France, 1782-1865, married Anne-Marie de Lasalle, had two daughters.
8. Halévy, Léon, Souvenirs de Saint-Simon.

XIV.

1. Saint-Simon et Enfantin, op. cit., VII, p. 163.
2. Reybaud, Etudes sur les Réformateurs ou Socialistes Modernes I.
3. Le Globe, Jan. 18, 1831.
4. Allemagne, Les Saint-Simoniens, Prédication de Transon, Le Globe, 23, mai 1831, p. 163.
5. Ibid. Prédication de Laurent, Le Globe, 28 mars 1831.
6. Ibid. Prédication de Baud. Le Globe, 6 juin 1831.
7. Ibid.
8. Halévy, Léon, Ode to Saint-Simon.
9. Saint-Simon et Enfantin, op. cit., VII, pp. 22-23.
10. Camp, Souvenirs littéraires, II, p. 90.
11. Allemagne, op. cit., p. 162.
12. Ibid., o. 265.
13. Ibid., p. 153.
14. Sauzède, Les Saint-Simoniens dans le Languedoc.
15. Camp, op. cit., II, p. 103.
16. Saint-Simon et Enfantin, op. cit., pp. 138-145.

XV.

1. Bouglé, Comment naît un dogme.
2. Engles, Herr Eugen Dührings Revolution in Science, p. 284.
3. Normano, Saint-Simon and America, p. 9.
4. Stark, Saint-Simon as a Realist.
5. Saint-Simon et Enfantin, op. cit., II, pp. 24-25.
6. Normano, op. cit., p. 8.
7. Neff, Carlyle and Mill, pp. 165-166.
8. Cofer, Saint-Simonism in the Radicalism of Thomas Carlyle, p. 17.
9. Neff, op. cit., p. 172.
10. Hainds, John Stuart Mill and the Saint-Simonians, p. 107.
11. Del Vayo, The Last Optimist, p. 143.
12. Normano, op. cit., pp. 12-13.
13. Ibid.
14. Hugo, V., William Shakespeare, II, p. 11.
15. Musset, L., Lettre de Depuis à Cotonet.

BIBLIOGRAPHY

This list of references includes works that have been consulted.

Allemagne, Henry-René d',
Les Cartes à Jouer du Quatorzième Siècle, I, Paris, Hachette et Cie, 1906.
Les Saint-Simoniens 1827-1837, Paris, Lib. Gründ, 1930.
Prosper Enfantin et les Grandes Entreprises du XIXe Siècle, Paris, Lib. Gründ, 1935.
Alméras, Henri d',
La Vie Parisienne sous le Consulat et l'Empire, Paris, Albin Michel, 1909.
La Vie Parisienne sous la Révolution et le Directoire, Paris, Albin Michel, 1925.
L'Amour sous les Verrous. Les Prisons Révolutionnaires. Paris, Albin Michel, 1936.
Anonymous
Almanach des Prisons, Paris, Michel, L'an III de la République, 1795.
Critical Remarks on Saint-Simonism, Dublin Review, January 1838, pp. 138-179.
Doctrine Saint-Simonienne, Paris, Librairie Nouvelle, 1854.
Doctrine de Saint-Simon, Exposition, Au Bureau de l'Organisateur, Paris, 1829, 1830.
Letter on the Doctrine of St. Simon, Fraser's Magazine, July 1832, pp. 666-669.
Saint-Simonianism, The Westminster Review (London), April 1832, pp. 279-321.
Saint-Simon And His Disciples, The Westminster Review (London), July 1, 1863, pp. 109-137.
Notice sur Saint-Simon et sa doctrine et sur quelques ouvrages par son ancien secrétaire. (in manuscript form) Bibliothèque de la Ville de Paris.
Anselme (le Père)
Histoire Généalogique et Chronologique de la Maison Royale de France. . . . Paris, Compagnie des libraires, 1726.

Archives
Archives Départmentales de la Somme, Amiens, 1761.
Registres Des Districts (1790 - an 4) District de Péronne, Imprimerie Modern, 1938.
Archives Nationales, carton C 2744.
Aulard, A.
Paris pendant la Réaction Thermidorienne et sous le Directoire, IV, Paris, L. Cerf, 1900.
Bailly, E. M. de Blois
Discours prononcé sur la tombe de M. Henri Saint-Simon. Paris, Aucher-Eloy, 1825.
Balch, Thomas
The French in America during the War of Independence of the United States, 1777-1783. I, II. Philadelphia, Porter and Coates, 1895.
Balde, Jean
A Propos d'un Centenaire. Le Comte Henri de Saint-Simon. Paris, La Revue Hebdomadaire, 1925, pp. 168-188.
Bawr, Mme de,
Théâtre, Comédies, Paris, 1813.
Mes Souvenirs, Paris, 1853.
Nouveaux Contes pour Les Enfants. Paris, 1867.
Béranger, P. J. de
Oeuvres, II, Paris, Arnier Frères, 1876.
Blanc, Louis
Histoire de Dix Ans, 1830-1840. I. Paris, Jeanmaire, 1882.
Boissy,
Poésies Saint-Simoniennes et Phalanstériennes, Paris, A. Patay, 1881.
Bonsal, Stephen
When the French Were Here, New York, Doubleday, Doran and Co., 1945.
Booth, Arthur John
Saint-Simon and Saint-Simonism, a chapter in the History of Socialism in France, London, Longmans, 1871.
Bouglé, C.
Comment nait un dogme, La Revue de France, Paris, IV, 1922, pp. 742-766.
Le Féminisme Saint-Simonien. La Revue de Paris, 1918, pp. 371-399.
L'Oeuvre d'Henri de Saint-Simon, Paris, Félix Alcan, 1925.
(with) Halévy, Elie,
Doctrine de Saint-Simon, Paris, Marcel Rivière, 1924.
Bourbonnais, Marc
Le Néo Saint-Simonisme et la vie sociale d'aujourd'hui. Paris, Les Presses Universitaires, 1923.

Bourquelot, Félix
La Littéraire Française Contemporaine 1827-1849, Paris, Delaroque, 1857.

Boutaric, Edgard
Institutions Militaires de la France avant les armées permanentes. Paris, Henri Plon, 1953.

Bowers, Claude G.
Jefferson and Hamilton, Boston, Haughton Mifflin & Co., 1925.

Brandes, Georg
Main Currents in Nineteenth Century Literature, V, New York, The Macmillan Co., 1906.

Brunet, Georges
Le Mysticisme Social, Paris, Les Presses Françaises, 1925.
Saint-Simon et Léon Halévy, Paris, Revue d'Histoire Economique et Sociale, 1925, pp. 164-165.

Butler, E. M.
Heine and the Saint-Simonians, The Modern Language Review, XVIII, 1923, pp. 68-85.

Cagny, de
Histoire de l'arrondissement de Péronne, II, 1869.

Camp, Maxime du
Souvenirs Littéraires, Paris, 1882.

Carnot, M.
Sur le Saint-Simonisme, Paris, Picard, 1887.

Casson, Herbert N.
Saint-Simon: The First American, The Arena, 1904, pp. 513-519.

Charavay, Etienne
Le Général LaFayette, 1757-1834. Paris, Société de l'histoire de la Révolution française, 1898.
Collection of Letters, Bibliothèque Nationale.

Charléty, Sébastien
Histoire du Saint-Simonisme (1825-1864), Paris, Hartmann, 1931.
Enfantin, Paris, Alcan, 1930.

Chateaubriand, François Auguste René
Mémoires d'outre tombe, I, Paris, Garnier, 1893.

Chenaye, de la, (ed.)
Dictionnaire de la Noblesse, VII, Paris, Schlesinger, 1872.

Cofer, David Brooks,
Saint-Simonism in the Radicalism of Thomas Carlyle, Austin, Texas, 1931.

Comte, Auguste
Lettres d'Auguste Comte à M. Valat, 1815-1844, Paris, Dunod, 1870.

Correspondance Inédite d'Auguste Comte, 4 volumes, Paris, Société Positiviste, 1903.

Constitution of the Union of Soviet Socialist Republics, printed in the Soviet Union, 1938.

Contenson, Ludovic de

La Capitulation d'Yorktown et le Comte de Grasse. Paris, Revue d'Histoire Diplomatique, 1928, pp. 378-399.

Deux Documents Sur La Guerre d'Amérique, Paris, Revue d'Histoire Diplomatiques, 1930, pp. 20-34.

La Société des Cincinnati de France, Paris, Picard, 1934.

Cuvillier, Armand

P.-J.-B. Buchez et Les Origines du Socialisme Chrétien, Paris, Presses Universitaires, 1948.

Dehove, Gérard,

Saint-Simon a-t-il été socialiste? Paris, Revue des Etudes Coopératives, 1935, pp. 121-143.

Doublet, E.

Une Entreprise des Saint-Simoniens, Revue Scientifique, 1932, pp. 560-563.

Dumas, Georges

Psychologie de Deux Messies Positivistes Saint-Simon et Auguste Comte, Paris, Alcan, 1905.

Durkheim, Emile

Le Socialisme, Paris, Alcan, 1928.

Saint-Simon, fondateur du positivisme et de la sociologie. Revue Philosophique, 1925, pp. 322-341.

Eichthal, Eugène d',

Les Idées de Henri de Saint-Simon sur la Paix Européenne. Paris, L'Académie des Sciences Morales et Politiques, 1925, pp. 350-361.

Ely, Richard T.

French and German Socialism, New York, Harper and Bros., 1883.

Emerit, Marcel,

Pauline Roland et Les Déportées d'Afrique; Alger, Edition de l'Empire, 1945.

Enfantin, P.

Mémoire Inédit Sur La Colonisation de l'Algérie, Revue d'Histoire Economique et Sociale, 1925, p. 196.

Mémoire Sur Les Relations Nouvelles Que La Colonisation de l'Algérie peut et doit établir . . . , Revue d'Histoire Economique et Sociale, 1925, pp. 197-200.

Oeuvres (see under Saint-Simon).

Engels, Friedrich

Socialisme Utopique et Socialisme Scientifique, Paris, Editions Sociales, 1945.

Herr Eugen Dühring's Revolution in Science, New York, International Publishers, 1939.

Faguet, Emile
Le Comte de Saint-Simon, Revue des Deux Mondes, 1894, pp. 856-882.
Politiques et Moralistes du Dix-Neuvième Siècle, Paris, Société Française d'Imprimerie, 1898.

Fournel, Henri
Bibliographie Saint-Simonienne, 1802-1832, Paris, Johanneau, 1833.
Fonds Fournel, Bibliothèque Nationale.

Gagne, Elise Mme., (Elise Moreau)
Madame de Bawr, Paris, Didier et Ce, 1861.

Gançon, Maurice
Grandeur et Décadence des Saint-Simoniens, Paris, Journal des Débats, 1930, pp. 394-397.

Garnier, Honoré
Invocation à Saint-Simon, Ode, Paris, 1931.

Genlis, Mme de,
Adèle et Théodore ou Lettres sur l'éducation, Paris, Lambert et Baudouin, 1782.

Gerathewohl, Fritz
St. Simonistische Ideen in der deutschen Literatur, München, Birk, 1920.

Gide, Charles and Rist, Charles
A History of Economic Doctrines, London, Harrap and Co., 1919.

Gilliam, E. W.
The French Colony of San Domingo, Magazine of American History, 1888, pp. 471-478.

Goncourt, Edmond et Jules de,
Histoire de la société française pendant la Révolution, Paris, Quantin, 1889.

Gouhier, Henri
La Jeunesse d'Auguste Comte, I, II, Paris, Vrin, 1933.

Grossman, Henryk
The Evolutionist Revolt Against Classical Economics, The Journal of Political Economy, 1943, pp. 381-396.

Guérard, Albert
Napoleon III, Cambridge, Mass. Harvard University Press, 1943.

Guigniaut, M.
Notice Historique sur la vie et les travaux de M. Augustin Thierry, Paris, Didot Frères, 1863.

Guthrie, William D.,
   General Count de Rochambeau, The Franco-American Review, 1938, pp. 230-243.
Hainds, J. R.
   John Stuart Mill and the Saint-Simonians, Journal of the History of Ideas, 1946, pp. 103-112.
Halévy, Elie
   La Doctrine économique de Saint-Simon, Revue du Mois, 1907, pp. 641-676.
Halévy, Léon
   Saint-Simon, Ode, Paris, Levavaseur, 1831.
   Souvenirs de Saint-Simon, France littéraire, 1832, pp. 521-546.
   Souvenirs de Saint-Simon, Revue d'Histoire Economique et Sociale, 1925, pp. 166-176.
Hayek, F. A. v.,
   The Counter-Revolution of Science, Economica, 1841, pp. 9-36, pp. 119-150.
Heilbroner, Robert L.
   The Worldly Philosophers, N. Y. Simon and Schuster, 1953.
Hoefer, Le Dr.,
   Nouvelle Biographie Générale, Paris, Firmin Didot Frères, 1862.
Hubbard, M. G.,
   Saint-Simon, Sa Vie et Ses Travaux, Paris, Guillaumin, 1857.
Hume, Edgar Erskine
   LaFayette and the Society of the Cincinnati, John Hopkins Press, 1934.
   General Washington's Correspondence Concerning the Society of the Cincinnati, Baltimore, The Johns Hopkins Press, 1941.
Hunt, H. J.
   Le Socialisme et le Romantisme en France, Oxford, 1935.
Isambert, Gaston
   Les Idées Socialistes en France de 1815 à 1848, Paris, Alcan, 1905.
Ivray, Jehan d'
   Le Centenaire de Saint-Simon, L'Illustration, 16 mai 1925, p. 485.
Janet, Paul
   Saint-Simon et le Saint-Simonisme, Paris, Ballière et Ce, 1878.
Janin, Jules
   Mme de Bawr, Journal des Débats, 14 janvier 1861.

Jaurès, Jean,
  Histoire Socialiste 1789-1900, I, Paris, Rouff et Cie, 1904.
Jenks, Leland Hamilton
  Henri de Saint-Simon, pp. 221-240. New York, Harper Bros.,
  1929. Essays in Intellectual History.
Josephson, Matthew
  Stendhal or The Pursuit of Happiness, New York, Doubleday,
  1946.
Jullien, Jean
  Saint-Simon et le Socialisme, Bordeaux, Cadoret, 1926.
Knight, M. M., Barnes, H. E., Flugel, F.,
  Economic History of Europe in Modern Times, Boston,
  Houghton Mifflin Co., 1928.
Kotzebue, Auguste
  Souvenirs de Paris en 1804, Paris, Barba, 1805.
Lafayette, Général
  Mémoires, Correspondance et Manuscrits, Paris, Fournier,
  1838.
Lambmert, Charles
  Suicides, de St. Simon. Papiers personnels de Lambert, 1835.
  (In manuscript form—not published) Fonds Enfantin, Bibli-
  othèque de l'Arsenal.
Larrabee, Harold A.
  Un chapitre peu connu de la vie d'Henri de Saint-Simon.
  La Révolution Française, 1929, pp. 193-216.
  Henri de Saint-Simon at Yorktown, The Franco-American
  Review, 1937, pp. 96-109.
Lavisse, Ernest,
  Histoire de France Contemporaine, Paris, Hachette, 1920.
Lenoir, Raymond
  Henri de Saint-Simon, Revue Philosophique de la France et
  de l'Etranger, 1925, pp. 179-222.
Leroux, Pierre,
  La Grève de Samarez, Paris, Dentu, 1863.
  Le Livre de Job, 1865.
Leroy, Maxime
  La Vie Véritable du Comte Henri de Saint-Simon, Paris,
  Grasset, 1925.
  Les Spéculations Foncières de Saint-Simon. Revue d'Histoire
  Economique et Sociale, 1925, pp. 133-163.
  La Coopérative Internationale, La République Française,
  1947, pp. 3-8.
Leroy, Stéphen
  Ternaux, Rouget de Lisle et Saint-Simon, Bulletin de la

Société Grayloise d'Emulation no. 6., 1903.

Loménie, Louis de
Galerie des Contemporains Illustres, II, Paris, René et Cᵉ, 1847.

Louis, Paul
Histoire du Socialisme en France 1789-1945, Paris, Rivière, 1946.

Louvancour, Henri
De Henri de Saint-Simon à Charles Fourier, Chartres, Durand, 1913.

Maistre, Joseph de
Considérations sur la France, Paris, 1796.

Mason, Alpheus Thomas
Brandeis, New York, Viking Press, 1946, p. 39.

Mason, E. S.
Saint-Simonism and the Rationalisation of Industry, The Quarterly Journal of Economics, 1931, pp. 640-683.

Mathiez, Albert
L'Arrestation de Saint-Simon, Annales Historiques de la Révolution Française, 1925, pp. 571-575.
Saint-Simon et Ronsin, Annales Historiques de la Révolution Française, 1926, pp. 493-494.

Maurois André
Lélia, The Life of George Sand, N. Y., Harper and Bros., 1953.

Maurice, Barthelemy
Histoire politique et anecdotique des prisons de la Seine, Paris, 1840.

Maury, Lucien
Les Oeuvres et les Idées: Le Saint-Simonisme, Revue Politique et Littéraire, 1931, pp. 414-417.

Michelet, Jules
Histoire de la Révolution Française, Paris, Flammarion, 1868.
Histoire du Dix-Neuvième Siècle, I, Paris, Flammarion, 1872.

Mill, John Stuart
Autobiography, New York, Columbia University Press, 1924.

Monzie, A. de
Saint-Simon et l'Instruction Publique, Revue d'Histoire Economique et Sociale, 1925, pp. 177-180.

Moréri, Louis
Le Grand Dictionnaire Historique, IX, Paris, Libraires Associés, 1759.

Mowrer, Edgar Ansel

Challenge and Decision, New York, McGraw-Hill, 1950, p. 22.

Muckle, Friedrich,
Saint-Simon und die ökonomische Geschichtstheorie, Jena, Fischer, 1906.
Henri de Saint-Simon. Die Persönlichkeit und ihr Werk, Jena, Fischer, 1908.

Murphy, Ella M.
Carlyle and the Saint-Simonians, Studies in Philology, January 1936, pp. 93-118.

Neff, Emery
Carlyle and Mill, New York, Columbia University Press, 1924.

Nicolaïevski, B. et Maenchen-Helfen
Karl Marx, Paris, Gallimard, 1937.

Normano, J. F.
Saint-Simon and America, Social Forces, 1932, pp. 8-14.

Ogg, Frederic Austin
Era of Social Speculation and Experiment, The Chatauquan, 1904, pp. 317-328.

Parodi, D.
La Philosophie: La Doctrine de Saint-Simon, Revue Politique et Littéraire, 1925, pp. 380-383.

Pearson, Hesketh
Tom Paine, New York, Harper and Bros., 1937.

Pereire, Alfred
Autour de Saint-Simon, Paris, Champion, 1912.
Des Premiers Rapports entre Saint-Simon et Auguste Comte, Revue Historique, 1906, pp. 57-102.

Picard, Augustin
Les Etudes classiques avant la Révolution, Paris, 1887.

Picard, Roger
Le Romantisme Social, New York, Brentanos, 1944.

Polinger, Elliot H.
Saint-Simon, the Utopian Precursor of the League of Nations, Journal of the History of Ideas, 1943, pp. 475-483.

Puech, Jules L.
La Société des Nations et ses Précurseurs Socialistes, Revue Politique et Littéraire, 1921, pp. 82-85.
Flora Tristan et le Saint-Simonisme, Revue d'Histoire Economique et Sociale, 1925, pp. 207-215.

Quérard, J.-M.
La France Littéraire, VIII, Paris Didot Frères, 1836.

Redern, J. E.
Mémoire sur mes anciennes relations d'affaires avec M. de

Saint-Simon, Au château de Flers, le 8 juillet 1812.
Reybaud, Louis
    Etudes sur les Réformateurs ou Socialistes Modernes, I,
    Paris, 1848.
Rochegude, Marquis de,
    Guide Pratique à travers le Vieux Paris, Paris, Hachette,
    1907.
Rodrigues, Olinde (editor)
    Oeuvres de Saint-Simon, Paris, 1932.
Romanet, J. de
    La Communauté terrestre et la marche vers l'unité selon
    Auguste Comte, II, Paris, 1945.
Saint-Beuve, Charles A.
    Premiers Lundis, II, Paris, 1851.
Saint-Simon, Louis, duc de
    Mémoires de Saint-Simon (editor, A. de Boislisle), Paris,
    Hachette, 1879.
Saint-Simon, Henri de
    (In manuscript form) Copies of two letters written to his
    father, February 20, 1782, October 16, 1782, Fonds En-
    fantin, Bibliothèque de l'Arsenal.
    Letter in reference to his supposed arrest, Journal de Paris,
    September 19, 1797.
    Lettres d'un Habitant de Genève à ses Contemporaines,
    Geneva, 1802.
    Introduction aux Travaux Scientifiques du Dix-Neuvième
    Siècle, Paris, 1808.
    Lettres au Bureau des Longitudes, Paris, 1808.
    Mémoire Introductif sur sa Contestation avec M. de Redern,
    Alençon, 1812.
    L'Industrie, ou Discussions Politiques, Morales et Philoso-
    phiques, Paris, 1817, 1818.
    Pétition à Messieurs les Membres de la Chambre des Dépu-
    tés pour demander l'addition d'un article à la Loi des
    Finances, Paris, 1819.
    Lettres à Messieurs les Jurés Qui Doivent Prononcer sur
    l'Accusation intentée contre lui, Paris, 1820.
    Système Industriel, Paris, 1821.
    Nouveau Christianisme, Paris, 1825.
    Oeuvres Choisies, edited by Lemonnier, 3 volumes, Brussels,
    Van Meenan, 1859.
    Lettre Inédite de Henri de Saint-Simon sur l'Organisation
    du Droit Public, Revue d'Histoire Economique et Sociale,
    1925, pp. 129-132.
Saint-Simon, Henri de, et Thierry, A.

De la Réorganisation de la Société Européenne, Paris, 1814.
Opinion sur les Mesure à Prendre Contre la Coalition de 1815, Paris, 1815.
Saint-Simon, Henri de, et Comte, Auguste
Système de politique positive (Catéchisme des Industriels), Paris, 1824.
Saint-Simon, Henri de, et Enfantin, P.
Oeuvres, 47 tomes, publiées par les Membres du Conseil Institué par Enfantin, Paris, 1865-1878.
Sauzède, Albert
Les Saint-Simoniens dans le Languedoc, Journal des Débats, Politiques et Littéraires, May 22, 1925.
Sée, Henri
La Notion de Classes Sociales Chez Les Saint-Simoniens, Revue d'Histoire Economique et Sociale, 1925, pp. 201-206.
Ségur, Louis-Philippe de
Mémoires ou Souvenirs et Anecdotes, I, Paris, Eymery, 1824.
Shine, Hill
Carlyle and the Saint-Simonians, Baltimore, The Johns Hopkins Press, 1941.
Sicard, Augustin
Les Etudes Classiques avant la Révolution, Paris, Perrien, 1887.
Sirven, Alfred
Les Prisons Politiques, Paris, 1869.
Stanton, Theodore
The Brotherhood of Saint-Simon, The Open Court, 1910, pp. 542-552.
Stark, W.
Saint-Simon as a Realist, The Journal of Economic History, 1943, pp. 42-55.
The Realism of Saint-Simon's Spiritual Program. The Journal of Economic History, 1945, pp. 25-42.
Stendhal, M. de, (Beyle)
D'Un Nouveau Complot Contre Les Industriels, Paris, Sautelet, 1825.
Stone, Edwin Martin
Our French Allies, Providence, 1884.
Thacher, James
Military Journal of the American Revolution, Hartford, Conn., Hurlbut, Williams and Co., 1862.
Thibert, Marguerite
Le Rôle Social de l'Art, Revue d'Histoire Economique et Sociale, 1925, pp. 181-195.

Le Féminisme dans le Socialisme Français de 1830 à 1850, Paris, Giard, 1926.

Thierry, Augustin
D'Après sa Correspondance et ses Papiers de famille, Paris, Plon, 1922.

Thompson, J. M.
The French Revolution, New York, Oxford University Press, 1945.

Vauthier, G.
Le Premier Mariage de Mme de Bawr, La Nouvelle Revue, 1908, pp. 355-369.

Vayo, J. Alvarez Del
The Last Optimist, New York, The Viking Press, 1950, p. 143.

Vinçard, P.,
Nouvelle Profession de Foi d'un Libéral, Chanson Saint-Simonienne, 1832.

Washington, George
Correspondence of General Washington and Comte de Grasse, 1781, U. S. Government Printing Office, Washington, 1931.

Weill, Georges
Saint-Simon et Son Oeuvre, Paris, Perrin, 1894.
L'Ecole Saint-Simonienne, Paris, Alcan, 1896.

Werner, Alfred
Poet of the Pleasure Principle December 1947 Marks the 150th Anniversary of Heine's Birthday, The Saturday Review of Literature, December 20, 1947, pp. 7-8, 29.

Wilson, Edmund
Origins of Socialism, Saint-Simon' Hierarchy, The New Republic, June 16, 1937, pp. 149-151.
Enfantin and the American Socialists, The New Republic, July 7, 1937, pp. 241-246.

Witt, Emmanuel de
Saint-Simon et le système industriel, Paris, Larose, 1902.

Yves-Guyot,
Saint-Simon et son école, Journal des Economistes, 15 juin 1925.

APPENDIX

Origin of the House of Saint-Simon as given in detail in Father Anselme's Genealogical History entitled:

"Histoire Généalogique et Chronologique de la Maison Royale de France, des Pairs, Grands Officiers de la couronne et de la Maison Royale de France; des Pairs, Grands Officiers de la couronne et de la Maison du Roi; et des Anciens Barons du Royaume; ainsi que les Qualités, Origine, Progrès et Armes de leurs Familles . . ." Paris, 1726.

A translation of the document follows:

Origin of the house of Saint-Simon as given in detail in Father Anselme's genealogical history:

"Genealogical and Chronological History of the Royal House of France, of the Peers, Grand Officers of the crown and of the Royal House of France, of the Peers, Grand Officers of the crown and of the King's House; and of the Ancient Barons of the Kingdom; together with the qualities, origin, progress and arms of their families; also the statutes and catalogue of Knights, Commanders and Officers of the Order of the Holy Ghost.

"The whole being drawn from original titles, from the registers of the Charters of the King, the Parliament, the Chambre des Comptes and of the Châtelet of Paris, cartularies, manuscripts of the King's Library and of other Curious Cabinets.

"By Father Anselme, barefooted Augustin monk, continued by M. de Fourny. Third Edition, corrected and augmented by Father Ange and Father Simplicien, barefooted Augustin monks.

"Second Volume, containing the twelve ancient Peerages ecclesiastical as well as lay.

"At Paris, by the Company of Booksellers, MDCCXXVI with the approbation and privilege of the King.

". . . Documents concerning the duchy-peerage of Saint-Simon,

Raising of the land and seigniory of Saint-Simon to duchy-peerage, in favor of Claude de Saint-Simon, At Paris, in January 1635. . . .

"Louis by the grace of God King of France and Navarre, to all present and to come, Greetings. . . . Considering the antiquity and nobility of the house of the said lords of Saint-Simon, descended in direct line from the counts of Vermandois, and having regard for the great and commendable services which several of this house have done for the defense and conservation of the rights of our crown and state; among others Jean de Simon, lord of Rouvroy, who in the year 1214 while serving King Philippe-Auguste in the Battle of Bouvine, distinguished himself through his courage and skill by the capture of the Comte de Boulogne, and Alphonse de Saint-Simon, also lord of Rouvroy, whose important function marks his fidelity and merit in the government of the Kingdom of Navarre, which was committed to him in the capacity of viceroy in the year 1340, in which time and year Mathieu de Saint-Simon de Rouvroy, his brother, was made a prisoner of war during a voyage to Haynaut, which was made by King Jean, then duke of Normandy, and, two sons of the said Mathieu de Saint-Simon having lost their blood and lives in the battle of Azincourt in the year 1415, their brother Gilles de Saint-Simon was left sole heir of their virtues and estate, and in the year 1419 so valiantly defended the State against the invasion of the English, whom he compelled to raise the siege of the town of Gisors, so that as a mark and token of his valor he was made a knight of his order and since then was employed in all the expeditions, in which during many battles and sieges of cities he perpetuated his name, prudence and valor for the glory of his descendants, who ever since have continued their services, fidelity and affection toward the kings our predecessors and ourself. All the said advantages of birth and services having by a legitimate succession been happily transmitted in the person of our beloved and faithful knight of our orders, counselor in our state and private councils, captain of a hundred armed men of our regiments, our first equerry, grand master of the wolf-hunt of France, governor and general lieutenant in our towns and citadels of Blaye, master Claude de Saint-Simon, lord of the said Saint-Simon, baron of Benay, viscount of Clastre, lord of the castles, lands and domains of Pont-Artan, Avennes, Gauchy, Voigny-l'Esquipée, Pontruet and other places, from his young years when he had the honor to be brought up near our person we noticed in him so much wisdom in his behavior, and so much ardor and zeal for our service that, esteeming him worthy of our singular affection, we raised him consecutively and by degrees to the highest functions, dignities and offices of our house, in all of which functions every one has been able to see with how much honor, prudence and fidelity he has conducted and acquitted himself in a worthy manner. For these reasons, desirous of showing the great contentment and satisfaction which we have of him, and, through a mark that will last with those of his house, wishing to give proof of our determination to treat him well and favorably in the future, we make known that, on the advice of certain princes of our blood and other great and notable personages of our council, and on our own accord, knowledge, full power and royal authority, to the said land and domain of Saint-Simon situated in our country and county of Vermandois we have united and incorporated, and by these present letters signed by our hand, we do unite and incorporate the baronies, viscountship, lands and domains, justices, châteaux, boroughs and villages of Benay, Clastre, Pont, Artan Avennes, Gauchy, Vigny-l'Esquipée, Thorigny, Pontruel, Savy, Rumigny, Pithou, Aubigny, Iverny, Corbeny, Dury, and the fees of the market places of Saint-Quentin and Saint-Prix, their appurtenances and appendages and other dependencies or those which we will add to them hereafter and which at present are fully dependent on our own fief by reason of our said county of Vermandois; and the whole of which we have created and erected, ordered and instituted, and by the present letters signed by our hand we do create and erect and order and institute in name, title and dignity of duchy and peerage: we command and it pleases us that the said lands, baronies and domains and places be said and called hereafter the duchy of Saint-Simon, to be enjoyed and made use of from the day of the present erection, perpetually and forever, . . . wishing the said master of Saint-Simon and his male heirs to be called and known as dukes of Saint-Simon and Peers of France."

The document in the Archives of Amiens dated December 1, 1798, gives the following data about the sisters and brothers of Henri de Saint-Simon: the oldest sister, Adélaïde-Blanche-Marie, born October 8, 1759, married to Claude-Charles de Saint-Simon Monbléru, February 1, 1781, was now a widow. She was five feet tall, had a long nose, a large mouth, round chin, oval face, medium brow, brown hair, and gray eyes.

Marie-Louise, born October 12, 1763, married to Louis, count de Montléart, May 29, 1786, was soon divorced. She was five feet three inches tall, had a long nose, medium mouth, long chin, brown hair, brown eyes.

Adrienne-Emilie-Joséphine, born November 14, 1767, married Joseph-Jean-Baptiste, May 20, 1793. Her height was five feet one inch, and she had brown hair, brown eyes, long nose, medium mouth, round chin, round forehead, oval face.

Of the boys, Eude-Claude born in 1766, died at the age of nineteen, June 5, 1785. Claude-Louis-Jean was born July 30, 1769, and admitted to the military school in 1782. Andre-Louis was born May 27, 1771. Hubert was the youngest brother.

INDEX

249